HEAR
ME
NOW

The Mark of One Ordinary Pastor

KAREN LYNN SYTSMA

I DEDICATE THIS BOOK TO

*Pastor Jerry Worsham and
Pastor Mike Matheson, shepherds who
have helped me hear God's voice
and follow him.*

TABLE OF CONTENTS

Foreword

I once heard it said that young pastors tend to *over*estimate what they can accomplish in a local church in a short period of time. I've also heard it said that they *under*estimate how God might use them in one local church over a long period of time. Jerry Worsham's pastoral ministry at Grace Church in Racine, Wisconsin, for more than three decades is a testimony to the truthfulness of that second statement and the faithfulness of God.

In the pages that follow, you will encounter numerous stories and anecdotes about the life, ministry, and lessons of Pastor Jerry. On one level, these are simply stories about one man and his faithful efforts over the long haul to follow Christ and help others do the same. You will either discover or be reminded of how he influenced his family, his friends, and his flock. But on another level, a much grander horizon, these are stories of God's own faithfulness, power, and provision as he used one man, multiplying his influence across churches and even continents, leaving a legacy of grace.

It is that legacy of grace that makes Karen Sytsma uniquely qualified to bring us these stories. I say that not simply because she was around for many of those years, though she certainly was. She was deeply involved in the life and ministry of Grace Church, alongside both Jerry and Jane. But the primary thing that qualifies Karen is that she embodies and continues the same legacy that Pastor Jerry personified: devotion to family, tenacious commitment to prayer, hunger for God's Word coupled with giftedness to teach it, sacrificial service, consistent mentoring, and an undying love for the people of Grace Church. Of course, like Pastor Jerry, in humility, Karen would object and tell us it's not about her; it's about Jesus. Which is true. And I'll probably have to fight Karen to get her to keep these comments in this foreword. Nonetheless, it's right for us to rejoice in God's faithful provision not only of Pastor Jerry, but his servant Karen, who helps us to remember and continue his legacy.

People sometimes ask me, "Pastor Mike, is it weird or difficult for you to hear all these great things people say about a former pastor of Grace Church?" Well, believe it or not, I can always answer with a resounding, "No!" Far from being difficult, it is a delight to hear about the loving relationship that existed between a senior shepherd and his congregation for thirty-five years. My hope is that the stories that follow will serve to encourage everyone—pastors, missionaries, ministry leaders, and church members alike—to emulate the very best of Pastor Jerry's ministry that we all might be used to leave a legacy of grace.

To God be the Glory,
Grace Church Lead Pastor Mike Matheson

Acknowledgements

Every book has a beginning and an ending, and this book began after Pastor Jerry's memorial service on September 12, 2020. A few good men got to talking and said, "Wouldn't it be great if someone would write a book about Jerry? Who do we know who could write a book about Jerry?"

Their conversation turned into a telephone call to me, and that telephone call to me turned into days of prayer, and those days of prayer led to God's "yes" and me moving forward to write this book about Pastor Jerry Worsham.

I chose the title *Hear Me Now* because Pastor Jerry used that phrase often in his preaching. I also chose the title because I believe God wants those who read this book to hear HIS voice through the encounters people had with Jerry Worsham. (At the end of the book, there is a link to Jerry's favorite songs as well as select sermons he preached throughout the years. So, you really will be able to *hear* Pastor Jerry *now*.)

I was assisted by a Book Team that included Jack Bell, Phil Adams, Debbie and Ric Palmer, and Jane Worsham. To my teammates, thanks for praying, brainstorming, and walking with me through this process. To Jane especially, thanks for digging up all the research materials I asked for month in and out, providing names and contact information, listening to countless sermons, and just being such an awe-inspiring source of joy and encouragement! You are brave. You are bold. You ooze mercy and grace. And you are featured on so many pages in this book because you were Jerry's wife, best friend, helper, and one in Christ. People simply could not talk about Jerry without talking about you, and this book would not be complete without your name on many, many pages.

To my praying friends, you know who you are, you are the wind beneath this book. Nothing happens without prayer. You all know it. I know it.

To every beautiful soul who let me ask question after question in interviews and via email, thank you for opening your lives to me and for sharing your recollections about Pastor Jerry. I know you all loved him and miss him like I do. I had to stop writing many times to wipe away tears while I put your memories into *Hear Me Now.*

To my prereaders Theresie Bode, Anne Hall, Diane Peterson, and my editor, Marie Monson, I appreciate all the time you took to make this book the absolute best it can be. Special thanks to Grace Church Director of Communications Melisa Scott and Grace Church Pastor of Worship Matthew Lautz for assistance with Jerry's sermons and favorite songs and to Grace Church Lead Pastor Assistant Michelle Jenks and Suzanne Schackelman for assistance with the cover.

To my family: Mom, Jim, Nicholas, Jeannie, Charles, Peter, and little Phoebe Jean—*Have you seen my granddaughter? That one was for you Pastor Jerry!*—you are all gifts from God, and I love you very much!

And to my faithful God, who promised to be with me until the very end of the age, may your name be glorified as people read about the life of your shepherd Pastor Jerry Worsham.

Introduction

Have you ever encountered someone who changed your life? Pastor Jerry Worsham did. At age eight he met God the Father, God the Son, and God the Holy Spirit. After praying with his father and a visiting speaker to receive Jesus Christ as his Lord and Savior, Jerry's life was no longer his own. Christ redeemed him from his sin and an eternity apart from God's loving and gracious presence. The old Jerry was gone and the new Jerry had come (2 Cor. 5:17). Thereafter, God influenced every encounter Jerry had with every person he met.

Pastor Jerry first influenced me through two women in his church before I even knew he was influencing me. The first woman was Loreen Radke who was a staff member at Grace Church. I started attending an exercise ministry Grace offered called Gracefully Fit, where Loreen occasionally taught and worked in the childcare area. At this time, I had two young sons, one who was very rambunctious. Now, when I say *rambunctious*, it may be a bit of an understatement. Childcare workers at other places would tell me how *active* he was, and in very indirect ways discouraged our return. Not Loreen. She loved my son and she loved me. She joyfully and graciously watched both my boys so I could exercise and get some adult contact. Years later after reading one of my social media posts, Loreen reached out to me, asked about my son, prayed for him, and followed up with me about him. She was a product of Pastor Jerry Worsham's shepherding, praying, and leading.

The second woman was Patti Booth, who was the teaching leader of the Bible Study Fellowship (BSF)[1] women's day class in Racine, Wisconsin. Patti was a loving, kind, and careful teacher of God's Word. She taught me how to study the Scriptures, and she gave illustrations that were easy to understand and apply—something she heard Pastor Jerry do masterfully every week. And like Pastor Jerry, Patti had one foot planted on the truth of God and the other foot planted on the grace of God. So much of Pastor Jerry's preaching came through in Patti's teaching and examples, and she led her BSF staff and leaders with love, with dedication to prayer, and with a laser focus on glorifying God. Jerry's teaching, praying, and shepherding marked her. You will hear both Loreen and Patti's voices later in this book.

When my family began attending Grace Church, we were coming from a church that was reeling due to a pastor's downfall. I came through the doors of Grace Church a bit skeptical and a bit cynical about leaders and churches. Pastor Jerry quickly restored my faith in the pastorate and the church. I knew he was a man I could follow because he followed Christ so very closely and prayer was at the forefront of everything he did.

During my public relations and journalism career, I have conducted many interviews, but I have never had to stop in the middle of so many interviews so the interviewees could stop weeping, get tissues, and compose themselves. As men and women shared their stories about Pastor Jerry with me, almost every single one shed tears of joy and love and gratitude for the many ways he marked their lives and pointed them to the Lord Jesus Christ. And I get it. Pastor Jerry left marks on my life too.

Hear Me Now is a book of encounters, a book of ordinary people telling their stories about an ordinary pastor who was led by an

---

[1] Bible Study Fellowship (BSF) is a global, in-depth Bible study designed to produce in its participants a passionate commitment to Christ, his Word, and his church. BSF uses a four-fold study approach including questions, small-group discussion, teaching, and exploring biblical commentary. For more information see www.bsfinternational.org.

extraordinary God. So, it is fitting for me to share just a few things Pastor Jerry said that have marked my life and my spiritual journey. He said:

- *I appreciate your heart for Christ.* When I first began attending Grace Church, I was part of the Care Team and was responsible for sending cards to the staff every month. As I set out to encourage Pastor Jerry, he encouraged me by telling me how he appreciated the notes I sent and the words I penned. Knowing he appreciated my heart for Christ was the best compliment ever!

- *Karen, you see the goodness of God because you look for it.* I am an excitable personality, get enthusiastic about worship, marvel at how God delights in answering prayers, and never tire of hearing how God leads his people in the most interesting ways. Jerry never squelched my exuberance but instead reminded me to keep on seeking God's goodness.

- *You are an overcomer in Christ. More than a conqueror.* During a sermon series on the letters to the seven churches in Revelation, Pastor Jerry stressed how we were overcomers, more than conquerors in Christ, and that conquering does not come in the way we expect. Christ conquered by suffering and dying. In God's sovereignty, he knew how many times I would need to be reminded of this truth in the upcoming years. Jerry's teaching helped me remember that I was an overcomer in Christ and that I could not be unseated. No. Matter. What. Came. My. Way.

- *Justification, Sanctification, Glorification.* Written in the back pages of my well-worn Bible are the definitions of these words just as Pastor Jerry detailed in a sermon years ago. His definitions were so clear and simple that I have gone back to them repeatedly in my personal study and when teaching women.

- *You are on my Thursday prayer list.* Pastor Jerry followed a prayer schedule, and on Thursdays he prayed for people who had urgent needs. I was going through an extremely difficult family situation, and it was a blessing to hear him tell me he was praying for me. I knew he would not just *say* he was praying but that he really *would be* interceding for God's kingdom to come and God's will to be done in my life.

- *Yes. I would love to be on the Prayer Shield.* One of the roles God gave me at Grace Church after Jerry's retirement was to lead a Prayer Shield for Pastor Mike Matheson. Mike became the lead pastor of Grace several years after Jerry's retirement. When I was praying for the names of people who God wanted on this Shield, the Holy Spirit brought Jerry's name to my mind. I hemmed and hawed, thinking Jerry would be "too busy" and have "too many other things happening" in his retirement years, but when I asked him, he gave me a quick, firm "yes." It was such a blessing to pray with Jerry and Jane and the rest of the Shield for Pastor Mike Matheson, and it was yet another demonstration of Jerry's great humility.

- *Karen, Jesus does not mind your tears.* My brother, Curtis, died unexpectedly at age fifty-one and just nine months later my only other sibling, Linda, died of cancer. Linda had a dramatic end-of-life conversion, and I shared this story at her funeral. When I spoke with Jerry beforehand and told him how I hoped I could get through my talk without crying, he looked at me with his kind eyes and big smile and said, "Karen, Jesus does not mind your tears." He and Jane stayed for the funeral and gave affirming nods as I got about thirty seconds into my talk and started to cry.

Pastor Jerry has been at home in Paradise with King Jesus for more than two years now and I miss him. So many people miss him.

One of the many leaders Pastor Jerry influenced, Pastor Mike Lueken, shared these words at Jerry's memorial service:

…Right about now I can hear Jerry saying, "Well now Mike, it's not about me, okay, it's about Jesus." Indeed, it is about Jesus. I get it. But Jerry showed us Jesus in so many wonderful and shaping ways.

I still remember a line from a sermon Jerry gave a long time ago. He was talking about how God wanted Israel to fully navigate various challenges and struggles and trials.

God invited the Israelites, and here I am quoting him "to walk backward into the future, to go forward with confidence into an uncertain future by looking backward into the past and remembering God's faithfulness and provision."

Jerry modeled this way of living. He lived this way through the various challenges of his life. When I heard he had died, I spent several hours alone in my backyard thinking about him, and I revisited this picture of Jerry walking backward through his life and ministry, walking backward as he loved his family so well, walking backward as he led Grace Church, walking backward as he invested in so many of us who wanted to learn to be pastors and leaders, walking backward through his life-long heart problems and through his retirement, and walking backward through his recent health challenges and speech difficulty, and then on August 17, 2020, as he walked backward through the final moments of his life.

I like to think he felt a gentle tap on his shoulder, and as he turned around, his Lord and King was standing in front of him with his arms wide open. He embraced Jerry and he said, "Well done my good and faithful servant. You fought the good fight and finished the race."

Well done, my pastor and mentor and friend.

Jerry is right now celebrating and laughing and worshiping and reveling in the presence of Jesus, and Jesus now means more to Jerry and is more real to him than ever before.[2]

As you read the accounts in *Hear Me Now* and walk backward through Pastor Jerry's life, may you hear not only his voice but the voice of God whom Jerry loved with all his heart and with all his soul and with all his strength and with all his mind (Luke 10:27a). May you encounter God and be found bearing the marks of a disciple of Jesus Christ just like Pastor Jerry Worsham.

---

[2] Pastor Jerry's memorial service can be watched at vimeo.com/457289802.

Chapter 1

THE MARK OF AN EXTRAORDINARY GOD: Face to Face

*When I was a child, I talked like a child, I thought like a child,
I reasoned like a child. When I became a man, I put the ways
of childhood behind me. For now we see only a reflection
as in a mirror; then we shall see face to face.*

1 CORINTHIANS 13:11–12A

Jerry Worsham wanted everyone he met to know that he was ordinary, nothing special, no rock star. He never wanted to touch the glory of God. Yet, those who knew Pastor Jerry saw beyond the simple pastor to an extraordinary, extremely special, and anointed man.

One man standing for God and doing his will, becomes extraordinary to those watching. Jerry let his light shine before men that they would see his good deeds and glorify his Father in heaven (Matt. 5:16). After Jerry met his extraordinary God, he grew to become more like him every day.

Growing Up Years

Lorain Worsham Evans: Jerry, our siblings, and I grew up in a wonderful family with wonderful parents in the Panama Canal Zone. We were all born in Panama. Jerry was first, I was second, Ralph "Easy" was next, and last came Arvin. Our dad, Virgil, was just getting out of the Army after World War II, when he met our mom, Alicia, a beautiful Panamanian. They got married and moved to San Augustine, Texas, where Mom took classes to become an American citizen.

People in Texas did not treat Mom well. So, she told our dad that she did not want to stay in America and suggested that they move back to Panama. Dad found a civil service job transporting Americans who were relocating to the Panama Canal Zone. Dad would transport their possessions and would make sure everything with their relocation went smoothly. It was during this time he got involved with the Gideons.[3]

Like most people born in Latin America, Mom grew up in the Roman Catholic Church. Dad, who was Methodist, gave Mom a Bible. She read the Gospel of John and became a believer.

At the military base we were on in Curundu, the church we attended could have a pastor of any Protestant denomination. When we were there, the pastor was Milton Leidig, a Methodist pastor who was evangelical and held to a Wesleyan[4] doctrine. (I think Jerry preached a lot like him.) Our church was very missional, and it set a foundation for Jerry's love of missions.

Mom and Dad became active leaders in the church. We had a born-again mother and father who lived out their Christian faith. My dad was a gentle man, a man of prayer, and an encourager. As children,

---

[3] The Gideons are a body of believers dedicated to making the Word of God available to everyone and, together with the local church, reaching souls for Christ. For more information visit www.gideons.org.

[4] Wesleyan theology is a theological tradition in Protestant Christianity based upon the ministry of the eighteenth-century evangelical reformer brothers John Wesley and Charles Wesley.

we saw our father pray for us, care for us, and live out the Christian life before us. My dad made sure we all knew Jesus. Jerry really admired and followed our dad's example, and he was so much like him.

Jane and her family lived in the next base. Her dad was an Air Force retiree working as a civilian. We were raised in the1950s on the Pacific Ocean side of Panama, and life was quite different back then. We grew up going to Sunday school and playing outside. Jane and I attended Girl Scouts as Brownies, and our brothers played sports together.

Jerry excelled in his school studies and he also played baseball like you would not believe. My sweet mom thought that we needed to know a bit of the Panamanian culture. So, one year she enrolled all four of us in the conservatory of music. Jerry was playing violin. Oh, did he play well! My mom wanted me to play the piano; I did not do well, and she wasted her money. Ralph played the trumpet. Arvin took up drums. So, there we went, off to Panama City weekly to get cultured. Mom also made us take singing lessons in a Spanish school.

Jerry became a believer in Christ at an early age, and the Lord was always extremely important to him. When high school came, we were bused to Balboa High School, which was the only high school on the Pacific side of the Canal. Our school was made up of students with family members serving in the Army, Navy, Air Force, Marines, and working for the Panama Canal. There were seventeen different bases around Panama. Our high school offered Reserve Officers' Training Corps (ROTC) and Jerry got involved and soared. He did so well that when it came time for college, he wanted to go to Texas A&M University and be part of the ROTC there. Dad decided we would drive him to college. We traveled on the Pan-American Highway.[5] Jerry saw more of the Latin culture and loved it.

As God would have it, when Jerry had his ROTC physical, they discovered he had heart problems, so he was denied entrance into the ROTC program and had to switch gears. Our pastor in Panama had gone to Asbury University, a Christian school in Kentucky. Jerry decided he would go there too. After he enrolled, there were six or seven of us from the Canal Zone who followed him and attended Asbury. Jane and I were two of them.

Different Than All the Other Kids

Ralph "Easy" Worsham: Jerry was unlike all the other kids we hung around with, and certainly me. I was known as the black sheep of the Worsham family. My personality was quite different from Jerry's; and growing up, he and I did not get along well. I had a horrible temper, and I got into lots of fights with my siblings and others. Jerry was five years older than me, took on the big-brother role, and took it very seriously. He always tried to be with me to make sure I did not get into trouble. Most of the time I did not want to listen to him. He wanted various aspects of who he knew I was to come out of me. He would ask me why I was behaving like I was. At the time I did not appreciate it, but looking back, he really did help me. I do see his efforts now as loving. Jerry always stepped in and helped when anyone was in trouble. He was a mediator and had good, wise words.

We called him the *golden boy,* a goodie-two-shoes because he couldn't do anything wrong in our eyes. We always thought of him as good. Period. Good. You could add all sorts of adjectives to that, but Jerry was just very, very, very good.

---

[5] The Pan-American Highway is a network of roads stretching across the Americas that measures about 18,640 miles.

He Influenced Me More Than He Knew

Allan Hesters: My two brothers, Jane, Jerry, his siblings, and I grew up together in the Panama Canal Zone. We were active in many year-round sports, church activities, and scouting, and we all graduated from Balboa High School.

Jane and Jerry were an item throughout high school. Jerry was in my Reserve Officers' Training Corps (ROTC) unit, and I had the pleasure of getting in my sister's boyfriend's face at times for some grievous delinquency, such as a uniform violation.

We were also active in the youth group at Curundu Protestant Church, a very mission-oriented church. That was probably where Jerry's passion for mission work developed. There was no second-guessing where Jerry and Jane stood on issues; they wore their faith openly. On the other hand, my faith waivered throughout my teenage years; and I ran with a rougher crowd. Jerry's example influenced me more than he knew at the time. Looking back, he influenced my activities and decisions. His positive influence continued throughout my adult life.

When I was a young Army officer, Jane came to visit me. She and Jerry were in college and had decided to let things cool and Jane was miserable. My job was to listen. It had been serious enough that Jane knew if they got back together, marriage was in the works. After some time, I finally asked her if she loved Jerry, and she confessed with an aching heart that she did. So, in my most serious older, wiser brother voice I said, "Well, go get him!" And the rest is history.

He Fired the Gun in the Air

Ralph "Easy" Worsham: In Panama there were jungles, swamps, and animals–Jerry, loved being out in nature. We were out in the jungle once and Jerry had a shotgun to play around with. He fired it up in the air and happened to hit a spider monkey. It was lucky he did not shoot one of us with his aim! I honestly know that he really felt bad about that monkey for a long time.

We Followed in Their Footsteps

Jane Worsham with Johnnie and Ruth Jenkins: "Johnnie and I came to Panama in March 1964 as missionaries," Ruth said.

"I was raised in the 1940s in a ministry-focused home," Johnnie said, "and people with strong evangelism and mission skills often stayed with our family. I shared many of my growing-up stories with Jerry, including our family's involvement with Youth For Christ[6] and Awana.[7] About two weeks into our time in Panama, we started attending Curundu Protestant Church; and that is when we met Jane and Jerry."

"They were dating at the time and were student leaders in the church," Ruth said. "They were dedicated to Christ and mature as teen-agers; both were fun and serious at the same time. Jane was the youth group secretary and Jerry was the president."

"I saw in Jerry a leader," Johnnie said. "He was very *others oriented*, and had deep concern, love, and kindness of speech toward people. The love of Christ and the love of people were driving forces in both of their lives. You can't separate the qualities I just described from those of Christ. And Jerry and Jane were a good team."

"Jerry had the big ideas," Jane said, "I helped him administer things."

---

[6] Youth For Christ (YFC) reaches young people everywhere, working with the local church and other like-minded partners to raise up life-long followers of Jesus. For more information visit www.yfc.net.

[7] Awana is a world-wide nonprofit ministry focused on providing Bible-based evangelism and discipleship solutions for those ages two to eighteen. For more information visit www.awana.org.

"In a way, Jerry and I just followed in the Jenkinses' footsteps," Jane said. "They were mentors to us not in a way that was intentional and structured but by example," Johnnie was a teacher, a youth-group sponsor, a preacher, and a missionary. He was very *with* the people, very gregarious, strong, and skilled. That is who Jerry ended up being.

"And then there is Ruth. She was supportive, helpful, best in one-on-one situations with people, not an up-front person. I am much more like her."

"We fell in love with Ruth and Johnnie and they became great friends and spiritual mentors for us," Jane said. "Jerry and I appreciated all their input in so many seasons."

"I remember us all trying to keep in contact through the years," Ruth shared.

"Every few months we would meet," Johnnie added. "Our interactions were always so encouraging. They were memory related and ministry related."

"Jerry felt a strong camaraderie to Johnnie and Ruth, there was a deep understanding between all of us, a like-mindedness, a sharing hurts with one another," Jane said. "They were so encouraging to us through some very tough times in ministry. Both of them were a presence, they prayed, and they were with us to give us perspective. They also had such a spirit of joy.

"Along with this we had a mutual common background of praying for our kids and grandkids. We just shared life and ministry with them," Jane said. "Jerry and I had lots of love and appreciation for what they poured into us."

"One of the unique aspects of pastoral ministry is that when you get together with another pastor, you immediately understand the pressures and you immediately identify with the issues that every pastor faces at one point or another: cantankerous people, division, the loss of a staff member, or whatever it may be," Johnnie said. "I always appreciated our relationship with Jerry and Jane. They were iron that sharpens iron (Prov. 27:17). And there is always that kind of sharpening when you sit down with like-minded people. There was a mutual identification. We all just wanted to please God with our families, in the way we treated our spouses, and in the way we loved and led our church family and other leaders."

"We were so honored to be a part of their lives and we joyously got to watch their ministry grow and grow," Ruth said.

"We also prayed for one another and we often talked about the hidden hand of God, his sovereignty. Jerry loved this topic," Johnnie said. "It is so deeply encouraging to know we helped Jerry and Jane in some way. We prayed that over our sixty-plus years of ministry that somehow, some way, we would touch someone's life."

"By influencing and pouring into Jerry, you poured into everyone he poured into and influenced," Jane said. "You cannot even imagine the number of people you have influenced."

God Called Jerry at a Young Age

Ralph "Easy" Worsham: God called and saved Jerry at an early age. As he grew, he was always in church and loved it. He liked to go. I did not. Growing up, I had better things to do, but Jerry always encouraged me, and Arvin, and Lorain.

Our dad was a strong Christian and very passive: not much could get him riled up. Jerry always looked to Dad for guidance on how he should live. Dad had a sense of humor and so did Jerry.

We went to Curundu Protestant Church in the Canal Zone, and our pastor, Pastor Leidig, really liked Jerry and saw something in him.

Along with my dad, if Jerry needed guidance or help on what to do, Pastor Leidig would help him.

Jerry and Jane were together as far back as I can remember. When Jerry met her, I was younger. Later I got introduced to Jane's family and her brother Billy became my best friend. I thought it was great that I got a good friend out of their dating!

My Life With Jerry Worsham

Jane Worsham: I grew up in a good, nurturing home that I am very thankful for. Military bases in the tropics were wonderful places to grow up, though some of them were far from impressive with old, wooden, stilted, World War II, temporary homes. I learned that those things do not really matter. As a military family, we moved around a lot. In fact, we had seven homes during my twelve years in the Canal Zone.

Military bases had just Protestant, Catholic, and Jewish church services. My dad took my brothers and me to the Protestant chapel of whatever base we were on. In 1959, when I was about eleven years old, my family started going to Curundu Protestant Church, which was a remodeled Quonset hut. Neighbors gave me rides to youth programs, Vacation Bible School, camps, and picinics. I could not get enough! Thankfully Curundu Protestant Church had a pastor who preached from the Bible and who shared the gospel. I got immersed in the church, heard the gospel at a beach youth camp, and responded to it at age twelve by praying with my sweet pastor's wife, Lois Leidig, to receive Christ as my Savior. Eventually others in my family followed Christ too. (I never even shared the gospel message with them but was praying for them!) Church and more importantly the Lord became a big part of our lives.

Providentially, the Worsham family ended up living just a few streets away from my family and attended Curundu Protestant Church as well.

Jerry was my friend Lorain's brother. He played baseball with my brothers, and he would always win the kids' Bible memorization competitions. Jerry's home was filled with lots of activity, energy, and independence. He told me it was loud, that he and his brothers would often fight (the three of them shared a bedroom), and that there was plenty of drama. I experienced some of this and could hardly believe it coming from my quiet, structured home.

Jerry's family was in church any time the doors were open. Early in their marriage, his mom, Alicia, started reading a Bible for the first time, and she gave her life to Christ. She was very social. At church she grew spiritually, learned English, and made lots of friends. I am positive that Jerry's love for the local church stems from all that Pastor Reverend Milton Leidig and the people of Curundu Protestant Church modeled and poured into him and his family.

Growing up, Jerry was a very mischievous boy. He was attending Jet Cadets for Jesus at our church, like the Awana program many churches use today, and he won all kinds of awards for memorizing Scripture. One year at the banquet, the presenter said, "Reluctantly, I am giving Jerry Worsham this award."

After many people attempted without success to redirect Jerry's behavior, eventually one church member sat him down and said, "Young man if you would just direct that energy to the Lord, you could do amazing things for the kingdom!"

He took these words to heart and did redirect his energy to the Lord. At about this same time, he wanted to start sitting by me in our classes. I was so not ready for that and communicated regularly in Pig Latin to my friends to please hurry and sit by me!

When we started dating in high school and Jerry was hanging out at our house, my parents realized quickly that he was a good guy. He had a newspaper delivery route, and my mom and dad felt sorry for the people he delivered to after us. He spent so much time "delivering our paper" that their papers were late.

When we were young high schoolers and being discipled by others, I saw in Jerry an open and eager heart to learn about and follow Christ. He was very teachable and a diligent student of the Word. He became the president of our high school youth group, often gave the devotionals at our meetings, and passed along everything he learned to others in our youth group. I was the secretary, so we were a team way back then planning things and growing with our friends. Amazing youth leaders and pastors like the Jenkinses, the Cottons, the Gustafsons, and the Leidigs poured into us and became our dear friends.

Jerry felt called to full-time ministry during high school in response to a Sunday morning message. He and I shared and prayed about these things as we talked on the phone for hours most nights.

Curundu Protestant Church recognized and encouraged Jerry's leadership and giftedness, and they allowed him to preach occasionally at the Sunday evening services. Later he served as the youth director when he was home from college in the summer months and became full time in the same position after college.

We dated through most of high school, I followed him to Asbury College, and then I broke up with him. After going our separate ways for a year and one-half, I realized that I did really miss and love him: his zest for life, his heart for God, his friendship, his desire for ministry, our spiritual sharing, his ideas, his leadership, his giftedness, his adventurous spirit, and the fun we had together. We complemented each other well and he loved me for exactly who I was. He loved to say that I finally "saw the light!"

Our decision to get back together was more like deciding to get married since we had already dated for so many years. Jerry proposed at a nice restaurant in Panama City while we were home for the summer. Though we had planned a longer engagement, our beloved pastor of fourteen years, Pastor Leidig, was leaving Panama, so we moved up our wedding six months so he could officiate. Jerry loved to teasingly say, "We had to get married!"

We were married on December 20, 1968. Since it was an evening wedding, Jerry spent long hours that day running, swimming, and playing racquet ball. I enjoyed hanging out with my bridesmaids.

The ceremony with our families and church family in the simple Quonset hut church building was so meaningful. A funny memory was how Jerry's Panamanian family in their typical Hispanic culture arrived at the church as we were walking out. They had totally missed the ceremony!

Our reception was nice but totally exhausting, and we did not think it was funny to find out our luggage had been locked by our "friends" when we finally got to our hotel room. We honeymooned at Santa Clara Beach and El Valle in the Cocle Province of Panama, and it was wonderful.

Right after our honeymoon, we were back to college in Kentucky and delighted to move into a new and cute basement apartment. (That basement had some issues later with mice and flooding, but none-the-less, we loved it.)

Our biggest adjustment was getting up early enough to both be at the same psychology class at 8 a.m. in the winter. We were always late and mercilessly teased.

We had a very joy-filled time as newlyweds, working, taking under-graduate and graduate classes, and spending time with great friends. To top it off, months before I graduated, Jerry and I were very blessed to be part of the 1970 Asbury Revival[8] and later to join teams that went out to share the gospel in nearby states.

From our teenage years on up, Jerry openly and transparently shared what God was doing in his life. I was a bit more private, but his example made it easier to open up.

We prayed together and discovered that sharing spiritually was the most important thing we could do to develop oneness and intimacy in our marriage. We also discovered how easy it was for busyness to push that aside. Reevaluating our priorities, time, and activities was constant. Scheduling our date nights usually included looking at our planners.

While I was finishing up my teaching degree at Asbury College, Jerry attended Asbury Seminary and then was set to finish up a graduate degree in biblical studies at Wheaton College in Illinois. I had a teaching position lined up in Wheaton. However, those plans changed when we found out I was pregnant with our daughter, Janna. In those ancient days, you were not allowed to teach when you were pregnant. Nevertheless, I was thrilled about the pregnancy; Jerry was sobered and then thrilled.

With this development, our home church in Panama, Curundu Protestant Church, asked Jerry to come on staff as the youth director. That year and a half of full-time ministry was outstanding; the Spirit

---

[8] https://romans1015.com/1970-asbury-revival/.

worked in all of us and in the church. This experience started to turn Jerry's heart toward ministry in the local church. Since we both grew up in Panama and knew Spanish and the culture, we previously thought a career in missions made sense.

We teased Janna years later that it was her fault that her dad was a pastor knowing full well that it truly was God's sovereign hand at work. As a pastor, Jerry was able to multiply in a greater way his heart for missions. He got to send missionaries, send short-term mission teams, and have 25 percent of a large church budget dedicated to missions.

While we were in Panama, our home was open to the youth. Jerry was full of ideas, and I helped make them happen. One time he needed me to be a camp counselor, and I was just weeks away from Janna's due date. Jerry knew it was risky to be so far away from the hospital so he arranged for a pilot friend to fly me to camp and back from camp in his single engine plane and to be on call.

I loved those times with the youth group girls, and I was privileged to pray with some of them when they gave their hearts to Christ. Jerry was a great leader and teacher, and loved to disciple, but he looked like he was sixteen! I still can't believe the parents entrusted those teenage kids into our hands.

Baby Janna was born on December 15, on the same day and hospital as Jerry. Janna was the youth group's mascot, and everyone loved her. She came with us everywhere and flew on that single engine plane a time or two, even over the Andes Mountains, much to Abuela's [Jerry's mom] chagrin.

When Jerry's time as the youth pastor ended, we were excited that God had not only helped us save enough money to proceed with Jerry's graduate school plans in Wheaton, Illinois, but he also provided him a part-time youth director job at First Baptist Church in nearby Elmhurst, Illinois.

We dove into ministry in Elmhurst in much the same way we did in Panama. It was a hectic and stressful couple of years; in addition to Jerry's job at Elmhurst, he earned a master's degree in biblical studies at Wheaton College and a master's degree in family counseling at Loyola University. He also worked as head resident at the Elmhurst University men's dorm where we lived in dorm rooms that were combined to make an apartment. At this same time, our daughter Jennifer was born. Our girls not only had a youth group to play with but also a dorm full of big brothers!

Jerry and I were still unclear about what specific vocational ministry God would have us serve in. In God's sovereignty, a letter sent to us about becoming missionaries in Costa Rica, never reached us; so, we were left to make other plans.

Jerry's youth director position at Elmhurst became full time, and we moved into a rental home. Jerry taught, discipled, and developed youth leaders and even got to preach occasionally.

Jerry was ordained at First Baptist Church in fall of 1975, and Pastor Leidig gave the ordination message. Soon Jerry became the church's associate pastor. At this time, First Baptist was between senior pastors, and Jerry quickly assumed additional church leadership roles including preaching. God anointed his preaching (especially one Sunday when dozens of people came forward to receive Christ in response to a message), confirming in Jerry's heart a call to local church ministry as a pastor.

Here is an account Jerry wrote in 2011 about God's sovereignty and how he was called to Grace Baptist Church in Racine, Wisconsin:

Jane and I were excited to stay at First Baptist Church in Elmhurst, Illinois, and share ministry with a new senior pastor. We had five years of relationships and ministry established at the church and we were not looking to move, especially to move north! Who would have thought that six months later I would be the senior pastor of Grace Baptist Church in Racine, Wisconsin? Well, God thought and God knew and God orchestrated this plan in his most sovereign way.

Winnie Johnson, a member of the Grace Baptist Church Pastoral Search Team, just "happened" to sit next to Don Bjork at a Moody Christmas Concert in Chicago. Don was the first senior pastor I worked with at First Baptist Church. Winnie discovered he was between ministries and asked if he could come to Racine and do some interim preaching. Grace Baptist wanted him to consider becoming its new pastor, but he was headed into an international mission position. Instead, "he highly recommended they check with Jerry Worsham about becoming their new pastor."

Much to our surprise, in September 1976, when I was twenty-nine years old, Jane and I arrived in Racine with our two little girls. We wanted our ministry in a church and a community to be long term, and God blessed and granted us thirty-five years of ministry at Grace Church in Racine!

Jerry always said that he grew as the church grew. From the beginning, he chuckled saying he had no clue what he was doing. This was true for both of us, but God knew what we needed; and along with his Spirit to counsel us, he brought us just the right books, conferences, pastors, personal studies, friends, and a loving and patient church to foster our growth.

Jerry and I were a normal couple who did lots of things right, but not always. We were open about our failures and how God used them and taught us over time. Let's just say, I provided some great material for his sermons! If he was preaching on marriage the next Sunday, we could count on marriage problems during the week before. The enemy tried hard to destroy our marriage, and we learned to recognize the attacks and battle them in prayer.

We also learned over the years how to love each other in ways that were meaningful to the other. For example, Jerry finally learned that for Valentine's Day I liked solid dark chocolate not the gooey chocolates he liked.

I did not think of him as my pastor most of the time, but I did really respect and pray for him and was proud of and thankful for how God was using him. He often wanted me to critique his sermons, but I just wanted to listen and learn from them instead.

It surprised me when people from church would hesitate to go talk to him. I encouraged them and reminded them that he is just a normal guy. Some, I guess, saw him more as the strong, driven, persuasive pastor. I saw him as my best friend, a loving husband, and a good-hearted man who planned fun family days and loved to play and laugh with his kids and grandkids.

Like anyone else, we were always adjusting to new seasons of life like kids leaving home, increasing medical issues, daughters' weddings, caring for elderly parents, and the birth and delight of grandchildren. To Jerry, our home was always a haven especially on hard ministry days.

The Lord knew that ministry would be demanding enough and graciously gave us an easy relationship and a great marriage even though we married young at ages twenty and twenty-two. We truly have an amazing and extraordinary God!

Chapter 2

THE MARK OF ORDER:
God, Family, Church

*... Everything should be done in
a fitting and orderly way.*

1 CORINTHIANS 14:40

**Pastor Jerry's parents modeled the importance of an ordered life: God
first, family second, church and ministry third. They stressed making
quiet time with God and prayer a priority. After God, family and
church were the two institutions for which Jerry poured out his life.**

GOD:
Uncompromising

Terry Kultgen: Whenever I think of Pastor Jerry I think of the real
deal. I don't know how it works in the scheme of things, but his love for
the Lord was uncompromising. Many people, me included, go through
life and make compromises. Jerry did not.

Is This God-honoring?

Chuck Dumars: Pastor Jerry was friendly, humble, humorous, and focused on being a fully devoted follower of Jesus Christ. He and Jane set a notable example of maintaining a Christian home, and loving one another, their girls, and their parents. Everything they did and became involved with was weighed in the balance: "Is this God-honoring and will it help others find a saving relationship with Jesus Christ?"

No Agenda of His Own

Jim Arndt: Many pastors came and left under Jerry's pastorship, and we have had several that we love since he retired, but for years he was the stable one—the foundation that held things together. This is because he had no agenda of his own. His agenda was always God's agenda.

Balancing Act

Cindi Stewart: Pastor Jerry was a very balanced man. You knew he loved his Lord and Savior first, his family second, and his church family third. We all learned so much just by watching him. He was a great leader and teacher, possessed wisdom, and yet remained an ordinary man. He would always say, "God uses ordinary people." He proved that to be true.

God Is First in Everything

Scott Demarest: I was humbled when I was asked to consider serving on the Grace Elder Board. As with all elders at that time, I was interviewed by a group of current elders including Pastor Jerry. In this interview he let all the other men speak first and then filled in any gaps. His presence was calming to me, and I remember that he exhibited amazing grace. Yet at the same time, I saw that he ensured the tough topics were addressed. God was first in everything, and he wanted to make sure the elders followed all the Word and put it into practice as obedient and good examples. Pastor Jerry emphasized our call to be like Jesus, who was full of grace and truth, and who came to obey everything the Father commanded.

FAMILY:
Husband and Wife ...

He Loved Me, Thanked Me, Prayed for Me

Jane Worsham: As his wife and the mother of his children, Jerry loved me, thanked me, and prayed for me. He made time for me, for us, and for the family. Jerry learned quickly that sharing and processing life with him was important to me as a wife. I was fine with his busy schedule as long as we could talk; it helped that I could join him in many ministries, like visiting new people who attended Grace.

Jerry encouraged me to be involved in ministries and often stayed home with the girls to make that possible. Monday (his day off and the day I substitute taught) was his day to cook. He occasionally came up with a winner, like Potato Chip Chicken.[9]

Their Relationship Was Unlike Others

Grace Harding: My dad, Gordon Gustafson, was a missionary in the Panama Canal Zone, and my mom worked with the servicemen. Dad later became the pastor of the church Jerry and Jane attended.

When I first met them, they were dating and were still in high school. It was so cool to witness a high school couple that loved the Lord, and it was obvious Christ was first in their relationship. Both Jerry and Jane were mature beyond their years and sensitive to God's heart.

---

[9] Jerry's Potato Chip Chicken: 1. Crush 2 cups of potato chips. Add ¼ tsp. garlic salt and a dash of pepper. 2. Dip 3 pounds of chicken pieces in butter. Roll chicken in chip mixture, place on a greased cookie sheet, and sprinkle chicken with any remaining butter and chips. 3. Bake at 375° for 60 minutes. (Do not turn chicken.)

They oversaw our youth group, and it was powerful seeing such a young couple that had a relationship unlike most teenage relationships. They made me want to have a relationship like they had. Jane was a complement to Jerry, so sweet and so caring. Watching them dating and then married was a fundamental foundational memory for my faith. They were a beacon of light to me and to many in the youth group. Under their ministry I committed and dedicated my life to the Lord Jesus Christ.

They were part of my thread to the Lord. Through their influence, I attended Columbia Bible College and met my husband, Bill. He pastored a church for five years and then we went to Ethiopia for seventeen years to serve as missionaries.

God used Jerry and Jane's marriage in my life and others' lives. There was a ripple effect from their faithfulness and availableness to the Lord.

They Marked Me in Ways
I Don't Even Know

Pastor Kent Carlson: Jerry and Jane brought me into their home and their lives. I was a young dude and not even aware that I was learning from them. I ate so many meals at their home, and they made me a part of their family. Their daughters Jen and Janna played lots of jokes on me including putting my boxers in the freezer and giving me a cold drink that turned out to be pickle juice.

I observed Jerry and Jane's marriage. It was the first time watching a married couple, except for my parents, and all my ideas, my understanding of marriage, how to do married life, and how to raise a family, came from watching them. I watched what a Christian wife did, what a husband did, and how they related to one another.

I watched how they raised their daughters and the commitment they had to them, how their family was central to everything. Watching them marked me in ways I don't even fully know. I witnessed the concepts of stability, loyalty, endurance, virtue, and integrity. They modeled how to live not based on what I will get out marriage but what I need to put into it.

A Beautiful Dance

Pastor Mike Lueken: I would listen to and watch Jerry and Jane interact with one another and get such a kick out of it! Jane was never as wound up as Jerry. Jerry was a little straighter and narrower; Jane was more relaxed.

Jerry would present a story, and later when I would get around Jane, she would have a much more down to earth, scuffed-up version of Jerry's polished story. Jane would get going and Jerry would say, "Ah, Jane's Jane." And Jane would be saying, "You know Jerry. He gets a little uptight."

They were a couple who had such a genuine love for one another. They grooved together in a way that created a beautiful dance. They dealt with each other's differences, and they were kind and very gentle with one another.

Integrity and Elegance

Pastor Rusty Hayes: Jerry was the picture of integrity. Jane was the picture of elegance. They had a wonderful relationship and a healthy marriage. I never worried about them.

They were extremely comfortable setting boundaries about who a senior pastor's wife is supposed to be, which impacted my wife, Judi, and me. The congregation can have all kinds of expectations about what a senior pastor's wife should be, you get two for one—she is supposed to be another senior pastor, the female version of the head pastor. Jerry did not embrace that. Jane worked with the kids' ministries, she was more behind the scenes, she saw her primary role as taking care of Jerry and the kids and making a stable home life. She was unapologetic about that. This had a significant impact on Judi.

When we were at Grace, it was a big church. We had seen large church pastors' wives in highly public roles, and there is nothing wrong with that, but Jane was a quieter power behind the scenes. She did not want to, nor need to be in the limelight. She was not hiding, she was grace under control, an extraordinarily strong woman. This was freeing for both Judi and for me. I am incredibly grateful for her example. Judi has been an outstanding mother and wife.

SOLER

Phil Adams: At a guys' retreat we learned how to communicate with our wives or those close to us using the acronym SOLER: Square off; Open up; Lean in; make Eye contact; and Relax.

This is what I always saw when Pastor Jerry was around Jane. He squared off and opened his body language to her, he leaned in, there was eye contact, and he was relaxed with her. She was never secondary to him. He loved her. They had a joint mission for Jesus that would not survive without this intimacy. Their close relationship also guarded outside forces from hearing about any of the tension that I am sure they had. Everyone does. We saw two people really committed to each other on all levels: spiritually, mentally, emotionally, physically. My wife, Laurie, and I would see them holding hands walking in the parking lot.

A Mutual Love

Pastor Brian Petak: I was able to see the oneness between Jane and Jerry and the love. Jane adored Jerry; Jerry adored Jane. It was such a mutual thing. You really saw it in the last few years of his life as his health was declining. She faithfully served, honored, and loved him as he loved her.

R-E-S-P-E-C-T

Dr. Robert Gullberg: Just watching Jane and Jerry interact influenced me. They had comical sparring at times, every couple has some of that, but they had incredible respect for one another.

A Biblical View of Marriage

Bob Magruder: Jane and Jerry had a fabulous relationship because they cultivated a biblical view of marriage. It formed the embryo of their relationship which was playful, tender, and magnificently devoted. Marriage to them wasn't commitment; it was about complete surrender—you before me. They were clearly best friends.

My wife, Patti, reminded me that they were always affirming one another even when the other person was not present. It was a relationship that was remarkably pristine and authentic. They did not put on facades. They were quite open about marital conflict and how to overcome ensuing problems. In other words, they were not scripted. They modeled tenacity, forgiveness, and fortitude. Together they epitomized the beauty and sacredness of marriage. To them, matrimony was nothing to be trifled with. It was to be honored and exalted. They modeled to Patti and me that the institution of marriage has not failed, but it is people who fail by prematurely throwing in the towel rather than working through conflict. They showed that conflict could be the gateway to greater intimacy.

How to Serve as Husband and Wife

John Czerwinski: Knowing Jerry and Jane profoundly impacted everything in our ministry and marriage. They demonstrated how to serve together as husband and wife, how to live a life devoted to ministry, and how to do it well.

Pastor Jerry told my wife, Sharon, and me often that we would never regret investing in the lives of our kids. We were and still are deeply impacted by their life of service together. They modeled that great kids could come from ministry families.

We regularly cite and quote Jerry and Jane as we encourage our kids in each of their ministries, and our entire family still quotes Jane. Once, after a particularly difficult season, when there was much weariness and some discouragement, Jane assessed the situation, smiled, and calmly said with a smile, "Well, that's ministry."

They Complemented One Another

Jessica Schultz: Jerry and Jane complemented each other well. When I saw them together, they were always happy and respectful to one another. Sometimes watching them, I would feel my marriage and children did not measure up, but even this was not bad. It helped me grow.

Today, we need more leaders to look up to who will hold out the biblical standards by which we can measure our marriages, our parenting, and our careers.

Go With Your Spouse

Trish Baccash: When I was on staff, I casually mentioned that my husband, Gerry, had an impending trip to Las Vegas for work. Pastor Jerry came around his desk, sat next to me, and kindly encouraged me to do all I could to accompany Gerry on the trip.

We got into a quite candid conversation about marriage. I had never had an experience like that. No one had taken the time to show interest in my life the way he did that day. Pastor Jerry balanced wisdom and pastoral instruction masterfully.

The Epitome of a Godly Couple

Denise Pipol: Even though Pastor Jerry and Jane are close to our ages, my husband, Jerry, and I always looked up to them as the epitome of a godly couple striving to live holy and pleasing lives before God.

They both dedicated their lives to God at an early age and followed through on their commitments to the Lord, which is not something you see very often. They are true examples to follow as they follow Christ.

He Supported Jane

Karen Smith: Pastor Jerry and Jane were always at events together, serving together. They built one another up. Once after Jerry was retired, while we had been visiting Grace after we moved, we witnessed how proud and supportive Pastor Jerry was of Jane's business. He was explaining Juice Plus+®[10] to us, what it was, and everything Jane was doing.

They Modeled Biblical Roles

Sheri Kobriger: Jane and Jerry really modeled many things for my husband, Joe, and me. I saw Jane firsthand because she served in women's ministry. She encouraged everyone and was a good listener.

When we watched the two of them together, there was no struggle for power in their marriage. Pastor Jerry was the spiritual leader, and he loved his wife like Christ loved the church. Jane lived under his spiritual authority, and she modeled for the women of Grace how to do this.

But Jane had a voice, Jerry wanted to hear her voice, and he listened to her voice. They really modeled what a woman was made for, a helpmate. Jane supported him so he could pastor and lead the church and pour training into the staff and volunteers.

---

[10] Juice Plus+® delivers plant-based, whole-food nutrition that helps bridge the gap between what people should eat and what people do eat. For more information visit jworsham.juiceplus.com. For information on the Tower Garden® (aeroponic growing of fresh, healthy food) by Juice Plus+® visit jworsham.juiceplus.com/tower-garden.

Pastor Jerry affirmed Jane in her role as a woman, wife, mother, and motherly role model of Grace Church. She never asked for the role and would not think of herself in that role, but nevertheless, she was, and he affirmed her. No matter how busy they were or how many people wanted their time and attention, they never seemed frazzled. They always seemed at great peace and very connected.

Jerry and Jane, Jane and Jerry

Melissa Lindsey: Jerry and Jane. I don't think I'll ever say one name without the other.

Before we officially moved to Wisconsin to be part of Grace Church, I heard many wonderful things about Jerry and Jane. Their gifts of leadership and service. Their kindness.

When thinking of all the adventures, gifts, and challenges of our years in ministry at Grace Church, one of the most beautiful blessings was getting to see the legacy of Jerry and Jane up close. Not only were they encouraging to Joel and me personally, but they always had the big picture in mind—the wisdom, patience, and insight of a lifetime of learning and working together. The more we got to know them, the more we saw their integrity, their humility, their love for Jesus, their joy, and again and again their perseverance. We got to see the fruits of prayers, conversations, and actions they started thirty-five years prior to our arrival working out in the incredible ways only God knew they would.

When Joel stepped back from ministry, we were no less important in their eyes. No less loved. I cherished our little under-the-radar place in the balcony together, chatting with Jane and Jerry after services.

I don't know how to think about Jerry without Jane or talk about Jane without Jerry. Their wisdom, love, thoughtfulness, kindness, humility, humor, and enthusiasm are one long, beautiful story of a life lived in partnership: Jerry, Jane, and Jesus.

They Made You Feel You Belonged

Maggie White: After church Pastor Jerry would walk up the aisles and greet congregants. He and Jane had a way of making people feel that they belonged and were wanted. My husband, Larry, and I are not special; yet they made us feel so special.

One Person, Yet Two Distinct People

Michelle Bush: Jerry and Jane had such a beautiful marriage. When Pastor Jerry was struggling because of his heart condition and having trouble speaking or finding the right words, Jane knew exactly what he wanted to say and spoke the words for him. That is only possible in certain marriages. I love how they were one person yet two very distinct people with their own interests and passions.

A Tender and Playful Relationship

Kirk Ogden: Jerry and Jane's relationship was tender, playful even. I got to see them on some international trips together, and that was fun. We did a centennial celebration for South America Mission (SAM) in Panama, which is where they got to know each other, and it was precious to see their joy in returning there.

The length of their real commitment to one another and the depth of their mutual calling was amazing. Increasingly, especially in the later years during Jerry's decline, I saw more of Jane's care, almost a guardianship of him.

Jerry always reiterated the importance of my relationship with my wife. He encouraged me to bring Emily along to be a part of SAM board trips, and he made her feel included.

Another thing I learned from Pastor Jerry about marriage was recreation. He and Jane did a fantastic job of taking an annual trip to Mexico, planning it way ahead, and making sure it was marked off on their calendars. I needed to learn how to set aside time during ministry for that kind of investment. I have done a much better job because of Jerry's influence.

Jerry Honored and Protected Jane

Pastor Greg Smith: There can be a lot of pressure on the pastor and the pastor's wife. Jerry set a healthy expectation of Jane. He told her to serve the Lord and use her gifts. She knew she did not have to be the main leader of the women's ministry, nor did she have to be a type of co-pastor.

Jane really impacted people's lives, but Jerry was careful that no unnecessary or extra expectations were ever placed on her. This paved the way for other pastors and wives to do likewise.

Jerry honored Jane and said "no" to a lot of things so he could be with her. They had a really sweet marriage. He spoke highly of her and modeled making her a priority.

He also honored and protected her and his kids in his preaching and his ministry.

Mutual Servanthood

Pastor Isaac Miller: I was at their house a few times and witnessed how Jane served Jerry and Jerry served Jane. Their interactions reflected mutual servanthood.

One Flesh

Pastor Danny D'Acquisto: Jerry and Jane were one flesh. Often ministry is seen as a barrier to the family as sometimes it keeps the pastor away from his wife and kids. Jane had plenty of opportunities to think of ministry that way, but she did not. I got the sense from her that she was with Jerry in ministry every step of the way.

Jane ...

By His Side

Debbie Arndt: I know this is a book about Pastor Jerry, but I think he would say that he could not have done it all without Jane. Their marriage was something to watch, and the gifts that God gave them that complemented one another were amazing, impressive. Watching them and the beauty of it was a treasure. I don't know how many times he would say, "Now, Jane." I can still hear him.

She Created Family Stability

Pastor Kent Carlson: Any weakness that Jerry had was made up for with Jane's peacefulness, her steadiness, her non-anxious spirit, and her presence.

They were an old-school pastor and pastor's wife. They filled traditional roles, and they filled them perfectly. Jane wasn't this big, dynamic presence in church. She did not play the piano and sing solos, but she was this constant presence that created so much of the family stability. I don't know one person who could ever conceive of saying anything unkind about Jane because she was so extraordinary, so very kind.

A Marvelous Navigation

Pastor Mike Lueken: Jane had a calling she pursued, and part of it was the recognition that the church was going to be almost like a mistress, if you'll forgive the metaphor. It is difficult when you are the spouse of a lead pastor because of the time and the energy it takes to meet the demands of the church. There is always something.

Jerry pastored a long time and led through some awfully hard things. This is a reality pastors and wives must deal with. Jane navigated it in a most marvelous way.

Fruit

Jerry Morrison: Jane was so important as Pastor Jerry's support system throughout his ministry. She was an incredibly special pastor's wife, and much of the fruit of Jerry's ministry can be attributed to her work and ministry as well.

A High Priority

Jack Bell: Jane was an extremely high priority to Jerry. He really loved her. He did not make many decisions without her. What a great model he was for Christian men.

Top Influencer

Pastor Jason Montano: Jane was the top influencer in my wife's life. Kristen was a young, wide-eyed, I-never-wanted-to-be-a-pastor's-wife woman who got thrown into ministry and wondered what had just happened to her.

Jane did for Kristen what Jerry did for me. It looked different, but Jane got the pastors' wives together and would connect with them to encourage them. (And Jane cared for my heart, too.)

I have never met another woman like her in ministry. How Jerry and Jane got hooked up is just unbelievable! How do you get the boy Michael Jordan and the girl Michael Jordan on the same team? They were a power couple!

I believe Jerry's longevity in ministry can be attributed to Jane. Her character, her support, her love, and her connection to people served her family well but also filled a role in the church very naturally and organically.

Love Your Wife as Christ Loves the Church

Scott Demarest: One of the things that impacted me most about Pastor Jerry was his love for Jane. You could see him light up and smile when he mentioned her. His words were always full of adoration, respect, and praise. Jerry's relationship with Jane was his priority after following God. He loved his family and would do anything for them, but Jerry truly put Jane first, even ahead of his beloved children and grandchildren. In a world where marital relationships are too often cast aside and spouses drown in conflict and anger, Jerry and Jane's marriage stood as a bright example of a marriage fully entwined with God—a cord of three strands. Their selfless and unconditional love in marriage was one of the primary things that gave Pastor Jerry the integrity that was recognized by others. He did his all to love Jane as God loves his church.

Meeting With Staff Wives

Don Amundson: You never saw Jerry and Jane apart. She was always supporting Jerry. I think they were just terrific role models for families at Grace Church through the way they managed their family.

One of the neat things that Jane did that impressed me was how she and the staff wives got together and met on a regular basis. Attention in the church is often focused on the staff and elders and what they do. The meetings Jane held gave a space for the wives to get together and to talk about their thoughts and struggles and pray. It was a place for them to get a broader view of the process of leading a church.

Inward Adornment

Amy Cape: Jane is just plain beautiful inside and out! She modeled the kind of woman described in 1 Peter 3:3–4, "Your beauty should not come from outward adornment, such as elaborate hairstyles and the wearing of gold jewelry or fine clothes. Rather, it should be that of your inner self, the unfading beauty of a gentle and quiet spirit, which is of great worth in God's sight."

Behind every successful man is a strong, supportive, and praying woman. Jane was this to Pastor Jerry.

The Complement to Jerry

Yvonne Manning: I know Jane would grumble at the accolades and attention, but she was the perfect complement to Pastor Jerry. She had a beautiful, loving, neutral stance; was not a gossip; was a prayer warrior; had a legitimate I-am-standing-beside-my-husband attitude, and focused on her own family. That is the ultimate pastor's wife. I am not saying she was perfect, but all of what I described made her the perfect pastor's wife for Jerry during his time at Grace.

Serving Me in Her Grief

Denise Pipol: I am so grateful to Jane who reached out to me amid her own personal grief and loss of Pastor Jerry. She has been a huge support and comfort to me in my husband's healthcare crisis, showing me kindness and understanding. It is hard to believe that she had the strength to do that so early in her own grief; this clearly comes from her close relationship with Jesus. She quietly, humbly, and faithfully served Jesus side by side with Pastor Jerry through the years. We all saw it and so has our Lord.

Still Loving and Giving

Karen Smith: I saw Jane at a wedding and shared that my husband, Lee, would need surgery for cancer. We talked a long time. This is Jane: always attentive, always caring. God surely used Pastor Jerry and Jane, and he's still using Jane.

The day of Lee's surgery, suddenly a message pops up on my phone from Jane asking me how things were going and telling me that she felt the Spirit leading her to pray. She had no idea Lee was having surgery that day. Jerry is now with Jesus, and Jane is still praying for, loving, and serving the people Pastor Jerry shepherded for decades.

The Robin to the Batman

Larry and Maggie White: "On their vacations," Maggie said, "Jane had Pastor Jerry doing crazy things like zip-lining that even healthy people without a bad heart don't do! Jane wanted him to enjoy life to the very end and to the fullest. I am sure many people questioned why she was doing what she was. She also continued to encourage him to be involved in South America Mission."

"And she was talked into letting him go to Cuba too," Larry said. "He could barely walk, and she let him go share the gospel there."

"Jane was absolutely amazing and supportive of Jerry until the day he died. She is an extraordinarily strong person," Maggie said.

"She was the perfect sidekick to Jerry," Larry said.

"She was the perfect pastor's wife," Maggie said.

"The Robin to the Batman!" Larry added.

"And she did not need to be…" Maggie said.

"…the star," Larry added.

God Will Be Faithful

Paul and Laura Kienzle: We recalled some of Jane's stories about their daughters Janna and Jen going to prom. So, when our three girls grew up, we remembered to encourage modesty, to let them be themselves, and to remember that they were young. Jerry and Jane gave their girls freedom and trusted them, but they trusted in God's faithfulness the most.

I'm Listening to a Love Story

Reannyn Bickle: To this day, if I run into Jane, we will sit and talk for fifteen minutes. She will ask about my kids. She will ask about my husband. She will ask about how life is going.

One year at a women's retreat, we were walking side by side and she asked me how I met my husband. At this point we were about to get married or had been recently married. And, of course, being excited to be a bride or a new wife, I told her the whole long story of how we met, how great my husband was, and I talked way too long about our relationship. At one point someone came up to Jane and said something and she said, "Just one moment. I'm listening to a love story right now. I'll be right with you."

I felt so special. I thought, *She is really listening and really wants to hear this.* Jane and Pastor Jerry always loved and accepted me.

The Family Unit ...

An Atmosphere of Blessing

Jane Worsham: Jerry was a very engaged expectant father. We learned Lamaze childbirth from a young doctor in the Canal Zone. Before I knew it, word got out and our living room was full of expectant parents and pillows, and Jerry was teaching!

As the girls grew, Jerry was great at baths and bedtime, reading books, and creating narratives about his make-believe character *Quacky Wacky* with a "lesson" usually related to something that happened that day.

He was committed to time with Janna and Jen at parks, playgrounds, museums, and at home watching "Little House on the Prairie" and having popcorn nights, leading family devotions and prayer, and eating together. He welcomed their friends, discussed anything and everything with them, cheered them on in their sports, and supported them in their college and career decisions. He was thrilled to get sons-in-law who could talk theology, and the birth of every grandchild was a source of sheer joy.

Jerry knew it was a gracious gift from God to have been given time (especially with his chronic heart issues that developed when he was just forty). Every season had its challenges and we were oh-so-normal, but throughout all the seasons and activities of life, Jerry's example and spiritual leadership set the "tone" in our home. There was an atmosphere of blessing.

Balanced

Yvonne Manning: Jane and Pastor Jerry had a profound impact on me as a young mom. They rejoiced over every baby born to Grace families, and Jane gave new moms a little spoon engraved with the baby's name.

I learned about family traditions and spiritual traditions from them. They embraced spirituality, but they embraced having a blast together too. They balanced their world so well. They were two people handcrafted for their God-given roles.

They went through hard things too, but the way they got counsel and resolved these difficulties was beautiful.

Family Over Ministry

Pastor Jason Montano: Jerry shared with me how he and Jane raised their girls: "I never missed anything for my kids. Things happened, sometimes I was out of the country, but one of us was always there," he said. "Jason, the time goes so fast. Don't miss a thing."

I quote this more than anything. Jerry really instilled this into me, and I see the fruit of it now. His advice got me to volunteer as a coach, it got me to attend every activity my kids participated in including band and tennis and ski races and plays. I did not miss a thing just like he advised.

Now, I sit on the horizon of my kid's growing up years nearing an end, and I smile and I think, *Thank you, Jerry. Thank you so much! I have not missed anything because of ministry.*

He also stressed that when I was home that I needed to be truly present with my spouse and my kids. Jerry worked hard, but he did not apologize for putting his family first. Not once. Not ever.

"Unless someone is dying, any emergency does not trump my family," Jerry told me.

What I did not know then, because I was so young in ministry, is how true that statement was. There are always ministry needs. There will always be ministry needs. Jerry was the head pastor of a large church and was needed all the time for so many things. Yet he deliberately put his family first and this honored God.

A Man of Character

Kirk Ogden: I would describe Jerry Worsham as someone whose stature was measured by his character, who had confidence in his voice because of his convictions, and who understood that discipleship was at the heart of the work of the Lord. However, he also knew that discipling relationships within his family came first and were the key to what he did with other discipling relationships.

He Lifted the Family High

Dr. Robert Gullberg: Pastor Jerry dedicated all our babies and the church's babies, and he would not give this up. This speaks volumes about who he was. He lifted the family so high. He made this one of his banners. He was a pastor who really loved kids.

Time

Jen Binkley (Worsham): Looking back on my childhood, I would say one word that comes to my mind about my dad is *time*. He always made time for me and was always available. Whether it was family nights on Monday nights, which was his day off, nightly family dinners followed by devotions, building forts for Janna and me, or playing hide and seek, Dad was never too busy to give me his time.

We took many family vacations during the summers and later took many beach trips and Disney trips with all the grandkids and family. We had lots of family time at my parents' house talking, connecting, and of course watching the Green Bay Packers.

A Discipleship Partner

John Binkley: Jerry prepared and discipled my remarkably godly wife, Jen. Besides the Holy Spirit through Christ, she has been the primary catalyst for progressive sanctification in my life. For this, I am eternally grateful to him.

Jerry was always present and living the incarnational life before his family. As a grandpa, he discipled our sons, Luke and Levi, right up until his journey heavenward, and he never missed a teaching moment. There were Christmas pageants in the Worsham living room; profound moments of prayer; hysterical belly laughing; and theological forums and debates between Jerry, my brother-in-law, and me "hosted" by the grandkids. He also dedicated and baptized our sons in crisp Wisconsin lakes. He was indeed a partner in discipling them.

I Became a Believer at Their House

Caleb Augustyn: I became a believer at Grandpa and Grandma's house. It was 2012 and I was going through a rough time. My cousin and I went into one of the bedrooms and we were talking. He told me,

"You need to become a Christian." I remember after making the decision to follow Christ that I came out into the family room and told everyone. They gathered around me, and we talked about the Holy Spirit and how powerful a feeling it is to have the Holy Spirit within you when he comes into your life.

Grandpa pulled out his Bible and began reading the Word. It was a special moment with my whole family gathered around and Grandpa leading our talk about Christ.

He Found Unique Connections

Levi Binkley: My grandpa and I had a great relationship, and he had a special relationship with each of his grandkids. They were very different because he would tailor things to each of us and find unique connections.

I did speech and debate, and I was into politics and the news. Grandpa and I would have all these intellectual conversations. We would debate theology and politics and the things of the world. My mom and my grandma would say, "Why are you two always arguing?"

My grandpa would say, "We are not arguing. Jane and Jen, you would not understand. We are debating; it is not an argument."

We looked forward to these. They were very intellectually stimulating. We built each other up and bounced things off one another. We would always end our conversation with love.

He was so wise, especially to me as a middle-schooler. I longed to hear his opinions and debate, much to my grandma's and mom's dismay!

We would also sit by the fire and play chess. My grandpa loved chess. Sometimes he would win. Sometimes I would win. When I won, Grandpa would get mad at me. He'd say, "You can't win! What are you doing beating me?"

On my chess team, I learned all the rules, but sometimes "Grandpa's rules" were different. He was competitive.

"I am not sure where you are getting these new rules from," I would say to him. "Chess has been around for hundreds of years."

"This is how the old timers play," he would say.

And of course, his rules would benefit him lots more!

My Bible From Grandpa

Caleb Augustyn: Grandpa gave each of us six grandchildren a Bible and wrote personalized messages in the front. I keep this Bible on my bedroom nightstand, and I read it every night.

This is what Grandpa wrote to me: "Caleb, you're named after a totally committed Old Testament man. Let it encourage you to be a wholly committed follower of Jesus. Joshua 14:8."

This message makes sense coming from Grandpa because this is the type of follower he was: totally and wholly committed. He always wanted to walk the walk, not just talk the talk. He set such a good example for all of us and honestly everyone he spoke with. When I think about what it means to be a good follower of Christ, I think of my grandpa.

Conversations With Grandpa

Luke Binkley: One of the most special memories with Grandpa came when I was eighteen. My cousin, Caleb, had just graduated, and Grandpa and Grandma took us on a trip to Mexico. It was just before he had surgery and his health became bad.

One night we sat down with Grandpa because we had a lot of questions about spiritual things, biblical things, and philosophical things. At this point we were young men. It was different than how he talked with us about Jesus when we were younger. This was a rich, deep discussion where he explained what he believed and why he believed it. There was so much wisdom in everything he said this night, and our discussion went to a whole different level. Caleb and I were both so blessed and blown away by our discussions.

We were both saved, we grew up in Christian homes, we knew the truth, but we were each on a journey to make our faith our own. We were both about to go to college and we had a lot of questions. Grandpa in a wise and upfront way shared with us and answered our questions with confidence. I don't know if I ever met anyone as sure and as confident in their faith as my grandpa. He was 100 percent convinced in what he believed. I was a believer, but I was starting to have some questions about what I believed and was trying to figure out the best version of my faith. I was questioning even some of the things my parents believed. Grandpa was so sure of everything and he really reassured my faith and helped it grow. I want that confidence one day.

Moments in Mexico

Caleb Augustyn: One favorite memory was a trip my cousin, Luke, and I took with Grandpa and Grandma to Cancun. As we got older, they upped the stakes in what and how they shared the gospel with us.

My cousin and I would hang by the pool during the day, and at night we would all come back together, eat, and talk. Grandpa liked to dive into the deep things of life. He questioned us on where we stood spiritually, where we were emotionally, and how we were mentally. We had conversations about God, our lives, where we wanted to go in the future, and how we could improve. I don't remember all the exact details, but I will never forget how we were all so engaged in the conversation.

I share with others that my grandpa was one of the wisest, most down-to-earth, people I have ever known.

His Son-in-Law Loved and Respected Him

Pastor Greg Smith: I found out about the Family Life Ministry job opportunity at Grace through Tim Augustyn, Pastor Jerry's son-in-law. He and I were on staff together at a church, and he relentlessly harassed me about the position at Grace. I told him, "I am happy where I am."

The only reason I considered the job at Grace Church was because of Tim's deep love for his father-in-law. He really respected him and so did Tim's wife, Janna, and her sister, Jen.

The Church Will Move On ...
Family Is Who You Have

Pastor Jason Esposito: Later in life, Jerry and I would sit down and right away I would want to ask him about a problem I was having. What do I do with this staff situation? What do I do with the board? What do you think of this idea?

He would say, "How's Amy? How are the boys?" (We have four boys.) He would say, "You know, Jason, in the end your family is who you have." He knew the church would move on, but his family was always going to be there. He would remind me to love my wife, love my kids, and this would lead into loving my grandkids one day.

He was so enormously proud of his grandkids, and he talked about the things he was teaching them, the Christmas Bible studies, the word of the year. He had all these formal things he did besides just being a grandpa. He was like a pastor to his grandkids.

I think he realized through retiring from Grace Church, that pastoring was important but that it ends. In our conversations Jerry was teaching me to prioritize my family because someday I would no longer be the pastor of CrossWay Church just like he was no longer the pastor of Grace Church.

He did not tell me this, another pastor did, but I think this is what he was trying to help me see: "Someday you are going to leave. Maybe you will get fired. Maybe you will decide it is time to leave. Maybe you will retire. Maybe you will pass away. As pastors, we are all going to leave. There are going to be some people who will cry. There will be some people who will be glad—finally he's gone! The rest will say they were so thankful for you and your ministry, and they will look at the board and will say, 'Who is next?' But your family is always your family."

Nurture Like Jerry Did

Dr. Robert Gullberg: We had three sons first and raising sons is a little different than raising daughters. Now, having a daughter, I've had the opportunity to nurture her just like Jerry did with his daughters. He was gentle, he spent time with them, he was very active in their events and athletics, and he was supportive. He incorporated Scripture with his kids young. So, I started with mine very young, teaching them the Bible on a regular basis.

His Family Was a Respite From Ministry

Pastor Danny D'Acquisto: Jerry loved his grandkids and they adored him. Ministry can make you unavailable to your family, but I did not sense that was the case at all with Jerry and his family. If you pit family and ministry against one another, it can have a poor effect on both. If you see them in concert and related to one another, the opposite is true. They both bear fruit. Jerry saw his family as a respite from ministry. He had such a safe place with Jane at home that when ministry was tough he could be cared for at home.

Family Was Vital to Pastor Jerry

Janine Carls: Jerry and Jane were always together, yet neither one of them was too dependent on the other. They were each dependent first on God. They clearly supported one another in a very balanced way— each seeming to give preference to the other so that each could continue to honor God, family, and our church family using their unique giftings.

We all chuckled whenever Pastor Jerry had the chance to put a picture of his grandchildren on the screen on Sunday mornings. It demonstrated how proud he was of his family, but it served a greater purpose than just a pride and joy moment. It spoke to the congregation about how important it was to highlight even the smallest, joyful moments in family life. Pastor Jerry also never missed an opportunity to ask people about their family and encourage them. Family was vital to him and he emphasized it everywhere.

Family First

Pastor Dan Petersen: Pastor Jerry was a man who put his family first, always. His family was his priority. His life centered on his Lord, then his family, and then his church. The way he elevated Jane and spoke about his daughters was proof of his priorities. He often told me that Jane was his stability and his girls were his motivator—motivating him to be an example of Jesus. This applied to his sons-in-law and grandchildren too. He was so immensely proud of every member of his family and their lives in Jesus.

Intentional

Paul and Laura Kienzle: Pastor Jerry impacted us by his example. We attempted to imitate him and how he loved Jane and his children.

We saw how he intentionally parented his daughters, how he asked them questions, and how he led them spiritually. I remember hearing how he sat with and talked to his girls when they were teenagers about their goals and helped them explore and make decisions. Later with his grandchildren, we saw this same intentionality.

Picture Plugs

Jeff Stewart: Periodically Pastor Jerry loved to show pictures of his kids, grandkids, and sometimes extended family members during Sunday services. His love for family was obvious, but he wasn't afraid to share anecdotes as part of his messages where he humbly admitted parenting mistakes or acknowledged that Jane sometimes knew better what to do than he did.

A Cherished Priority

Jim Kerkvliet: Pastor Jerry and Jane were significant role models for married life, parenting, and sharing adventures with grandchildren. I noticed how each new grandchild's photograph would become a part of Pastor Jerry's Sunday sermon.

When I was serving in the production booth, Pastor Jerry would go over his notes before the first Sunday service. He went into great detail about where each photo of a grandchild should be shown to the congregation.

It is not surprising that there are many stories of how Pastor Jerry influenced people's lives. He took time with everyone, including his family members. He was warm and inviting and highly personable.

Two things I appreciated most about Pastor Jerry were his examples of humility and dedication to members of his family. In the early years, I remember how he and Jane attended different school events for both Jen and Janna. I can remember so many of the stories he shared throughout the years during his sermons about his grandchildren. Family was clearly a highly cherished priority.

CHURCH:

The Church Is Where the Action Is

Pastor Mike Lueken: Jerry was a guy who relentlessly emphasized the importance of the church. He would always say, "The church is where the action is." I can hear him saying that phrase, and now I hear myself saying it.

Love for the Church

Phil Adams: If you go to the heart of Pastor Jerry, his love was for the church. His drive to build leaders and his passion for mission was all about the church. Whether it was the universal church or his church, he would protect it from anything he felt would be hurtful and was willing to put in place anything that would be helpful. If he deemed something might hurt it, no matter what it was, it would not win out against the church. He was about the church and he was going to protect it. That is not a personal agenda; that is an agenda for God and that is a good thing. He was fiercely protective of God's church, his people, and their spiritual well-being.

He Lived Out John 15

Pastor Greg Smith: When I started overseeing the Family Life Ministry at Grace in 2001, the church was in a sermon series on John 15. Jerry emphasized how apart from Christ we can do nothing (John 15:5c). I saw Jerry live out John 15. His example impacted me so much that I'm still wrestling with it today.

I've Got to Preach Tomorrow

Yvonne Manning: I was part of so many weddings with Pastor Jerry; he preached and I sang. Once the reception band would start, I got fired up because I love music and dancing. At this time Jerry would say, "Well, you know, I've got to preach tomorrow. So, we had better get going."

I remember thinking, *How challenging leaving must be and how boring!* It hit me later in life that Pastor Jerry made the better choice just like Mary (Luke 10:38–42). There I was dancing when I had to lead worship the next day. The next morning it likely showed that I was leading tired.

I've never seen a more disciplined person than Pastor Jerry. His routine was to the minute. Some might say this is legalistic. You can say whatever you want, but I saw how he loved God's church and sacrificed for it. I saw him as a man of God who loved God so much that he was going to be a clean vessel, ready to be used.

Everyone Welcome

Cindi Stewart: Pastor Jerry created an incredible church under God. Everyone was welcome, everyone was important, and everyone could be used in some way, experienced or not—which I wasn't. But it felt great to be on a committee and learn how to serve God from Pastor Jerry and others.

Church Discipline

Scott Demarest: Occasionally behavior of church members was brought before the elders. Pastor Jerry always made it clear that when we dealt with a situation that involved sin, repentance by those involved was the goal. Spiritual restoration was most important.

Pastor Jerry and the elders reread and discussed the passage in Matthew 18:15–17 before moving forward. We usually asked those involved if they had followed the steps of this process. When this was done, issues were often resolved through confession, repentance, forgiveness, and conflict resolution.

Unfortunately, there were some incidents that required immediate elder involvement. The nature of these situations was always unpleasant and painful. When necessary, Pastor Jerry led the conversation laying out an action plan and the specific communication needed. He was always full of grace and hope, but he ensured that we followed the instruction of the Bible and the direction of the Holy Spirit when dealing with church discipline.

He Loved the Local Church

Craig Vaughn: Over the years Jerry and I served together making hospital visits and home visits to people who were ill, had surgery, or who were recovering. He would talk and pray with them. He loved to do this.

As the church grew, the numbers of people who had cancer, surgery, or other issues grew. I sometimes tried to exclude Jerry because of his schedule and his other responsibilities. I did not want to put more on him to do, but if he found out about it, he would want to join. One of his passions was for ministering to and serving people. Serving was his joy. He simply loved the local church.

One-to-One Membership Class

Joan Gorton: Pastor Jerry was loyal to the church and committed to his responsibilities. When I wanted to become a member of Grace Church, the last of three membership classes was held on a Wednesday evening. I was teaching at Kid Zone that night and could not make it. Pastor Jerry knew this was why I did not show up for the class. He invited me to an appointment in his office to finish the membership classes so I could realize my goal of becoming a member of Grace.

That demonstrated his commitment to his church and to people who wanted to become members.

Part of Life as a Believer

Debbie Palmer: Pastor Jerry encouraged us to get involved in small groups at church. He stressed that doing life with the church was part of life as a believer.

My husband, Ric, and I have now been doing life with the same people for more than twenty years. Pastor Jerry loved the church and he taught us to love the church and the people in it.

If We Are the Body ...

Phil Adams: Pastor Jerry had the Elder Board read *The Body: Being Light in the Darkness,* by Charles Colson. I felt we should do something with what we had read. At this time, many area churches had issues with some of the new things Grace was doing. I wanted to have an event for as many Racine churches as possible to dispel notions that we were selling out the gospel.

Many people told me that an event like this could not happen, that it had already been tried. Pastor Jerry said to me, "If you think you can do this, I am behind you." He convinced the Elder Board to let me try it. If it wasn't for him being supportive it would not have happened.

The event ended up being held at Festival Hall in the marina because sixteen or seventeen churches and a few thousand people were involved. All the churches took ownership, and it was a really healing time for the city and the body of Christ.

After Retirement

Pastor Isaac Miller: Only one in a thousand lead pastors could stay at the church he led after retirement and do it as well as Jerry did. He supported the new pastor and the church unwaveringly. I remember someone asking him a question and he said, "I'm not the head pastor."

He was hands off, and this was huge for me to see. He had a commitment to the church of Jesus Christ. It was not about him or his comfort or his desires. I imagine he had opinions—we all do—but he never to my knowledge let his opinions get in the way of worshipping at Grace as a congregant. He knew Grace was not his church, but the Lord's church and that it always would be no matter who the head pastor was.

Chapter 3

THE MARK OF PRAYER:
First of All, Pray

*I urge, then, first of all, that petitions,
prayers, intercession and thanksgiving
be made for all people ....*

1 TIMOTHY 2:1

Pastor Jerry knew the power of prayer. He knew it worked and he made it a priority in his personal life and in how he led Grace Church. More than any other discipline, prayer was something Pastor Jerry stressed with his family, Elder Board, staff, congregation, the people he mentored, and in mission.

Every January Pastor Jerry would spend a month preaching on prayer. When the calendars turned, he wanted his congregants to refocus on their prayer lives. He impacted many people in many ways, but almost certainly where he gained the most ground for God's kingdom was on his knees in prayer.

Our Dad Was Jerry's Example

Lorain Worsham Evans: Our dad would go into another room, shut the door, and pray. He was a man of great faith with a quiet spirit. Everyone knew how much he cared for them. He was a doer of the Word and demonstrated faith to us when we were growing up. He made sure we all knew the way to the Lord. Jerry became so very much like Dad.

When we went to the United States, Dad took us to old-fashioned revivals. In fact, I became a Christian at one.

My dad also took us to hear Billy Graham at a crusade in the Canal Zone. Dad appreciated and practiced prayer and worship, and so did Jerry.

Jerry Benefited From
His Father's Prayer Life

Jane Worsham: Jerry's dad, Virgil, led him to the Lord at age eight and always encouraged him spiritually. Jerry benefited his whole life from the deep prayer life of his father who was the praying patriarch for generations of Worshams. Prayer was a high priority throughout Jerry's life too; he emphasized it strongly in his personal life, in the youth groups he led, at Grace Church, and at South America Mission.

Jerry became the praying patriarch of our family and extended family. The security and protection I felt from his deep prayer life was noticeably shaken when he went home to Jesus. He is missed in so many ways.

Dad Influenced Jerry's Prayer Life

Ralph "Easy" Worsham: Jerry and our dad never missed a Wednesday night prayer meeting at our church in the Canal Zone. Dad believed in prayer and his example certainly influenced my big brother Jerry.

When I was in high school, my dad would stay awake and wait for me because I would not be home by curfew. I would come home to him kneeling and praying about me. Dad prayed about everything, and Jerry did too.

We Had Been in the Presence of Evil

Allan Hesters: Our church in Panama was very mission oriented, and Jerry, Jane, and I were involved in a youth group that wanted to do mission work in a Panamanian village. It was close to the Canal Zone, but it still retained a small village atmosphere, unlike many neighboring villages that had evolved into what we considered small towns.

We arrived at the village in the afternoon, broke into teams, and set about going door to door inviting residents to that night's service. There was a strange air about the place. Many people we talked to were curious and receptive, while others would not even come to the door or completely avoided us. We noticed strange symbols and markings on a number of those doors and gates. Without knowing for sure, we suspected these were some type of cult symbols, and we did not feel comfortable.

That night we gathered at a communal thatched-roof structure in the middle of town. It could seat about fifty people on well-worn, wooden benches. We were pleased with the turn out. As our adult leader's talk continued, a stirring and restlessness among everyone began. We noticed an older villager standing in one of the rear doorways. He stared at us blankly with an evil expression on his face. He said nothing. He just stood there staring. Slowly, one by one, the villagers began to leave while being careful to avoid the older villager.

Suddenly a huge storm hit and a heavy blackness settled in over us. It was obvious that there were principalities of evil and darkness at work. Jerry opened his Bible, knelt, and began praying. He commanded in the name of Jesus Christ that the dark forces leave. He repeated his prayers until a noticeable difference occurred. The storm lifted. The air became light and breathable. The older villager was gone. And slowly those who had left earlier returned. After what took place, they were receptive to the Word of God.

Later as we were traveling home, everyone was very quiet, and we began to process what had happened. One thing was clear to us all: We had been in the presence of evil. It was real and tangible, but the Word was more powerful.

We never dwelled on it, but when Jerry, Jane, and I spoke of this event over the years, it was always with a knowing nod or smile of God's greatness.

Praying for Our Girls' Husbands

Jane Worsham: Since our daughters Janna and Jennifer were strong, independent, capable young women who loved God, Jerry and I prayed for strong, godly men for them who would love them in their giftedness. God more than answered those prayers by giving them Tim and John—life partners perfect for them.

Iron Sharpens Iron

Julie Lueken: My dad, Dr. Don Cohill, and Pastor Jerry became accountability partners soon after we started attending Grace Baptist Church in the 1980s. For years and years, they met every Wednesday morning to talk and pray. I don't think they ever missed a Wednesday unless one of them was out of town.

Pastor Jerry had a huge influence on my dad and my dad also influenced Pastor Jerry. They sharpened each other as they prayed for one another and each other's families. They also liked to talk theology and would often be found debating. Both loved the book of Romans.

So much of my life and my family's life was impacted by the life and prayers of Pastor Jerry. He married my husband, Mike, and me and did our premarital counseling. We went on a mission trip with him and he trusted me to mentor his daughter, Jennifer. He shaped my husband throughout his life and during his time at Grace as a youth and associate pastor.

When my brother died tragically in January 1992, Pastor Jerry and Grace came alongside of us and supported us. Pastor Jerry's steadfast love and commitment to Christ and to the leadership of the church continues to have an impact on my life to this day.

This Guy Figured It Out

Pastor Rusty Hayes: When I went to Dallas Theological Seminary, it was a cessationist school, meaning they believed the miraculous gifts like prophecy, speaking in tongues, and miracles were not in operation today and ceased to exist with the Apostolic Age. It was tough because I needed to see it scripturally, and they could not prove it to me. I was rebellious in that way when I was at Dallas, and I remember someone asking me what my dream church would look like.

"I want to go to a Baptist church that teaches the Bible like Baptists, but worships like the charismatics," I said. "If you took the charismatic ways of worship and prayer and married them with sound biblical teaching, you would have a complete church." Grace Church was the first church where I saw this.

During my initial visit to Grace, I knew I wanted to work there. I thought, *This guy, Jerry Worsham, figured it out.* He had charismatics leading worship and he had solid theology coming from the pulpit. So, it was charismatic but not weird.

Jerry was always open to the charismatic. His attitude was, "If you can show me legitimately that you have this gift and are speaking in tongues, go for it."

Grace had a prayer ministry with full-on charismatic folks, and Jerry welcomed and appreciated that. We saw healings. In fact, I experienced a miraculous healing at Grace Baptist. I had a ruptured disc that could be clearly seen in my MRI scan. The Grace prayer group prayed for me, and I was healed. Bob Gullberg was my doctor, and he said, "I can't explain this."

He Was Fully in the Spirit

Pastor Brian Petak: A lot of churches and pastors diminish the role of the Holy Spirit. He sits in the back seat. Not so with Jerry, he was Spirit dependent. In fact, that could be one descriptor of his life.

I have not listened to his sermons for a long time, but I know he taught on the Holy Spirit often, and in January he would preach on prayer. These sermons always focused on the Holy Spirit's role in our lives through prayer and dependence.

I don't know that I witnessed the sign gifts, like tongues and interpretation, in Pastor Jerry's life. Although not sure, I would not doubt if he had a prayer language with his Heavenly Father. He was fully in the Spirit and the gifts of the Spirit were fully in operation in his life; he was not a cessationist. He wanted to elevate the role of the third person of the trinity in the life of a believer and for everyone to know that we don't move forward in our Christian life without the work of the Holy Spirit.

Prayer Is the Hard Work

Pastor Jason Esposito: I learned from Jerry that prayer is not the last thing; it is the first thing. It was never, "Well, we're going to try to do it on our own, and if we can't, then we will pray."

Jerry always put prayer in the forefront, and it is a huge reason why God used him in the way he did. We saw the movement of the Holy Spirit at Grace through him championing prayer and never putting it on the back burner.

Jerry really believed in prayer and God poured out his blessings through this. He led with prayer in the overall planning of events and meetings. He made prayer and solitude part of his sermon prep, and he wrote his sermons after his prayer times.

He was a very hard worker, but he recognized that prayer is the hard work. I need that reminder. This is why the *First of All, Pray* card is still on my bulletin board. This is why I journal my prayers. It was Jerry who advised me to take a half day or full day of solitude. We did this when I was on staff, and then we would come back together as a group and share what we learned from God. I have incorporated this in similar ways with my staff today.

Pray for God to Fill Every Space

Chris Booth: I was overseeing the parking lot expansion at the church on Northwestern Avenue. At the time, the church only wanted to put in a small parking lot. I told Pastor Jerry I thought we should build a parking lot as big as we could and then pray for God to fill every space. He agreed, and that is exactly what we did. It was amazing to watch what God did in response to our prayers. We marveled at how God filled every single lot spot and how people were still parking on the streets.

A Big Thing We All Struggle With

Dr. Robert Gullberg: Pastor Jerry realized that prayer is the biggest discipline that Christians need and the one we all struggle with the most. If we are honest, we know we do not spend the time we should praying. So, Pastor Jerry brought it into the light and emphasized prayer big time with his church. He did a sermon series on prayer every January and he would break things down in detail for us. The *First of All, Pray* cards he gave out represent who Jerry was. From him I learned the priority of prayer.

We Learned to Pray for Our Girls' Spouses

Lori Vaughn: Joining Grace Church early in our early marriage was a blessing; my growth as a Christian was huge. I was raised Catholic, and I did not even have my own Bible. God used Pastor Jerry's ministry and preaching to really change me.

Prayer was so important to him, and my husband, Craig, and I were influenced by this. He prayed for his girls' future spouses. So, early on in our three girls' lives, not knowing who their spouses would be, we started praying for them.

Our girls grew up at Grace, and Jerry left an impression on all of them. He was special to and instrumental in the lives of everyone in our family.

We Were Praying for You

Lorain Worsham Evans: I was a prodigal in the 1980s. My sweet brother Jerry prayed for me when I was far away from the Lord, when my marriage was not good, and through my husband's unemployment. Jerry was my anchor and was always supportive.

When our dad and brother Arvin both got cancer, I went to help care for them. God was using their illnesses to bring me close to him. Seeing the faith of my father and Arvin fighting cancer brought me back to the Lord. I told my husband we were going back to church; we are going to have children; we will go to counseling.

"We were praying for you," Jerry told me.

I wanted a child, and my husband and I found out we could not have children. I wept, came home, picked up the phone, and called Jerry.

I told him everything and he just listened to me. He and Jane prayed and prayed, and God was so good to us. We adopted the most beautiful little girl, Jessica, who we raised to know the Lord Jesus.

Jerry and Jane were always listening, always praying, always involved.

God Heard His Prayers

Janna Augustyn (Worsham): On the night our second child, Caleb, was born, I was having trouble with his delivery. He was stuck and his heart rate kept dropping and got dangerously low. The doctor told us she needed to take some drastic steps to get him out as quickly as possible. Before she took those measures, however, she said we would try one more time. On that push he came out!

My dad later told us that he felt prompted at about the same time (in the middle of the night) to get on his knees and pray for the delivery. I believe God heard his prayers.

Always on His Knees

Pastor Brian Petak: Pastor Jerry's weekly prayer times were open to everybody, but very few people came. Despite this, Jerry was there praying on his knees, always on his knees. I almost always pray on my knees today; I don't feel comfortable sitting in a chair praying. I can picture Jerry on his knees in his office praying, and I know this is what influenced me.

Prayer Partners

Karen Smith: When our daughter Kaylee was born, she was never assigned a prayer partner at Grace so Pastor Jerry and Jane filled the role.

Prayer partners are supposed to partner with the parents and pray for the baby during his or her first year of life. Jane would check in with us and tell us how she and Jerry were praying. Kaylee is now an adult, and Jane still checks in and prays. She went well beyond her one-year commitment!

Remain in Him Through Prayer

Caleb Augustyn: Grandpa had a very structured prayer life and was always in the Word. He talked to us grandkids about prayer often and encouraged us. He stressed the importance of talking to God and how this would keep us on track with everything else that happened in our lives.

He told us to let God talk to us through the Bible and then we talk to God through prayer. Grandpa said prayer was foundational for everything else that would happen in our lives; committing to spend this time with God would help us remain in him and be grounded no matter what happened to us in this world.

Pray! God Does Not Think or Act Like Mankind Does

Pastor Dave Kehrli: One of the major things Pastor Jerry impressed on both Mary and me was the need for prayer in all parts of our lives— big things, little things, and every in-between thing. Early on in our walks with the Lord, we learned from Pastor Jerry to take time to fast and pray earnestly about decisions so God would order our steps.

This became evident when I was offered a pharmacist position in Rhinelander, Wisconsin. Mary and I were new Christians but had been trained well by Jerry in prayer. He emphasized that God does not think or act the way mankind does (Isa. 55). Even though everything about this job appeared positive from the worldly view, we had to really pray about it. In doing this, we sensed a clear answer of "no" from God.

The same thing happened in 2006 when Grace Church offered to change my pastor position from part time to full time. It seemed like a no brainer to just accept this gracious offer and move forward with the church where we became born-again Christians and where we were raised in the faith. Once again, going back to Jerry's words to always seek God and his answer in prayer, we sensed a clear "no" to this offer. We knew this meant real change was imminent as to where we would be going and what we would be doing next. Pastor Jerry always inspired people to pray and then go where God directed them knowing he would take care of all the details.

Psalm 63

Terry Kultgen: Pastor Jerry shared with me that on Sundays before every service he would enter the sanctuary and pray, "O God, you are my God; earnestly I seek you; my soul thirsts for you; my flesh faints for you, as in a dry and weary land where there is no water. So I have looked upon you in the sanctuary, beholding your power and glory" (Ps. 63:1-2 ESV).

A Living Room Prayer

Pastor Chris Amundson: My mom felt a pull to get us to a church where we would be more enthusiastic about going. We had a cookout with some family friends who invited us to visit Grace Baptist Church, and so we did.

In those days Jerry and Jane would make house visits to new church attendees, and I have a vivid memory of Jerry and Jane coming to our house. As a young kid I remember thinking that it was strange, yet a good thing. I had a sense that their visit was different; it caught my attention and made an impression on me. I remember Jerry and Jane praying with our family and that was weird because we never did that besides meals or bedtime, and then we said rehearsed prayers like, *Come Lord Jesus be our guest and let this food to us be blessed. Amen.*

It was completely new to have prayer together in the living room with Jerry and Jane praying over us.

Don't Pray Too Small

Phylis Hessenthaler: Once Pastor Jerry shared with the congregation in a sermon on prayer, "God told me that I pray too small." He shared that after this, he began praying very differently.

I have never forgotten this. Pastor Jerry said he started taking God at his word and praying accordingly. Now, I do too!

"Now to him who is able to do *far more abundantly than all that we ask or think*, according to the power at work within us, to him be glory in the church and in Christ Jesus throughout all generations, forever and ever. Amen" (Eph. 3:20–21 ESV, emphasis added).

He Needed Jesus So Much

Maria Rosa Griffin: Pastor Jerry's example of prayer was so impactful. During church services he would come up front, kneel, and raise his hands. I saw him and watched him, and his example really affected me.

He never tried to get people to think he was more spiritual because he was the pastor or because he was praying more. He always wanted his church to know that he was praying more because he needed Jesus so much.

He Saw Prayer Work

Jack Bell: Pray! Pray! Pray! He flat out did it. I am a disciplined guy, especially when it comes to making disciples and being in the Word, but that deep commitment of Pastor Jerry's to pray, pray, pray has changed me. I now spend a half day a month alone with the Lord to pray Scriptures.

Pastor Jerry saw that prayer worked and he believed that God responds to prayer. I heard him quote Jeremiah 33:3 many times, "Call to me and I will answer you and tell you great and unsearchable things you do not know."

At one of our Elder Board meetings, we told Jerry that we sensed we needed to follow his example and pray for the church and its leaders.

I asked him, "What do you think about the elders taking four or five hours to walk and pray for the church and missionaries?"

He absolutely loved the idea and we went through the church halls and prayed for members, the staff, and all our missionaries. We did this often and saw God work in amazing ways.

Prayer was part of who Pastor Jerry was, and by example, he helped us make it part of who we were as a church. My prayer life does not always measure up with his, but his example as such a deep man of prayer is always in the back of my mind.

The Work Begins With Prayer

Pastor Greg Smith: When I was overseeing the Grace Family Life Ministry, Pastor Jerry had us read and discuss *E.M. Bounds on Prayer.*

He shared with us things about his early years as the pastor of Grace when it was a growing church and how he quickly found himself working like a dog and how he got to a place where he said to himself, *This is all I can do. I have taken this church as far as is humanly possible. The next year must be all God.*

My understanding is that reading that book really firmed up what his ministry rhythms were going to look like. He drew a line in the sand where he said, "I am taking Mondays off, period. I am not coming into the office until the afternoon on Tuesdays, and I am going to commit the morning to prayer—praying over the text I'm preaching on, praying for the church, praying for the staff, and praying for ministry."

This helped Pastor Jerry have a healthy balance—not working one hundred hours per week. That was very impactful for me because I watched Jerry keep that schedule when Grace was a large church with very impactful ministries.

Lots of pastors get stuck in what they can do and do not look at what God can do. They don't recognize that the church is God's, and if he doesn't move, it is going nowhere.

At Grace I was told by leaders, "Go home, chill out, work less."

I don't hear that in the environment I am in now. It is not a bad thing, but it could be a bad thing. Jerry really recognized that God is the one who does the work, and work begins with prayer.

Pastor Jerry Prayer Hour

Nancy Henkel: I would often wake up at four o'clock in the morning. Pastor Jerry taught me to pray when I woke up in the middle of the night. I started calling 4 a.m. the *Pastor Jerry Prayer Hour.* He would say, "Nancy, God is waking you up for a reason. Pray!"

Christmas, Easter, Prayer

Michelle Jenks: During my time at Grace, there were a lot of sound biblical teachings that came from Pastor Jerry, particularly when it came to prayer. He started every new year with a series on prayer. I don't know if he did it throughout his entire career, but certainly throughout the last third of his career.

Prayer was so important to him that he found a way to teach it every single year. Think about that. We talk about Christ coming to earth as a baby every year at Christmas and Christ being crucified every year at Easter. Pastor Jerry wanted to teach us about our connection with Christ through prayer just as often. Sitting under his teaching, you could not help but realize how important prayer was to his faith and to our faith.

His Essence

Geri Baumblatt: We knew we could always count on Pastor Jerry praying; he was a man of prayer. We could call him and ask and he would pray for anything. He emphasized prayer in his sermons, and he made it a central part of every Grace team and committee. He came up with the idea of having the leaders of the church and someone always praying for him. Prayer was his heart, part of him, his essence.

When we were building the new church, I talked with Pastor Jerry about having a prayer room. It is small, but it is there. He always wanted Grace Church to be a house of prayer.

A Hedge of Protection

Tim and Stacie Rush: Whenever Pastor Jerry did child dedications, he would often pray for a hedge of protection over each child. We had never heard this phrase, and through Pastor Jerry's use, it stuck with us and we often use it in our prayers now.

(Author's Note: The phrase "hedge of protection" does not appear in the Bible in this exact way, but the concept is evident throughout Scripture. Job 1:10a reads, "Have you not put a hedge around him and his household and everything he has?")

A Prayer Warrior

Pastor Dan Petersen: Pastor Jerry's godly character flowed out into every aspect of his life, but most of all, it was evident in his devotion to the Lord Jesus and his passion for prayer. The man was a prayer warrior! No decision was ever made that he did not first take to the Lord in prayer.

When You Fast and Pray

Jim and Debbie Arndt: "I can think of so many examples of Pastor Jerry's compassion for and acceptance of all people, his integrity, and his humility. His compassion for me and my family was astounding. We had five to seven very difficult years. Our daughter was engaged once (almost twice) to the same person. It tormented us because we genuinely believed she was not with the right person. A lot of people would say, 'I will pray for you,' but Pastor Jerry and Jane really prayed for us all the time. And they even fasted for us. This made an enormous impact on me," Jim said.

"They actually fasted for one whole week for our decision," Debbie added. "This was when he was retired and at the beginning of his congenital heart failure. Yet, he fasted for us. It touched us in a way that is hard to describe. Jane told me the idea to fast was all Jerry's. He told her, 'Jane, we fast. That is what we do at times like this. We fast.'"

"He practiced what he preached. He did sermons on fasting. How many people fast? We did it because of Pastor Jerry. If he was doing it, we were doing it," Jim said.

"And *fasting* would be one of the words I would use to describe Pastor Jerry to someone," Debbie said.

Apart From Me You Can Do Nothing

Pastor Greg Smith: While I was on staff at Grace, I saw Jerry's drive to make prayer a significant part of the staff and church life.

There was a small group of people who would gather to pray for the church. Jerry also set aside one staff meeting a month for the staff to pray for one another and to pray for the church. He really wanted us to recognize that "apart from me you can do nothing" (John 15:5c).

Praying at a DC Talk Concert

Jeff Stewart: The first time I met Pastor Jerry was at a DC Talk concert at Memorial Hall in downtown Racine. He was there serving on a team that was praying for new believers or anyone who needed prayer. He impressed me as a man of small stature but noticeable integrity and kindness.

He Prayed With Me

Rob Jacobsen: Fifteen years ago, a very good friend of mine was seriously injured at our lake house. I was devastated and met with Pastor Jerry. He prayed with me and helped me. He shared with me a verse from Isaiah: "So do not fear, for I am with you; do not be dismayed, for I am your God. I will strengthen you and help you; I will uphold you with my righteous right hand" (Isa. 41:10).

I memorized that verse and repeated it over and over hundreds of times. I still do.

I have also shared this verse and how Pastor Jerry prayed for me with others who have had challenging times in their lives. They have memorized the verse too and experienced God's help.

Prayer = Essential

Scott Demarest: Pastor Jerry was a man of prayer. He did not necessarily know how God would choose to work, but he knew God would answer prayer, and that it was essential in every situation. He started and ended every meeting with prayer. On occasion he would ask the elders to pause during tough decisions to pray for guidance. This strengthened my own commitment as a leader to bring everything before the Lord in prayer.

Communion With God

Dr. Robert Gullberg: Jerry was regularly in touch with God. I know what his habits were—not in detail like Jane—but I know he spent time in communion with God every day and prayed for hours.

The Lord would speak to him through his study of the Word. Jerry would use the statement, "The Lord is showing me this through the Word and prayer." He was serious about his walk with Christ.

Prayer Peek

Jeff Stewart: I saw the importance of prayer in Pastor Jerry's life and how it was the base of everything he did. I had an inside peek into this on Saturday mornings once a month when I assisted with preparing communion. I would pass by Jerry's office and see him in prayer, sometimes on his knees, as he prepared for the Sunday sermon.

More Than Lip Service

Pastor Chris Amundson: Pastor Jerry had a role in my conversion and his preaching left a lasting mark on me. But what made the biggest impression was how he was disciplined in the essentials. And it wasn't lip service.

When I think of Jerry's shepherding, his value of the discipline of prayer is clear. His relationship with God in prayer was always the driving force in his shepherding. This was very apparent in how he applied and preached on prayer. When he would talk prayer or preach on prayer, there was an air of authority, and it was powerful because everyone knew he did it. Everyone knew: This is a guy who really lives this out. Listen to him!

Any day, if you caught him at the right time, you would catch him praying. He did not make a show of it. His office was just where he prayed and everyone knew it. He was never too busy to pray even as the church grew and doubled in size.

First of All, Pray Cards

Janine Carls: Pastor Jerry often had me laminate the words *First of All, Pray* from 1 Timothy 2:1 on cards as sermon take-away tools for Grace congregants and for use in places where he was a guest speaker on the topic of prayer.

You could find me at Grace on a Saturday morning tending to one thing or another, and I can tell you Pastor Jerry was praying every Saturday. He lived out the words *First of All, Pray.*

Chalk It Up to Prayer

Kirk Ogden: I saw Pastor Jerry's emphasis on prayer throughout his life, but I think it took on the weight of legacy shaping in his years of suffering. There were times when his physical abilities did not reach his desires, yet he kept going. I chalked that up to prayer, love for the Lord, and zeal for the Lord.

During this time, he gave his *First of All, Pray* sermon. We used it at South America Mission and gave out the same cards he gave out at Grace. Now the name of our prayer ministry is *First of All, Pray.*

Always Pray

Pastor Jason Montano: I still have the *First of All, Pray* card Jerry gave to the congregation in my Bible. It was formative to me because it is completely counterintuitive to my personality and leadership style—both of which are counterintuitive to being a disciple of Jesus Christ. For me it is *Last of All, Pray.*

At Mosaic Church, I am committed to dedicating the first month of the year to preaching on prayer because Jerry always did and it changed lives. His message penetrated deeply into our mentality and has so influenced my wife, Kristen, and me that we created a family motto: *Always Pray.*

Our son, Caleb, will text and say, "Dad, can you please pray about...?"

"Absolutely, Caleb," I say. "We *Always Pray.*"

And Jerry did not just teach us random, catchy slogans. He modeled prayer. This is discipleship: "Follow my example, as I follow the example of Christ" (1 Cor. 11:1).

Super busy on Saturdays, I would buzz by his office and see him kneeling in his office, praying. He did what he encouraged his congregation to do, and it still affects me deeply today.

Same Time Without Fail

John Czerwinski: One thing I learned from Jerry that we quote often is, "We don't know how prayer works; we just know it does."

What moves me most to this day are the years of walking through the Grace Church offices as we wrapped up our worship rehearsals on Saturday mornings. Pastor Jerry was always in his office kneeling in prayer. Every Saturday. Same time. Without fail. Always there. His dependence on the Lord was so evident.

Go Deeper and Higher

Michele Gipp: Pastor Jerry was faithfully part of every Thursday noon prayer meeting, corporate prayer meeting, and special staff prayer times. He was always challenging us to go deeper and higher with the Lord through prayer.

Nighttime Prayer

Jessica Schultz: I remember Pastor Jerry telling staff how he was often awakened in the middle of the night to pray for his children or grandchildren. Once he told me he was praying fervently during the night for one of his daughters. In the morning when he called her, she was in great distress. I do not remember the details, but I was amazed at how God worked and used Pastor Jerry in this way.

Emulate Jerry and Know You're Following Christ

Phil Adams: I don't know how many hours Pastor Jerry was up praying before everyone else or how much he was in the Word. These were primary and organic for him. In every case by watching him, I saw it was important to pray. You could emulate Jerry and know that you were following Christ. This is an exceedingly high order.

For all the years I knew him, he was on his knees praying before meetings. On Wednesday mornings with Dr. Don Cohill, they would pray for hours. On Sundays our Worship Team would get to Grace at 6:30 a.m., and he was already in his office praying on his knees.

Sometimes life crowds out spiritual disciplines and you need a person to push you. I learned from Pastor Jerry that if you want a deep prayer life, you must just keep going at it.

Once I had a severe infection in my leg. Dr. Cohill was my doctor and it was so bad, he thought he would have to remove my leg. He and Jerry prayed through the night for me. If they hadn't prayed, I really believe my leg would have had to come off. This was the kind of prayer life Pastor Jerry had.

Remember the Basics

Don Amundson: Every January Pastor Jerry preached a series on prayer. He kept repeating these messages on prayer because everyone needs to remember the basics. He needed to repeat because we needed to hear.

Never Fancy

Yvonne Manning: Pastor Jerry was always so gracious when our Worship Team sang. His face would get a crinkled look, and he would say, "I really feel the Holy Spirit when you sing."

He would pray for us before we led worship. He would say just a few words, never fancy, just genuine and straight forward. It was clear he wanted nothing but God's presence and glory in the service.

Prayer Was Our Dialect

Chuck Dumars: Grace was neither a church of prayer, a house of prayer, nor a strong praying church when I first arrived in 1978, but it became one.

In the years I served on the Elder Council, our ministry initiatives were biblically focused and the dialect we communicated in best was prayer. Pastor Jerry laid the groundwork for all of this, and prayer was the spiritual breath we began to breathe. As we grew in prayer, we grew in evangelism.

Pastor Jerry also had the elders take turns praying for the offering and for communion. In this way, the congregation was tutored in prayer through dozens of different examples throughout the calendar year.

A Man in the Corner Praying

Amy Mathew: Although I never sat under Pastor Jerry's direct pastoral teaching, he still taught me lessons by how he lived his life and how he prayed.

Pastor Jerry and I first served together on a Grace prayer ministry called the Prayer Furnace. I remember walking into the prayer room and noticing a man I had never met on his knees in the corner. He was truly, fervently praying for Grace Church. When someone told me that he was the retired pastor, I was humbled that he was still dedicating his time to care for and pray for the church.

He was fully dependent on prayer and no matter what the answer, he knew God was in control. By watching him and getting to know him during his retirement years as we served together in additional prayer ministries, I learned to focus on prayer—he taught me to pray, let go, and put my faith in Christ. He never made it seem like he was a "better prayer" than anyone else. He encouraged, welcomed, and was always ready to pray.

During a Convoy of Hope event in Racine, I was in the prayer tent with Pastor Jerry and Jane. I got to sit and talk with him about his passion for helping the community know Christ. As I watched him interact with people, it was clear this was his heart. He welcomed everyone into the tent, prayed over those sent his way, and shared the gospel with everyone. He had a smile that never disappeared, despite the long, warm, and tiring day.

I am grateful that God brought us together, even if it was for a brief time.

Jerry Wasn't a Starving Baker

Pastor Greg Smith: Dr. Tim Elmore wrote a series of books called *Habitudes*®.[11] His first book is on the art of self-leadership, and he uses the example of a starving baker. The starving baker's bakery is quickly becoming known in town as the place for the best bread you'll ever taste. Soon, the baker is barely sleeping, working all day, making bread for others; but in the meantime, he is killing himself, withering away.

Jerry was not the starving baker. Jerry had intimate, deep prayer times with the Lord that fed him; and because of this communion, what he shared was fresh.

The Sacrificial Life

Joan Gorton: A sacrificial life is what we are called to as Christians. And we saw the sacrificial life in the way Jerry ministered and shepherded. When he preached on fasting, the focus was not on refraining from eating, but instead his emphasis was on praying.

"Pray first" was his motto and I still have a card he gave out during a sermon on the side of my refrigerator. That sermon's emphasis on prayer has influenced me immensely throughout the years, especially

---

[11] Habitudes® is a breakthrough way to teach leadership principles to the post-modern student.

in praying for family members. I pray consistently in front of them and with them in hopes that they would pray before every decision they make.

I also take Jerry's motto as a challenge for how to start my day. I set aside morning time to pray first.

I Knew What to Do

Karen Smith: In his later years, Pastor Jerry talked about praying a lot because he was not able to sleep. This struck me and stuck with me. It helped me in my own times of suffering. I knew what to do—pray—because that is what Pastor Jerry did.

The Prayers of the Saints Carried Him

Jane Worsham: Jerry shared openly about his struggles. God used the prayers of the saints to get him through the ups and downs of life and church ministry, his worry, his pride, and his health struggles. Even as top tier medications and procedures for his heart issues kept slowing him down, he pushed forward by God's grace.

Planted by God to Pray

Chris Booth: On September 8, 2005, I went to visit Pastor Jerry in the hospital after he had a stroke. While I was by his bedside, I recognized he was having another stroke and dropped to my knees and prayed. It was a special God assignment. I never got over it and neither did Jerry; he often referred to the way God placed me in his room to pray at just the right time.

We Prayed Like He Taught Us

Craig Vaughn: In 2005 Jerry was hospitalized after having two strokes, and I gathered the elders together for an impromptu meeting at [Grace attender] John Henkel's office. I remember watching the other elders walking in one by one. There was a somber mood and many men were in tears. We did not know if Pastor Jerry was going to make it through these strokes. His condition was very serious.

We joined in a circle like we had during many elder meetings in Jerry's basement. We started singing praises, and we were on our knees praying and pleading with the Lord for Jerry's recovery. Then we had a discussion on next steps, contingency plans, and what ifs.

Meanwhile, the whole church was praying for Pastor Jerry including a twenty-four-hour prayer vigil. He was so admired and respected by other pastors, that they put him on their church prayer chains as word got out.

God heard our prayers; the next morning he was alert and asking for the newspaper and coffee!

He Set the Bar High

Pastor Isaac Miller: Pastor Jerry's commitment to prayer was one of those bars that was set high. When I am convicted of my lack of prayer at times, Pastor Jerry and his commitment to prayer pops into my mind. It is clear he was at the place and in the position he was in because of his dependence on God and his commitment to regular prayer.

Praise as a Weapon

Terry Kultgen: The Apostle Paul says to pray continually (1 Thess. 5:17). How in the world can you pray continually?

The only way you can do it is if your life is a prayer, and Jerry's life was a prayer. He knew how to praise and how to use praise as a weapon. When praise becomes your weapon, you speak differently, you pray differently, and your prayers are powerful.

Jerry impacted thousands of people in many ways and in various degrees through prayer and teaching the importance of prayer.

His Prayers Were Clear

Jane Worsham: After Jerry's two brain surgeries, if he was asked a direct question, he could not answer. He knew the answers in his mind but could not give them aloud, and conversation was difficult too. This is called aphasia and occurred because the language part of his brain was damaged in surgery performed to remove an abscess. This abscess had to be treated or it would have been fatal.

Even so, Jerry loved to pray. And as he did, often his words freely flowed. When missionaries and friends would stop at our home to see him, he would struggle to communicate with them, but when he prayed for them as they left, his speech was nearly perfect. He would look at me as if to say, "Jane, I did it!" He knew it was a miracle from God to bless all of us. One of our grandsons, Caleb, observed that if prayer was involved, Grandpa's speech was almost flawless.

He Linked Himself to My Ministry

Pastor Mike Matheson: I think Jerry's service on my [lead pastor] Prayer Shield was the piece that really opened our relationship. It was no longer just him popping into my office now and then and giving me his opinion, it was him deliberately linking himself to me and my ministry by praying for me. When that happens, it forms a certain kind of relationship between people. I think there were times, through prayer, that he would discern situations and he would ask me about them.

It was a huge blessing to have Jerry and Jane shielding me. They did not need to do that! They could have just as easily said "no" to serving me and Grace Church this way and no one would have blamed them. It was a significant ministry to me, and it was a huge encouragement to know they were in my corner. But I did not just need cheerleaders. They were on their knees, setting aside time to pray for me and my ministry.

Best Way to Spend Your Time

Jane Worsham: Jerry faithfully spent time in the Word daily using his favorite devotionals, reading through the Bible in a year, or by reading through books of the Bible slowly. Meditation and prayer were important to him, and his sermon ideas often stemmed from his quiet times with God. Jerry had a prayer routine that he fervently maintained until the end of his life. It included:

- **Daily**: family and family needs
- **Monday**: life groups, church staff, Grace needs
- **Tuesday**: extended family and neighbors
- **Wednesday**: those in authority, government (national, state, local), South America Mission board, Grace elders
- **Thursday**: individual needs and intercession
- **Friday**: missionaries
- **Saturday**: churches (local, United States connections, global, persecuted)

Each of these categories had lists of people and needs under them. Jerry had it so memorized that when he could no longer read following his brain surgeries, he continued to pray as fervently and even more fervently than ever before.

He spent so much time in worship and prayer the last two years of his life in our home, on our patio, or out in nature. His times with God always ended with his arms lifted high. There was so much he couldn't do, but he focused on what he could do and that was to pray. He was a blessing and beautiful example of allowing God to bring good and joy out of great loss. I learned so much from him, and I witnessed the reality and genuineness of his walk with Christ. There is absolutely nothing more important that he could have done for all of us than spend time in the Word of God and in prayer!

Chapter 4

THE MARK OF PREACHING AND TEACHING: Not by Bread Alone

Preach the word; be prepared in season and out of season; correct, rebuke and encourage— with great patience and careful instruction.

2 TIMOTHY 4:2

If Pastor Jerry were here right now, he would tell you that he did not think he was the greatest preacher, but that he was faithful to the text and diligently prayed and prepared his sermons.

His messages stuck with people because he made difficult topics and words easy to understand and digest. He repeated concepts he wanted his congregation to internalize, and he was clear. Very, very clear.

In the early years of his pastorate, his preaching was a bit more confrontational and his later preaching years were characterized by gentleness and love. In this way Jerry reminds me of the Apostle John, whom Jesus deemed one of the two "sons of thunder" in Mark 3:17. John, too, mellowed with age and used terms of endearment like "my dear children and dear friends" (see 1 John 2) when addressing those he taught.

He Helped Mom

Ralph "Easy" Worsham: Scripture was everything to Jerry. He always tried to counsel us and others. Our mom could speak English, but it was not her first language.

I remember in our kitchen Mom had a stand on which she would put recipes. One day I came up into the house from the carport, and there was a Bible on that stand. Jerry, who was a freshman in high school, was reading to Mom from it, explaining it, and interpreting it for her.

He never said, "Mom you are doing it wrong." He would say, "This is what I think Jesus was saying." He was very polite and loving.

Mom was saved, but the English language gave her trouble. Jerry later found and bought her a Spanish Bible to help her.

Radio Devotions

Lorain Worsham Evans: Our grandparents lived in San Augustine, Texas, and our dad would work for three full years without a vacation so he could accumulate enough vacation days to take off three months in the summer to take us to the United States. While we were vacationing, we rented a house right across the street from our grandpa, Virgil Worsham. Our grandma had died earlier.

The church we attended while we were in San Augustine had a radio station affiliate. Jerry, a recent high-school graduate, got really involved in the church. They recognized his giftings and invited him to come on the radio and lead devotions and teach. He absolutely loved this.

He Put His Heart and Soul Into the Preparation

Allan Hesters: In the summer of 1967, Jerry was attending Asbury College and was visiting his parents (and Jane, I am sure) in Panama.

We were serving as staff for a church camp in Santa Clara, Panama. I am not sure how it came about, but Jerry was asked to deliver the sermon that Sunday. I believe it was his first "from scratch" sermon. He put his heart and soul into the preparation and did a fantastic job. One of our adult leaders, Reverend Gustafson, complimented him afterward. You could sense even then that this was the first of many sermons to come.

A Life Changed

Fay Clark: Before Jerry Worsham was the Grace Baptist Church pastor, he was a youth minister in the only civilian church in the world located on a military installation. More than fifty years ago, Pastor Jerry and his bride, Jane, were at Curundu Protestant Church [now Crossroads Church] in the Canal Zone at a crossroads in my life.

Through his preaching and teaching, the soil of my thirteen-year-old heart was plowed. The Word he helped plant in my heart germinated, grew, and is bearing fruit for Christ. I am a life that was changed through Jerry giving himself to the work of the Lord.

Life and Death

Pastor Kent Carlson: I have memories of Jerry up front in the sanctuary preaching. I enjoyed the meticulous way his sermons were put together. I was being trained by watching his faithful and diligent preparation, his logic, and his consistency. I remember who he was so much more than the things he preached.

Every week he would get up there, preach his heart out, give an altar call inviting people to come forward and follow Christ, and pray. It was life and death to him, and he would have the most anguished face when he prayed.

I remember Jane talking to him and saying, "Jerry you've got to quit looking so serious and smile more."

Sovereignty of God

Pastor Mike Lueken: Whenever Jerry preached or talked about the sovereignty of God[12] it was clear he had a conviction seeped deep within him that God ruled over everything because he was sovereign: God was aware of everything, had power over everything, and everything was going to work out in God's time and in his way.

Jerry's firm belief in God's sovereignty was rooted in his own recognition of the frailty of life. It was evident that he lived the truth he believed when he sought God's will as he struggled with worry, control, and all his health issues.

He drove home the message of God's sovereignty to his congregation because he wanted people who were hurting and suffering and going through hard things to lay them down at the feet of a God who was able.

The Word Is the Power

Pastor Jason Esposito: Jerry was a solid preacher. He did not try to dazzle. He was just real, consistent, and authentic. The Jerry you saw preaching was the Jerry in the pew and the Jerry in the office and the Jerry in his home.

He was a very meat and potatoes preacher, and that is positive. You will always get naysayers about certain preaching styles. Listeners don't always need to have an ah-ha moment in a message.

Preaching on the shepherds during the Christmas season, I found myself thinking, *I must find the angle.* Jerry would say, "No. Just preach the Word. The Word is the power."

---

[12] The *Holman Bible Dictionary* defines the sovereignty of God as "the teaching that all things come from and depend on God." The *Easton's Bible Dictionary* defines it as God's "absolute right to do all things according to his good pleasure." Pastor Jerry defined it as: "God is in control and is working. He is all powerful, wise, loving, and is working for our good."

I Heard, I Received, I Could Apply

Pastor Jason Montano: We first attended Grace Church when the new building had just opened. My family lived in Waukesha, Wisconsin; I had just graduated from Trinity; and Kristen, my wife, said: "We'll move here," pointing to Racine on a map.

I grew up in southeastern Wisconsin, and I was like: *Racine?* I had no desire to live in Racine!

At that time, I was the typical, "I love Jesus, but I'm done with church" guy.

"Well, we really need to go to church," Kristen said.

"I am not going," I said. But she was very insistent, so I finally agreed. Grace was near where we were living, so we went to a service.

I remember so vividly hearing Pastor Jerry speak the first time. He was clear. His words made sense. He spoke and I could hear, receive, and apply immediately.

"I have never heard anybody like that," I said to Kristen.

Looking back, that comment is interesting because Jerry was not a dynamic preacher by any means in terms of dynamic by today's standards.

Yet, for the first time in a very long time, I was hungry to come to church and take notes. I would complete the inserts from the worship bulletin, and I would use them for my personal study time. I had a three-ring binder, and I kept all my notes.

I had super strong faith in high school. I was in a public school, and I had to live out my faith. Then I went to Trinity and my faith got rocked, my church split, and I had a crisis of faith. Jerry Worsham brought back everything to me that I had lost.

Pretty soon I was telling Kristen, "We have to go to church on Sunday!" Kristen loved it too and was growing.

He Lived It

Debbie Arndt: *Bible* would be a word I would use to describe Pastor Jerry because the Bible is what he lived. He lived every part of it until the day he died. Nothing speaks louder or stronger than that.

In his retirement years his health was failing, yet he was at church every week in the balcony, meeting new people, asking everyone how they were doing, and hugging people. What speaks of living out God's Word more than how you live your everyday life even when you are suffering?

I Made Homelife a Priority

Nan Arnone: Jerry's preaching had an enormous impact on me as a wife and mother. I intentionally dedicated my time and talents to our homelife and made it my priority. As our son grew older, I was able to spend my time serving the women at Grace through various teaching, writing, and prayer ministries.

Giant Man of God

Al Boscha: Pastor Jerry's life can be compared to a cottonwood tree planted by a stream. The tree had a huge canopy of branches and leaves under which many people sat and were taught God's Word. The roots run deep and spread. The stream of living water continuously nourished them. They held the tree firm as the storms of life came and went. The tree gave off many seeds, which were carried by a rushing wind. They were scattered around the world, creating more life.

Pastor Jerry Worsham was a giant man of God, and he made a profound impact for him.

Duty to Be Joyful

Pastor Rusty Hayes: If you asked Billy Graham about himself, he probably would have said, "I'm just a country preacher." But there was an anointing on him. Jerry would have probably said something similar about himself, but he had an anointing from the Lord too. It was very special and very unusual.

Delighting in God was a frequent theme of his sermons. "As a Christian you have a duty to be joyful," he told us.

I thought it was such a strange way to say this, and that statement really stuck with me.

I Want to Suggest ...

Jerry Morrison: As a believer from age twelve and a Bible teacher, I was surprised at how much I grew under Pastor Jerry's ministry and preaching. His sermons were so simple, short, and to the point, yet powerful and applicable. He had several main points, and always ended with, "I want to suggest to you...." He made his applications through this phrase. He did not ram the application down throats; he suggested that we take in what he had preached and make it a part of how we lived.

A Message for Everyone

Terry Kultgen: Even though I believe I made a genuine confession of faith in 1977 during a Billy Graham crusade, I had no Christian friends, I wasn't reading the Word, and my life spiraled out of control. It was like a train wreck. I started using alcohol, and my wife, Deb, and I separated.

I got invited to go to Grace Baptist and that was the first time I encountered Pastor Jerry. I snuck into the church and went to the back row to be able to get out quickly. Deb had been attending Grace, and Jerry and Jane were discipling her and praying for our marriage.

(Author's note: Debbie shared that throughout their seven-year sep-aration, she and Terry would go out on dates or be together and have an enjoyable time, but Terry just could not come home. Jerry and Jane coun-seled her to "kill him with kindness," something she said she had the ability to do with her personality.)

When I saw Jerry I thought, *Who's the little guy up front?* Then Jerry started preaching. I wasn't familiar with a Protestant service. He had no robe on or anything to distinguish him. I am an emotional per-son and as the service went on, I thought, *What in the world is going on?* I was really affected by his preaching. I knew two men who were attend-ing service that day, so my plan to get out of church without anyone seeing me failed. They simply told me they were glad to see me.

Several weeks later I went back to Grace to investigate the emo-tional response I had to Jerry's words. I felt Jerry was preaching just to me. I asked Deb, "What are you telling him about me, that he is speak-ing so personally to me?"

Finally, one Sunday I told Deb, "I think I want to go talk to Pastor Jerry."

It was my first real introduction to Jerry Worsham. I wanted to know more about what he was talking about in his messages. I told him how I thought he was speaking just to me.

"A lot of people feel that way," he told me. "The message is not just for one person but for everybody."

After I got to know him, I learned I was emotional during his preaching because the Holy Spirit was transforming me to see things through a new lens.

Glistening Integrity Graced His Life

Bob Magruder: Pastor Jerry sought to be a holy vessel in the hands of Almighty God. He knew instinctively that he was not a sil-ver-tongued orator, but he also knew this was not the most important thing for ministry. It is highly overrated, if not all together exaggerated. The most important thing for ministry is a pure heart and a praying spirit. Jerry was deeply blessed with both. These two attributes working in concert formed the glistening integrity that graced his life. How refreshing it is when you meet someone so incredibly good. Jerry was an extremely good man. And contrary to popular opinion, it is not boring to be good; it is exhilarating. Goodness ignites power for living. Jerry was effective in ministry because he was genuinely good. And this goodness flowed from his integrity. And of course, his integrity flowed from the Lord Jesus Christ.

His impact on my life will never recede or diminish with time. He has unknowingly secured the unending respect of countless multitudes. He was a true man of God of the highest order.

Seized Heads and Hearts

Dr. Robert Gullberg: In my twenty-five years under Pastor Jerry's leading, he had a huge influence on me as a believer, and I grew a ton in my walk with Christ. He taught me the Word. I was a note taker, and Jerry encouraged that. I have attention-deficit/hyperactivity disorder (ADHD), so I needed to take notes, or my mind would have gone everywhere. I took sermon notes during his entire career and authored a book on them called, *Wisdom from the Word: A reference with 700 unique topics to enhance Bible Study for students and teachers.*

He and I would talk about his sermons afterward. It was not formal; it was just casual. I loved and appreciated the way he orchestrated his sermons over the years. He did sermons on prayer, the Old Testament, the New Testament, and worship, rotating things year in and year out. He was a wonderful teacher, and he simplified the gospel—never dumbed it down—and made it very palatable. He did not do the "fire and brimstone" type of preaching much when I was at Grace, instead he focused on the grace and love of God.

He always thought about what would be helpful to the flock in his sermons. He had an ability to encourage people in the Word but not get so intellectual. God used his preaching to seize heads and hearts. I love storytelling, and Pastor Jerry was excellent at telling God's story. He was also good with respectfully incorporating Jane and his family into his preaching. We knew him as the proud husband, dad, and grandpa. He was never afraid to let us see the flawed human side of himself.

What I Learned About Being a Wife, Mother, and Pastor's Wife

Jane Worsham: Some of the biggest lessons I learned about being a wife, mother, and pastor's wife came from Jerry's preaching. He taught me:

- The sovereignty of God rules.

- God sits on the throne in the center of the universe.

- The purposeful hand of our sovereign God is always at work.

- The key is God's glory—always!

- A strong marriage is made of two strong people each giving 100 percent.

- The best thing you can do for your kids is to have a thriving marriage.

- God works best in our brokenness and can give us joy.

- Celebrate and worship God. He alone is worthy.

- Nothing will defeat Jesus. Death is conquered in his resurrection.

- *First of All, Pray.*

- When we are weak, he is strong.

- Be generous.

Not Like Pastor Jerry Did

Patti Booth: When we moved to Racine, we settled on attending Grace because of the way Pastor Jerry preached. At that time, the church had a choir and an organ. We had none of that in Texas or Wheaton, Illinois, where we had previously lived. Our other churches both taught God's Word and people carried notebooks and pencils to write down what they were learning. These were sound Bible churches, but they did not teach the way Jerry did.

Pastor Jerry had a great love for God's Word. My teaching at Bible Study Fellowship [as the Racine class teaching leader] was a lot like his. His illustrations were easy to follow and stemmed from God's Word. He had us open the Word. He was simple, yet deep. You always came away with a strong message and something to apply. His sermons were not just giving a talk on the passage and us walking out. He always wanted us to apply, apply, apply!

God Was Cementing His Grace in My Life

Jack Bell: I will never forget a sermon Pastor Jerry preached when we were at the old church on Northwestern Avenue on the topics of grace and truth because I was really struggling.

I had just started a study of Galatians, and what Pastor Jerry said made so much sense to me. He talked about the Pharisees and teachers of the Law of Moses and how they were all about the truth of Scripture. He told us that people usually fell into one of two camps—they are either all about grace or all about truth.

He said, "You know, Jesus was always all about both grace and truth. Keep in mind that wherever you are serving God, you can beat people over the head with the Scriptures, but you really need to season your ministry with grace."

As a leader, it was helpful for me to think about grace and truth this way. I learned that it was not about how many Bible verses I could spout off which I was good at and which got people's attention in the church. It was a critical lesson for me, a time when God was cementing his grace in my life.

Names of God

Pastor Jason Montano: Jerry did a sermon series on the names of God. At that time, I had never heard anything like it. His explanations were influential in helping me identify who God is. Like everything, he made the names very concrete and easy to understand. My wife, Kristen, and I now have a big picture hanging in our home listing the names of God.

What Are You Doing With Jesus?

Pastor Dave and Mary Kehrli: On Easter morning 1981 we first walked through the doors of Grace Baptist Church. It was a warm, welcoming place where the Bible was being preached. The people were friendly and genuine, not afraid to reach out to a young couple who had no idea that they needed a life with Jesus. One message came through: *What are you doing with Jesus?*

In July 1982 during Pastor Jerry's sermon, the Holy Spirit was convicting us of our need to trust in the Lord for forgiveness of our sins. In the quietness of our hearts, we accepted the gift of salvation God offered to us. We were both baptized the next month.

Soon after, Jane and Jerry started us on a discipleship process. We met in their dining room and went through a book series entitled, *Operation Timothy.*[13] This series kick-started our growth in Christ followed by involvement in Sunday school, small groups, mission teams, and serving as a deaconess and elder.

---

[13] *Operation Timothy (OT)* is a relational disciple-making tool. Pastor Jerry used the two OT books to help people grow spiritually. The original version of *OT* was published in 1970. For more information visit www.cbmc.com.

Jerry and Jane were our spiritual parents, and they knew of our pregnancies and our two sons' births as soon as our natural parents did. Jerry dedicated and baptized both our boys.

Jerry also helped us discern God's calling on our lives to serve full-time as missionaries. This came about after the Holy Spirit used another one of Pastor Jerry's Sunday sermons, and he suggested we check out a mission group he was familiar with from his days growing up in Panama called HCJB.[14] We checked them out and they were a perfect match for us.

When we left the mission field in 2002, Jerry and another pastor at Grace helped guide our re-entry back into life in the United States by inviting [Dave] to become Grace's mission pastor. During this time, I was ordained as a pastor with the North American Baptist Conference under Jerry's guidance and mentoring.

Later we returned to Grace after pastoring another church for ten years, and I was asked to lead the seniors' ministry. Pastor Jerry wrote me a glowing letter of recommendation. He included details that even we barely remembered. It's amazing that Pastor Jerry had the same involvement with so many other people he shepherded as he did with us. We thank Jerry for giving to the Lord. Our lives were changed.

Look What God Did

Lori Vaughn: From the pulpit Pastor Jerry spoke truth and his humility was amazing. When a church grows from 300 to 1,200 attendees, many pastors might say, "Look at what I did!"

Jerry never puffed himself up nor wanted people to look at him. His message was always, "Look at what God has done!" He always pointed the glory back to Christ.

---

[14] HCJB stands for Heralding Christ Jesus' Blessings. It started as a radio ministry and branched out to health care and community development.

How Many Times Do We Hear and Not Act?

Debbie Palmer: One of Pastor Jerry's sermons stressed that when the Holy Spirit tells you to do something you need to do it, to act.

One morning I was getting ready for the day and the Holy Spirit brought some words from Pastor Jerry's sermon back to me. I had a friend in the hospital who had cancer, and it was clear God wanted me to go and see her. When I got there, I encountered lots of obstacles just to get into her room. And once I was in, it was quite an ordeal! The phone kept ringing, people kept interrupting our conversation, and there were lots of distractions, but I just kept on telling her about Jesus because of Jerry's sermon. I shared with her and prayed with her and she accepted Christ. Afterward I told the doctor who said he had been praying for someone to come and share Christ with her because he could not in his position.

How many times do we hear and not act? God used Pastor Jerry's sermon to make the difference between life and death for my friend.

Preaching Calendar

Pastor Rusty Hayes: Jerry had biblical values that he thought Grace Church should be organized around: worshipping, caring, reaching out, learning, and praying. He would incorporate these values into preaching themes and would come back to the themes throughout the year. He would preach a theological series, one expository series from the Old Testament and the New Testament, a topical series on things like marriage or parenting, and then he would mix in sermons on the biblical values.

Jerry challenged the "expository preaching only" mindset; he believed there were times a congregation needed to hear from God on a particular topic. He would pray and ask the Lord, "What are some topics my congregation needs to hear from you on?"

His preaching calendar was an effective way to organize things because it allowed him to deal in real time with what people were experiencing. He was very instrumental in how I plan out my annual preaching calendar.

Jerry's Preaching Style

Pastor Jason Montano: Pastor Jerry's preaching was always so clear, and this is the greatest compliment.

My preaching style is different than Jerry's, but my methodology is similar: I take my congregation back to the culture and history to make the text clear and understandable. I compare Pastor Jerry's preaching to news reporting. He would go through the who, what, when, where, how, and why, so we could hear the intent of the text, internalize it, leave church understanding it, and go and tell others.

He Had a Whole Talk Prepared

Jen Binkley (Worsham): When I was planning my wedding to John, I knew I did not want my dad to marry us and be the pastor that day. I just wanted him to be my dad. So, Rusty Hayes married us. When Rusty asked who was giving me away, my dad just couldn't say "her mother and me." He took the microphone and had a whole talk prepared!

Will They Know You Are Christians By Your Home?

Dr. Paul Durbin: "If a person walked into your home, would they know it to be a Christian home?" Pastor Jerry asked during one of his sermons.

I would admit my wife, Jen, and I were secular in our thinking when we first started attending Grace. We had parties where alcohol was served; we had decorations up that were very secular. One decoration was this incredible picture of The Beatles that we bought in Door County, Wisconsin. This beautiful picture of the four of them was the first thing you saw when you came into our home. My wife and I were convicted by Jerry's sermon and realized that if someone walked into our home, they would have no idea that we were Christians. Well, down came The Beatles picture that we loved, and we replaced it with a Psalm print. Also, we stopped serving alcohol at gatherings we hosted.

If you walk into our home today, you will see many scripture verses, crosses, and Christian symbols adorning our walls. You will know we are a Christian family without us ever opening our mouths. Jen and I feel this honors God. We are so thankful that Pastor Jerry communicated God's truth to us.

(Author's Note: Dr. Paul Durbin is now a Grace Church elder.)

No In-Between

Joe Kobriger: Pastor Jerry shared in many of his sermons about his struggles with anxiety and worry. Of course, I wasn't happy he struggled, but his sharing made me more comfortable with how I struggle. Oh, how I miss him!

I also remember him saying many times that there are no grey areas when it comes to God's truth. There is black. There is white. There is right. There is wrong. There is holiness. There is evil. There is no in-between.

A Workman Approved

George Gorton: One Sunday in church listening to Pastor Jerry preach I thought, *He is a workman approved.* A workman is someone who rightly divines the Word of Truth and this is important. Pastor Jerry would say something and then quote Scripture. He spoke and lived out the Word of God.

I Was Poured Into So I Could Pour Out

Debbie Palmer: We were attending another Racine church and my kids were bored teenagers. We would come home and they would not even know what the sermon was about. When we went to Grace, they sat in the pews engaged.

Pastor Jerry shaped the church to apply and carry the messages that he gave on Sundays throughout the week. No matter what he taught, we could hold it and use it. He changed many lives, and he changed my life week by week through his preaching.

He also lived what he preached. He taught us all to go the extra mile, to be kind, to be good examples. I would talk to people during the week about what Pastor Jerry taught me on Sunday. I was poured into so I could pour out into others. Pastor Jerry's preaching met me where I was at and filled a hole deep inside of me.

Packers Game Starts at Noon

Larry and Maggie White: "I remember one time when we were at the old church and Pastor Jerry was getting ready to get up to preach. I was sitting right behind him, and I asked him, 'This isn't going to be a long sermon, is it?' Then I wrote him a note that said, 'Packers game starts at noon' and slid it on top of his Bible.

"When he got up to the pulpit he said, 'I just got a note that said the Packers game is starting at noon. I want you all to know you will be late.'

"There was nothing I could do," joked Larry. "He was already up front."

"What is ironic about that story," Maggie added, "is we told Pastor Jerry that when we were at another church they would shorten the sermon for any reason, a birthday party, a game, whatever. Pastor Jerry said there was nothing more important than the sermon and the preaching of the Word of God because it is what changes lives."

His Preaching Bridged Cultures

Pastor Jason Montano: Jerry gave the staff Randy Alcorn's book *The Grace and Truth Paradox,* and it was the most influential book he ever gave me. He often preached on these topics; and I learned from him that you could be full of both grace and truth because Jesus was both.

Jerry was a master at making topics like grace and truth, which seemed so far off and difficult to grasp, understandable and applicable.

In my preaching class, our professor taught us that our job as preachers is to take people over a bridge and into a 2,000-year-old, non-existent culture and immerse them in it so they can experience it. Then we are to give them a souvenir to take home with them to their world. The souvenir must help them make sense of that 2,000-year-old, non-existent culture so they can share it with others.

This is what Jerry did. He bridged cultures in his preaching, which is one reason why he influenced so many people from the pulpit. Stylistically, he wasn't dynamic except when he would go bounce on his toes on the edge of the stage! There were thousands of more interesting speakers, but because I knew he cared, I cared what he knew.

He Helped Us Remember God's Word

Craig Vaughn: I grew up in the church and came to know Christ at an early age. When my wife, Lori, and I moved to Racine and became members of Grace, my faith kicked into another category under Pastor Jerry's shepherding.

His preaching was different than what I was accustomed to, and I was challenged to get to another level in my spiritual walk. This was a game changer for me in many respects.

Years later when Jerry and I were talking about one of his sermons, he said to me, "Well, my preaching is just okay. I give it a C."

Jerry was not a flashy guy; he was not going to get up there and hit it out of the park like some top presenter. He did everything with acronyms, three T's, or three P's, or whatever to help us remember. What was beautiful about his preaching style was the content and the heart behind it.

He impacted many people through his "Grace and Truth" sermon. He told us we are not 50 percent grace and 50 percent truth, but we are 100 percent of both grace and truth. To this day my family challenges me with his sermon. They say, "Dad, you are more truth. You are supposed to be 100 percent of both grace and truth."

I was just having lunch with a guy at Olive Garden and told him how the restaurant reminded me of Pastor Jerry because he preached on God's grace. Jerry said from pulpit, "God's grace is like the bread sticks at Olive Garden; they just keep coming and coming and coming."

Pastor Jerry, of course, was being humorous, but it was something to help us remember the nature of God's grace. He then developed his point further by saying, "Imagine you are at a beach. You are watching the waves hit the shore and go back out and hit the shore and go back out. The waves will never stop coming in and going out. This is a picture of God's grace. It just keeps coming."

Heaven

Pastor Danny D'Acquisto: There were a few weighty topics that gripped Pastor Jerry's life. He gave most of his life to thinking about, preaching, and teaching on those topics.

I remember a series he did on heaven, and I remember him talking a lot about a book on heaven by Randy Alcorn. Along with the driving forces in his life of prayer and dependence on God, I think he also really had a heart of longing to be with Christ. And that really shined through.

He Diligently Prepared

Pastor Isaac Miller: In his preaching, Jerry communicated well with the people, and it was not overly emotional. Some preachers are explosive and command attention. In demeanor and in his choice of words, you could tell he had diligently prepared to bring the Word of God to the congregation. He had a purposeful preparedness about him and specificity with his words.

A Plainspokenness

Pastor Chris Amundson: When I heard a sermon from Jerry, it always really resonated. He had a plainspokenness about him, much more than I was used to at other churches. He used a lot of illustrations in his preaching, and I remember being really engaged as a kid; his illustrations helped me grasp things. In fact, I think in illustrations today more than the rest of the Grace staff because of Jerry. I soaked in what he did; and when I went into ministry, I realized you need great illustrations to get people's attention on what you are talking about. Illustrations connect the text and the content to what you are teaching about and this is important for your audience.

His Sermons Were Like a Basketball Clinic

Jim Kerkvliet: I was inspired by Pastor Jerry's Sunday sermons. I would frequently rush to the information table to get cassette tapes of the messages. In my early years as a basketball coach, I attended many basketball clinics and took detailed notes on effective coaching techniques. Pastor Jerry's sermons were like a basketball clinic, but instead of coaching techniques, I was learning how to follow Jesus.

As the [Washington] Park High School girls' basketball head coach, I discovered that I had been narcissistic in my dealings with players, other coaches, parents, and the media. I walked around with loads of pride. At that time, I put my heart and soul into coaching basketball. I wanted the players to put forth great mental and physical effort to be better than their opponents. Our Park girls' basketball team eventually began to experience success, and the more success we experienced, the more my narcissistic traits increased. I became obsessed with the sports section newspaper articles about our games, and I would get upset when I thought that a cross-town rival was getting more coverage than my team.

It was interesting to discover that when my narcissistic traits diminished, the basketball program had more post-season success. I learned to give God the glory instead of taking all the credit.

Reflecting on those times, I appreciate the access that I had to Pastor Jerry. I could listen to his message on a Sunday, I could listen to the message again with a cassette tape, and then I could listen to his instruction and comments during our couples' Bible study. I felt comfortable enough to be able to give him a call when I was struggling with something, and he instructed me about the danger of comparing myself with other people. Over time, the way I compared myself to rival coaches gradually shifted toward increased humility, and I even learned to share some responsibilities with my assistant coaches.

During the 1996–97 basketball season, the Park High School girls' basketball team was making its third state tournament appearance. We won both the quarter-final and the semi-final games on Thursday and Friday. On Saturday morning the day of the state championship game, I was feeling anxious and nervous. In the hotel room I started fumbling through one of those hotel Bibles looking for something to calm me down. I did not know it yet, but I was seeking wisdom, and I did not know where to find it. Getting nowhere, I decided to telephone Pastor Jerry. After a little bit of small talk, Jerry guided me through the book of James.

After my conversation with him, I felt energized. My team had a good walk-thru practice and watched some motivational movies. Later that day we ended up winning the state championship game. A major accomplishment!

A week or so later, Pastor Jerry and Jane presented me with a framed copy of James 1:5–6, "If any of you lacks wisdom, you should ask God, who gives generously to all without finding fault, and it will be given to you. But when you ask, you must believe and not doubt...." Following the Scripture were the words "Girls Basketball – State Championship – 3–15–97."

I had indeed found wisdom that day. That verse and the memory of Pastor Jerry leading me to it continue to inspire me.

He Talked About the Love of Jesus

Hannah Nobles (Czerwinski): Being a worship pastor's kid was simply fun. My brother and I fondly remember playing in our dad's office, doing cartwheels during worship rehearsals, and playing hide-and-seek in the sanctuary. I remember when Pastor Jerry would practice his messages for Sundays. Often my brother, Jack, and I hid in the sound booth and listened to snippets of his sermons. It was as if we were over-hearing a secret conversation he was having with the Lord.

I don't remember the specific sermon message that Pastor Jerry spoke when the gospel was presented to me. I do remember him talking about the love of Jesus so profoundly that all within my little six-year-old self just wanted Jesus. I wanted to belong to that kind of love and go on adventures with Christ. So, when Pastor Jerry prayed for people to receive Christ, I told Jesus I would follow him.

I could go on and on about so many little things I witnessed Pastor Jerry do or say when I was growing up. There were interactions with my dad that had them both doubling over in laughter. There were other moments when he would encourage my heart for work on the mission field. Then there was the tenderness he exhibited as he loved on families.

The highest honor I can give Pastor Jerry Worsham is that because of his labor, I now know Jesus. Through his leadership, love, and joy, our family has been impacted significantly on how to go about serving God together. Because of Jerry's example, we understand how to lead with compassion and righteousness in our own ministries. And like Jerry, I pass the baton of faith to others, including my three-year-old daughter, who will be the fourth-generation believer in my family.

What Do I Do Now?

Sheri Kobriger: During my first year at Grace, Pastor Jerry did a sermon series on marriage and family. I saw him in the parking lot and talked to him about the sermons.

"I have to tell you, it is very hard for the single, divorced people in the congregation," I said. "It is hard for me to hear these messages. I know what the Lord requires of me in marriage and that I was supposed to stick with it, but what do I do now that I am divorced? My ex-husband is remarried."

"That marriage is severed," Pastor Jerry told me. "Now you move forward."

I thanked him for doing the series because I wanted to know how to do it right if marriage should be something God would bring to me in the future.

He took time to talk to me and answer all my questions, and the next week he referenced our conversation from the pulpit and said in a fatherly and kindly way, "You know who you are."

He let me know that it meant something to him for me to thank him. And I appreciated that he took the time to explain things to me.

Take the Pen Offered You

Samuel Stewart: I grew up thinking of church service as synonymous with listening to Pastor Jerry. And, as I grew in height very slowly, he was always an encouragement and a reminder to me that God uses short people too!

One Christmas Eve service, my family sat in the front row so my grandparents could hear. (They always enjoyed hearing Pastor Jerry.) In the sermon, he equated the gospel, the gift of God, with a pen. He said all that someone must do to receive salvation is to accept Christ as if reaching out and taking hold of a pen. For illustration he reached out and handed me a pen in front of the packed church.

I have lost that pen, but I will always remember that I have received God's true gift of salvation through Jesus. Pastor Jerry taught me about that gift every time I heard him preach.

Used in a Unique Way

Debbie Palmer: In his sermons, Pastor Jerry would remind us that our job was to obey what the Holy Spirit said, share the gospel, and then leave the rest up to God. We could not save anyone.

When our kids would have friends sleep overnight, we would bring them all to church with us. From Jerry we learned that getting them there was our job and all the rest was God's.

Another phrase from one of Pastor Jerry's sermons that really impacted me was, "Don't judge other people just because they don't practice Christianity exactly the same way you do."

At the time, I was having some conflicts with close co-workers. I did not agree with the things that they were doing. Two questions Jerry had us ponder were, "Do they love God?" and "Do they love Jesus?"

In my co-workers' cases, the answer to both was "yes." That sermon helped me so much and impacted me deeply and totally changed the way I looked at things. From then on, I used it in my life and shared it with a lot of people.

Where There Is Faith, There Is Life

Diane Peterson: I was at Grace Church about two years and had not even met Pastor Jerry. I just knew him as my godly pastor.

Until I heard one of his sermons in spring 2000, I did not pray for or even think about praying for a baby because I thought it was God's will that I wasn't getting pregnant. It just seemed way too big. I knew time was running out for me physically; I was in my late thirties.

Every week Pastor Jerry would teach me to trust Jesus more in the hidden places of my heart—places I did not even know or understand. My desire for a baby was a perfect example of this. I held it somewhere deep inside, and I couldn't give it over to Jesus.

And in one sermon—*How long is a sermon?*—Pastor Jerry completely changed my being. With Holy Spirit-filled preaching, he took me out of a ten-year journey of barrenness, feeling unworthy to ever be a mother, and another broken dream never to be fulfilled. I walked out of Grace Church knowing that I would trust in Jesus fully and that I would have a child. I just knew it.

Instead of brokenness, I felt hope that I would be a mother for the very first time in my life—big, huge hope. Within a few months, I was pregnant! I learned where there is faith, there is life. Pastor Jerry was a faith giver; he brought me toward what Jesus had for me all along. I don't think anything can be more significant than your worst, saddest situation being reversed.

I told Jane this story and she brought Jerry over so he could hear. I wasn't comfortable because my story was, "Because of your husband, I have a baby!"

Pastor Jerry heard my story and gave me a humble, beautiful smile when I finished. It was always the beauty of Jesus that Pastor Jerry would see and hear in any story. You knew that he knew it was all about Jesus and his grace work.

"But hope that is seen is no hope at all. Who hopes for what they already have? But if we hope for what we do not yet have, we wait for it patiently" (Rom. 8:24b–25). "If God is for us, who can be against us?" (Rom. 8:31b).

It Drew Me In

Lee Smith: When Pastor Jerry spoke the Sunday we visited, I knew Grace was to be our church. There was just something about hearing him teach and preach that drew me in. And when I got to know him and saw the way he lived, his preaching and teaching were even more impressive.

I took notes on all his sermons so I could go back and look things up. He not only preached on things like grace and truth, but he lived them out. A couple of times he corrected me and the way he did it was so cool because it was grace and it was truth in action.

You Never Knew What He Was Going to Do

Cindi Stewart: I remember someone in my family asking me why I liked going to Grace Baptist. I told them it is because I never knew what Pastor Jerry was going to do on a Sunday! One week it would be a skit, the next week he would be up front on his knees praying, the next Sunday singers would be walking down the aisles, and yet another week he would ask a question and talk with someone in the pews. My list of examples could go on and on. Before attending Grace, I had only known *ritual* Sunday services.

Pastor Jerry and Grace Baptist Church took me in when I was young, single, and felt wounded by my home church. Looking back, it sometimes feels like someone else's life. But what I remember most was a warm welcome that has kept me at Grace for decades. And though it took me years of listening to Pastor Jerry's preaching, I was able to find a whole new God who loved me in ways I did not know I could be loved.

I only knew of a *conditional God* from *conditional people*, a challenging thing to shake. Though I questioned things at Grace, Pastor Jerry always answered my questions, and his answers were always biblical.

He Loved to Preach

Jon Nelson: On occasion Pastor Jerry would invite me to participate in ministry with him or preach at Grace Baptist Church. I remember the first time I preached when the church started to have three Sunday services. After preaching, I was spent! It was shocking to me that Jerry did this every week, and it gave me a new appreciation for him, his call to preaching, his preparation for preaching, and his love of preaching.

He Connected the Dots

Dr. Paul Durbin: I started attending Grace in 1999 when a fellow doctor, Bob Gullberg, invited me to an outreach event at Grace where Mike Singletary [a former linebacker for the Chicago Bears] was speaking. Growing up in the Chicago area, I witnessed the Bears win the 1985 Super Bowl, and I was interested in hearing what Mike Singletary had to say. That night the Holy Spirit was working on our hearts as my wife, Jen, and I walked into the church.

I was raised Catholic, Jen was raised Methodist, and we got married in 1995 in a Catholic church. When we moved to Racine, we tried many different Catholic churches, but we were not really connecting with people nor were we growing in our faith. And then came that night at Grace. We were blown away! Pastor Jerry spoke and he was so down to earth and presented things in a way that just made sense.

My wife and I left wondering if we should start attending church at Grace. We decided to visit the following Sunday and we never left. At first, attending Grace was a struggle because it was vastly different from the Catholic Church. But Pastor Jerry made it easy. He kept drawing us in with his sermon messages. We listened week after week to foundational sermons. I often found myself crying as Jerry seemed to be speaking directly to me. God used him in a powerful way. He explained the gospel so clearly.

Growing up I had heard and read about Jesus. I knew who Jesus was, but I did not have real clarity on the storyline of the Bible and how things connected. I had lots of dots in my brain, but they did not connect, and I did not know how to connect them. I heard of Abraham, Isaiah, Paul, and Matthew, but I had a poor understanding of how the Old Testament connected to the New Testament, and I did not understand God's plan for redemption. Pastor Jerry helped connect those dots for me, and I finally got it. After listening to him for six months, the Holy Spirit convicted me of my sin and my need for a Savior. I put my faith and trust in Jesus Christ as my personal Lord and Savior. What a glorious moment that was! I eventually got baptized at Village Creek Bible Camp,[15] a camp in which Grace Church was a key partner during Pastor Jerry's leadership.

Pastor Jerry taught me how to understand the Bible and why it is the most important book ever written. It is our guidebook to understanding life and who God is. He also helped me develop a love of reading and studying the Bible, something I never did prior to coming to Grace.

I Realized I Was a Sunday Christian

Al Boscha: I first came to Grace in January 2002. It was just a matter of taking a left-hand turn out of my driveway instead of a right. What a difference that turned out to be!

During our membership classes, Pastor Jerry took time to get to know my wife, Kimmy, and me. He knew my family and my Christian Reformed background through my sister Tina's friendship with his

---

[15] Village Creek Bible Camp is a year-round ministry offering camp experiences to people of all ages. For more information visit www.villagecreek.net.

daughter Jen. It was obvious he believed wholeheartedly in his calling and mission. Kimmy and I found him to be humble and sincere.

Pastor Jerry approached me where I was, not where he wanted me to be. I realized that I was a Sunday Christian, not a real Christian, and through his preaching and other efforts, I became a real Christian man.

I hunt with some men who attended Grace when Pastor Jerry was the lead pastor, Jerry Bloodworth and Garret Smith. In our hunting camps, whether in the mountains of Colorado or the woods of Pepin County, Wisconsin, we often recall things Pastor Jerry said like, "Walk true north...be willing to swim upstream, not downstream with everyone else...for married couples, remember the 'stand up and speak up' rule...raise your children in grace and truth—100 percent of each..." and my favorite, "the most important thing you can do is pray."

I am thankful Pastor Jerry spoke and acted knowing that Jesus and the Bible are real, not just history to be studied. Pastor Jerry was and still is a giant of a man, and I am forever grateful for him.

He Asked a Series of Questions

Patti Booth: In his preaching Pastor Jerry challenged us to love like Christ and come against a selfish spirit. In one sermon he asked us: "What kind of heart are you going to have? Are you going to give your wife the kind of candy she likes or the kind you like?"

Then he said, "If you really love your wife, you will give her what she loves." This stuck with me.

Basic, Simple, Profound

Heidi Jundt: I perused my journals and pulled out the one from 2001 to 2002. In it were notes from Pastor Jerry's *First of All, Pray* sermon from January 6, 2002. Our son Jacob was diagnosed with cancer in December 2001, just weeks before Pastor Jerry gave that sermon. His words came back to me repeatedly during Jacob's illness.

To remind us of the priority of prayer, Jerry gave the congregation cards with those simple words *First of All, Pray* imprinted. Our card was up on the fridge for so long that it finally got full of food, and I had to throw it out! This sermon gave me a basic, simple, yet profound message at a time I really needed one. That sums up Pastor Jerry's preaching: basic, simple, profound.

Jerry taught me to apply the Scriptures to my life. He was so clear. It was not like you were trying to figure out what his point was and how it related to life. He was always right in line with what Scripture was teaching. I could trust him.

He was a man of integrity. If he preached about spending time with Jesus early in the morning, you knew it was because that is what he experienced. He wasn't just telling you to go and read Scripture in the morning and pray. He was telling you to do it because he had spent two or three hours reading and praying. Many people saw him praying—it was his mode of operation, praying on his knees, in humility, grounded in Christ.

Through his preaching during Jacob's illness, I started to understand God's sovereignty (a big church word I did not really understand until we walked though Jacob's illness), and with this, how to give glory to God in all circumstances—even something so difficult as our young son dying of cancer.

Nativity Scene!

Lee and Karen Smith: "We are really into traditions," Karen said. "During one Advent sermon series, Pastor Jerry made a casual mention about riding along in the car and looking for Nativity scenes with your kids. He wanted us to take the focus off Santa Claus and secular things and put the focus on Christ. His suggestion was like the slug bug game, but instead of looking for Volkswagen Beetles you were to look for Nativity scenes."

"She's right," Lee said. "And our kids who are now adults still play the game during Christmas and shout "Nativity scene!" when they find one.

His Character

Joan Gorton: More important than Pastor Jerry's preaching was his overall character. As a preacher, he was not dramatic; he stuck to his notes, and he was prepared. To me, his preaching was always worthy of note taking.

Our Father in Heaven, Hallowed Be Your Name

Phil Adams: One sermon Pastor Jerry preached on the Lord's Prayer (Matt. 6:9–13) has governed my thoughts, my actions, and my view of worship from the moment he gave it. This sermon was more effective than any worship seminar or any training on leading worship.

He preached on the first words of the Lord's Prayer and then broke it into two sections. In his first section, he showed us how the prayer talks about an intimacy of worship. It says *our Father*. This intimacy is a snapshot of us crawling into the lap of God as a lamb does with a shepherd. It is just total intimacy where we are vulnerable and speak in Abba [Daddy] language.

Then Pastor Jerry said something else; he simply said the words *in heaven*—it makes me tear up when I think of it. He said, "Never forget the transcendence of God while you are being intimate with God. It is easy to get too familiar with God and lose sight of his majesty, his glory, and his transcendence."

When I go to lead worship or sing at other events, I am always thinking about this sermon. Most churches have the intimacy part down well: God is my buddy; God is my friend. But many churches lose sight of the transcendence of God and the fear quotient of being in the presence of a holy God.

I kept all my notes from this sermon, and I have it in my heart. I knew the moment Pastor Jerry preached this message that it was the missing link for me. No worship service I conducted after this was without both components.

What's at the Very Center of the Universe?

Phylis Hessenthaler: During a Wednesday prayer meeting, Pastor Jerry had us open our Bibles to Revelation 4, and he asked us, "What is at the very center of the universe?"

He paused as his eyes sparkled and then he answered, "A throne. God's throne!" Next, he read: "At once I was in the Spirit, and there before me was a throne in heaven with someone sitting on it" (Rev. 4:2).

The point of Pastor Jerry's message was very much like what I was learning in Bible Study Fellowship at this same time. He said, "Let's live each day with an awareness of that throne in the center of the universe—not just for believers but for every living creature. Everyone and everything belong to God and he is at the center. When you live in this awareness nothing can defeat you."

He Lived Out Grace and Truth

Jim Kerkvliet: One year the topics of grace and truth were a focus of many of Pastor Jerry's sermons. Those messages had an impact on me because I was raised with contrasting teaching that focused on doing good works.

In my youth and young adulthood, I would feel so guilty when I made mistakes. I don't believe that I was exposed to much of God's amazing grace in my formative years. Pastor Jerry stressed that grace and truth were not a 50–50 model, but instead, Christians should strive for 100 percent of both grace and truth. By this, Pastor Jerry helped demonstrate God's loving character to me.

Not only did he do an excellent job teaching his church about grace and truth, he also modeled grace and truth in the way he dealt with people and approached situations.

His Preaching Formed Who We Are

Lee Smith: Pastor Jerry started off every January talking about prayer because he said that it is first and foremost. My wife, Karen, and I had that little tan card on our fridge for years that he gave out that read *First of All, Pray*. But it wasn't just a card, it was a tool for Pastor Jerry to remind us that prayer was very important.

I had struggled with prayer for a long time, and Pastor Jerry made it clear it was a hump I needed to get over. It was a discipline he taught, so it was one of those things I worked at, still do, and one of the things that have helped me grow in my walk.

There were other disciplines he preached on like the concept of a quiet time, having an accountability partner, and getting involved in small groups. He preached and taught and instilled truths, and we started doing them. His preaching formed who we are now.

A Serious Worrier

Jim Arndt: In a sermon Pastor Jerry gave on growing your faith, he confessed to the church that he was a worrier. I would not have thought that was an issue for Pastor Jerry. He had what I saw as the strongest possible faith and trust in Jesus a person could have. But even with that faith and that trust, he still worried. He called himself a "serious worrier." When he preached this message, Jane sat in the pew and nodded her head.

As I go through cancer, it is comforting to know that someone like Pastor Jerry worried about things because I find myself worrying about things even though I am trying to leave it all in God's hands.

Giving *Is* Worship

Don Amundson: One of Pastor Jerry's sermons on giving was very impactful. He impressed upon the church that giving *is* worship.

He and I had a similar style for getting things done. I refuse to spend money unnecessarily. I manage a substantial portion of the Grace budget [as the Grace Church director of facilities and grounds], and I think everyone knows I am very frugal. Part of this comes from Pastor Jerry. I can hear him asking, "Do you *need* that?" and saying, "Remember, you are managing worship funds."

When you pass the offering baskets, you are worshiping. It is bigger and deeper than just giving money.

Spiritual Truths

Amy Cape: Pastor Jerry was one of the most influential people in my life. Many margins of my *New International Version Bible* have sermon notes and quotes from his preaching. Here are some of my favorite spiritual truths from Pastor Jerry:

- Pray First! Prayer is powerful and effective. (Jas. 5:16)
- Sin clogs the conduit of communication with God.
- Swim upstream! (Rom.12)
- Keep your focus on the True North.
- Only God is awesome.
- Be humble. (Jas. 4:6)
- Because you said so, I will! (BYSSIW) (Luke 5:5)
- Fix your eyes on the mountain mover not the mountain. (Heb.12:22)
- Win…Build…Equip.

I not only admired Pastor Jerry's wisdom and advice, but his example was a powerful influence. He truly practiced what he preached.

Funerals

Pastor Dan Petersen: Pastor Jerry was at his best when conducting a funeral. He would clearly lay out the gospel message point by point. He told me funerals were the best opportunity to present the gospel.

"You have a captive audience of people who may have never heard the gospel message before, and I am going to give it to them," he told me.

The Battle Belongs to the Lord

Kiyomi Bryson: I remember Pastor Jerry's sermon on how the battle belongs to the Lord (2 Chron. 20:1–30). I was going through great personal trials at that time, and his preaching reminded me that even though there is a vast army against me, the battle belongs to the Lord. From him talking about Ebenezer I remember that no matter where I am, "thus far the Lord has helped" me (1 Sam. 7:12).

What It Said, Meant, and How to Apply It

Denise Pipol: My husband, Jerry, and I had regularly attended church throughout our lives. I really wanted to stay at the church I grew up in because I believed that most Protestant churches were alike. But then we started attending services at Grace.

Even though we loved our former church home, we could tell God was moving us out of our traditional church to Grace where he could grow our faith and our knowledge of him through biblical preaching.

When Pastor Jerry preached, his sermons totally opened God's Word to us. He taught us not just what the Bible said, but what it meant, and how to apply it to our personal lives. It was shocking to discover just how little we really knew about God's Word! Pastor Jerry's clear and solid preaching left us wanting to know more and more. I remember being disappointed when his sermons ended.

In the Storms of Life

Dr. Paul Durbin: Pastor Jerry preached on how to handle storms in your life, and this became a key lesson for me. He said, "You may find yourself right now with a calm sea, but the storms will come. How will you stand when that happens? How will you cope?"

He emphasized that it is critical to have God in your life to persevere, and that no matter the storm, you can have hope as a believer in Christ. He assured us that God is working in every situation for his purposes (Rom. 8:28). I remember thinking at the time, *Things are pretty good for me; I am not really experiencing a storm.*

All that changed in March 2001 when our son Brian, born a healthy child, contracted RSV (respiratory syncytial virus) when he was a month old. He got extremely sick over the course of three days; was admitted to a Racine hospital; and within hours, he was put on a ventilator. He had to be flown via helicopter to Children's Hospital of Wisconsin in Wauwatosa. He was very sick and was admitted to the Intensive Care Unit (ICU). We were told his life was in great danger and that he may not survive.

We were new at Grace, but we let the church know what was happening, and we had a tremendous outpouring of support. I will never forget Pastor Jerry's visit to us in the ICU. He prayed over us and Brian, he prayed that God would heal Brian, and he prayed for us to stand strong in this storm and trust in our sovereign God.

His prayer made me recall the sermon he preached about the storms of life. My wife, Jen, and I grew so much in our faith during this time. We determined to trust in God no matter what, even if it meant Brian would go to heaven at that moment.

Brian stayed in the ICU for a week and made a miraculous recovery. He is now twenty-one, a godly young man, attending Grand Canyon University, and studying pre-medicine with the hope of being a doctor someday and serving others stateside and on the mission field.

A Bracelet, A Stone, A Button

Janine Carls: "True North" was one of the most impactful sermons I have ever heard, and I have those words engraved on my identification bracelet as a reminder. Jerry preached the sermon at a time in my life when I had only recently come to know the depths of God's mercy and grace. I really needed direction and needed to stay on course. The sermon series emphasized doing everything "as unto the Lord."

Pastor Jerry reminded us that we set goals that honor the Lord because they serve his purpose or demonstrate thanksgiving. As we move forward in this life, we should have one purpose: "to draw nearer to God in all we do."

In his sermons Pastor Jerry used tools we could take along as reminders. For one sermon on Ebenezer from 1 Samuel 7:12, he gave us all a stone with the name *Ebenezer* on it to remind us that God is our helper, our protector, and our victory.

Another time he gave us buttons that read "Because You Say So I Will" taken from Ephesians 6:10. It was a reminder to put on the full armor of God every day and to walk in God's steps.

He Spoke to My Soul

Karen Amundson: At age nineteen I turned my life over to Christ and moved to Racine not knowing a single soul. Brian Petak [a staff member] invited me to Grace, and the first time I heard Pastor Jerry speak, I was in tears. I continued to come to Grace and would cry every time he preached because God was using him to speak directly to my soul.

Pastor Jerry and Grace had an enormous impact on me in my young adult years transforming my rebellious previous life into a life of faith, hope, and trust. I fell in love with the family of Grace, and eight years after I began attending, I met the love of my life and now husband, Mike.

Fasting

Karen Smith: Pastor Jerry stressed fasting before a big decision. He stressed it, he lived it, we applied it, and we still incorporate his preaching on fasting all these years later.

My Soul Glorifies the Lord

Jessica Schulz: I remember Pastor Jerry preaching on how Jesus' mother Mary prayed and glorified God. He stated we are made for glorifying God. This really impacted me because reading Mary's prayer fills you up and makes you think, *I need to give God all the glory!*

> And Mary said: "My soul glorifies the Lord and my spirit rejoices in God my Savior, for he has been mindful of the humble state of his servant. From now on all generations will call me blessed, for the Mighty One has done great things for me—holy is his name. His mercy extends to those who fear him, from generation to generation. He has performed mighty deeds with his arm; he has scattered those who are proud in their inmost thoughts. He has brought down rulers from their thrones but has lifted up the humble. He has filled the hungry with good things but has sent the rich away empty. He has helped his servant Israel, remembering to be merciful to Abraham and his descendants forever, just as he promised our ancestors" (Luke 1:46–55).

New Wine Skins

Phil Adams: For one Sunday night service, Pastor Jerry sat down on a stool; he had never done this before in front of the congregation. It was symbolic of what his message would be. He told Grace Baptist Church that we were going to drink out of new wine skins.

He never wanted us to sacrifice the truth of God's Word—the truth does not change—but he wanted us to begin to embrace new methods of worship and sharing the gospel, new wine skins.

As the worship directors, my wife, Laurie, and I were encouraged by this sermon because we knew what we were bringing to the table from a worship standpoint was going to rattle cages. People particularly important to the church were accustomed to a very traditional and conservative worship style with an organ and a choir. This was a church that would have never considered doing a Saturday night service. We asked to have it after the "New Wine Skins" sermon, and in a month, we were doing it. I could go on and on about things like this. Pastor Jerry embraced change.

We Never Looked Back

Pastor Dan Petersen: On our very first visit to Grace Baptist Church, Pastor Jerry made a profound impact on my wife, Shirley, and me. We were there for no other reason than wanting a place to attend that Sunday because the pastor of our church was not in town. We saw in the newspaper that the preaching topic at Grace that day was "family."

After service we left our other church and never looked back. We were not upset with the church we had been attending, but we knew that we would grow spiritually under Jerry Worsham's teaching. We were excited and could hardly wait for each Sunday message anticipating what we would learn from the Scriptures Jerry would illuminate.

Soul Space

Kim Kind-Bauer: I often recall a sermon where Pastor Jerry taught that something is going to occupy the space in your soul—either God or Satan. It struck me to keep my guard up and to always keep my spiritual armor on.

A Special Charisma

Jeanne Ferraro: Jerry Worsham was a man of the Word. When he spoke or preached, there was a charisma that drew in all types of people and everyone wanted to hear what he said. This was not just a one-Sunday thing. Every single time he spoke he really impacted me. And it was not just me. I brought my brother, Bob, with us to Grace. He had grown up in the church and had fallen away from the Lord. When he heard Pastor Jerry's message he said, "He is talking right to me."

I said, "Yes, Bob. The Holy Spirit is speaking to you through Pastor Jerry." My brother was drawn in by Pastor Jerry and back to the Lord.

Thursdays With Jerry

Gerald Baccash: My wife, Trish, and I first attended Grace Baptist Church in August 1992. We immediately made a connection with Pastor Jerry after service that day as he was standing in the church entrance greeting congregants.

In subsequent weeks, it was clear he remembered us. He knew I was not a believer and invited me to a weekly Thursday morning prayer gathering he held in his office. I accepted and started attending with three or four other people. I came with great anticipation and was immediately and lovingly accepted.

It was in his office that I first learned of Pastor Jerry's incredible passion and love for the Lord, for prayer, and for his flock. It was also clear to me that although my own father was passionate about the Lord and prayer, I never really knew how to pray. As time passed, I was able to truly connect with our Father in Heaven in ways I could never have imagined. From Pastor Jerry I learned how to praise God; ask and receive answers and guidance from the Lord; and how to remain in God's presence.

Pastor Jerry's impact on me was immediate, momentous, and lasting. I miss him dreadfully and anxiously await our reunion!

Choose Joy Everyday

Yvonne Manning: To make us tune in and to get his point across during a sermon, Pastor Jerry would say, "Listen up. Hear me."

Once he gave a sermon on joy, and I remember the moment he said, "Hear me. You must choose joy. You have to choose joy every day."

I had thought that as a Christian, joy would just naturally bubble up in me, and if I did not have joy, I probably was not walking with Christ. This concept of the responsibility of choosing joy stuck with me. Every single day we have a choice to make.

Pastor Jerry shifted our thinking on ordinary topics like joy. He did the same thing during special sermons for Thanksgiving, Christmas, Maundy Thursday, Good Friday, and Easter. He would take familiar stories and explain them in ways that made everyone hear differently and do differently. He would give us something so unique that we had to make a change in our thinking.

His Favorite Topics Represented Who He Was

Patti Booth: Pastor Jerry was consistent in the pulpit and outside of the pulpit. There were not two sides to him. He was what he appeared to be, and this was why people were confident in coming to him.

He was a unique pastor. He was always willing and wanted to be there for people. His favorite preaching topics represented who he was: humility, prayer, the sovereignty of God, grace and truth, praising God, and overcoming.

Hallelujah!

Pastor Dan Petersen: Many of the things Pastor Jerry did that made me laugh were things he did not even intend to be humorous. For instance, when he preached, he did what we deemed the chop. While he was making points he would chop with his hands, raise his leg, and say, "Hear me!" or "Listen!"

Once while preaching an Easter sermon, he came to a spot that called for one of his chops. He raised his leg and somehow stepped on Worship Director Brian Petak's foot lever causing the "Hallelujah Chorus" background music to blast very, very loudly!

Jerry calmly said, "Hear me now. That was just to emphasize the point I am about to make."

The congregation could not stop laughing. Pastor Jerry waited a few minutes to allow things to settle down and then very stoically continued with his sermon.

He Could Not and Would Not

Scott Demarest: Pastor Jerry was a student of the Bible and knew it well. He would constantly reference Scripture to guide us. I recall one time when a leader within the church felt a strong conviction about a controversial subject [alcohol consumption] and brought this before the elders several times. Eventually this came to a head, and the leader demanded a specific decision. Although his concern was well intentioned and had merit, most of us felt that making it a mandate fell too close to legalism.

I remember Pastor Jerry addressing this individual and the Elder Board with tremendous grace and empathy. He shared that he had made a personal decision years ago to follow the advice that was now being advocated by the leader, and he encouraged other elders to do the same if they felt led. However, he shared numerous Bible passages that addressed the concern and declared that he could not and would not support mandating something that the Bible clearly did not prohibit. He articulated this calmly and peacefully, but with the conviction of a man who was confident and obedient to the Word.

Pastor Jerry constantly taught us integrity through his actions and reliance on the Lord. He never took credit for himself but enthusiastically and in a reverent way gave all the glory to God.

Preaching Practice

Jeff Stewart: I saw Pastor Jerry's love for sharing his messages with the congregation through the preparation he did on Saturdays. His routine was to run through delivery of his whole sermon from the pulpit. He would wait until the volunteers were done setting up communion in the sanctuary before starting. He was always polite about asking when we expected to be done, without saying directly to hurry up; and he was faithful in thanking the Communion Team for doing setup and cleanup every month.

I also saw an example of his great grace when he was practicing his sermon. His preference was to practice when the sanctuary was empty to avoid distractions, but for a time a family with special-needs children was stocking the pews with pencils and offering envelopes. The two special-needs children would sit and listen to Pastor Jerry practice his sermon just like it was Sunday morning. I always smiled when I saw this, knowing that he preferred the sanctuary to be empty.

No Big Secrets

Heidi Jundt: Pastor Jerry was not just preaching the Word to his congregation; he was living out the Word and helping us live it out.

His daughter, Jen, was in our small group. There were no big, dirty secrets about Pastor Jerry. He was just an ordinary guy. You knew who he was by hearing him preach and by hearing about him from his family.

Look at the Mountain Mover

Patti Booth: There were so many things that Pastor Jerry preached that changed me. I have lots of *Jerry notes* in my Bible. I sat under his preaching for more than thirty years.

I always think about one sermon he gave where he encouraged us to keep our eyes fixed on the mountain mover, not on the mountains. It made an impact on me because we tend to do just the opposite. It was a straightforward way to remember and reframe my focus.

What Matters in Life

Pastor Kent Carlson: Jerry was earnest, and there is a danger in being earnest. Pastors talk way too long, way too often, and way too much about things we know very little about. Every statement we make about God is really an approximation, and souls hang in the balance. The temptation to earnestness can make you take yourself way too seriously. In reality, most people forget what you've said by the afternoon after you've preached or sooner. What they really remember more than your words is who you are, how you spoke truth, and your integrity. Jerry did a fantastic job of talking about what matters in life.

A Message Just for Us

Luke Binkley: From the time I was little, every Christmas we would do a family pageant and enact the Nativity scene. Grandpa would give us lessons and parts to play. Every year as we grew, the pageant grew deeper and more elaborate.

After Grandpa retired, he really made the Christmas message a focus. He would spend months working on it for an audience of eleven. It meant a lot because we knew at one time Grandpa preached to thousands of people, and now, he prepared a special message for just us.

He was so wise. I just loved to sit and listen to everything he said and soak it in. Not just spiritually, but everything. He really led a morally pure life.

Yearly Theme

Caleb Augustyn: In addition to giving us in-depth, low-key, sermon-style messages every year on Christmas, toward Grandpa's later years, he would create an annual family theme. I remember the one he was most excited about was *joy*. He was really big on that and being joyful in all seasons of life no matter what you were going through.

He gave this sermon and had this family theme right before he got aphasia, the condition that caused him to struggle to speak. It was certainly the sovereignty of God that caused him to focus on joy not knowing what the future held for him.

A Congregation of Eleven

Levi Binkley: My grandpa went from preaching to and pastoring the whole congregation of Grace Church to giving Christmas sermons to a congregation made up of his six grandkids and our parents and our grandma. He did not care about numbers. His desire to preach and share the gospel never changed.

The Proclamation of the Bible Has Power

Pastor Mike Lueken: I spent many years imitating Jerry as a preacher—the hand gesture, the bouncing on the toes, the "now I want you to catch this" line. He liked to walk around when he preached, so I walked around.

One of my earliest duties at Grace Baptist Church was to preach at the Sunday night service. I remember talking to Jerry about my sermon because I was having trouble figuring out what passage to use.

"Mike, the Bible is rich and there is always a passage to use," he said. "You have a book of gold in your hand. All you must do is open it."

Those words stuck with me. He wanted me to remember that I was not dealing with an ordinary book. The Bible is a book filled with power and truth.

I was trying to sort out how to prepare my sermons, and Jerry showed me how he prepared and let me see his yellow notepads. He had tons of pages, he did not write on the lines, and he had quotes and illustrations. It wasn't messy, but by no means was he using a full sheet of paper. I did my preparation in a similar, but slightly different way.

The biggest mark about preaching Jerry left on me was that the proclamation of the Bible has power. He never stopped believing that, and sometimes that becomes a challenging thing to hang on to when you pastor for a while. You must get used to people not paying attention or not caring when you are talking. It really hits when you cycle back around to how often you say and repeat things.

There was a purity to Jerry's faith and devotion that remained unstained by his years in the ministry. Preaching was one of those things he remained enthusiastic about and was not cynical about. That also left a mark on me.

Chapter 5

THE MARK OF LOVE:
In Every Season
Without Reason

May your unfailing love be with us, LORD,
even as we put our hope in you.

PSALM 33:22

By the time Jesus started his ministry, the Jewish people were following more than six hundred laws. When asked, "Teacher, which is the greatest commandment in the Law?" Jesus replied: "'Love the Lord your God with all your heart and with all your soul and with all your mind.' This is the first and greatest commandment. And the second is like it: 'Love your neighbor as yourself.' All the Law and the Prophets hang on these two commandments" (Matt. 22:36–40).

Pastor Jerry followed his leader Jesus. He loved his God with all he was. And loved his neighbor as himself.

Jerry Bled for Me

Ralph "Easy" Worsham: Jerry was a very loving person. And holy macaroni, that is an understatement! He would listen to people and he cared. Growing up I never saw my brother Jerry upset. Even when I stabbed him with a sword...yes, I did!

Mom and Dad left Jerry to babysit me, Lorain, and Arvin while they went out. I was poking at Arvin with a sword. Jerry got in the middle of us, took the sword away, and was trying to settle us down. He had his Reserve Officer's Training Corps (ROTC) saber in the corner, so I grabbed that and said, "On guard!"

"Listen, put that down," Jerry said to me. "You are going to poke someone in the eye!"

"Like this?" I said as I lunged out at him and thankfully missed his eye but cut him in the hand. I did not mean to cut him. It bled like crazy.

And you know what? Jerry never told Mom or Dad. He knew I would be in big trouble and they would get the switch out. Instead, he patched up his wound, and when he got asked about it, he said, "I got injured by my sword." Which was true. He just did not say *how* he got injured or *who* did it. Jerry bled for me, never complained about it, and never again brought back up what I had done.

Everything He Did Was for Our Good

Pati Cole: My parents did not go to church and therefore my siblings and I were not allowed to go to church services as middle school students in the Panama Canal Zone. However, my parents did allow us to attend youth group. It was at youth group that I was discipled by Pastor Jerry, who was the youth pastor.

Jerry was known for his strict rules, especially at camp, and we gave him a tough time about these rules. However, he also had a smile and a laugh that made me feel loved and accepted. I remember telling him years later about his strictness, and he was surprised. I knew later that everything he did was for our good. He and Jane were both such good role models to the youth. I am thankful God put them in my pathway. Due to their influence, I am walking with the Lord today.

Unmerited Favor

Pastor Kent Carlson: I was watching Jerry and Jane's home when they went on vacation. I thought I would make some popcorn on the stove while I was watching a television show. I walked away from the stove, and when I came back, flames were shooting up out of the pan! I had no idea what to do, so I took the pan of popcorn with the oil and flames to the sink and poured water on it. The water caused flames to shoot up even higher and started the curtains on fire. I opened the back door, carried the pan over, and threw it into the yard, and then I went back inside and put out the fire on the curtains.

There were smoke stains all over the ceiling; oil spilled onto the floor and burned their linoleum; the alarm was going off, and their cat, Patches, was running around crazily.

I spent the rest of the evening washing the ceiling, calming down the cat, and trying to make their house look as though nothing had happened, but the marks on the ceiling, the burnt linoleum, the burnt curtains, the burn mark on the lawn, the smell of smoke, not to mention the now neurotic cat, gave it all away.

The marvelous thing was that the Worshams trusted me to take care of their home the next time they went on vacation. This was certainly an expression of their love and unmerited favor.

One of Jerry's Kids

Pastor Jason Esposito: I knew Jerry really loved me and cared about me. Some people jokingly called me one of Jerry Worsham's kids. I really was in many ways, and I'm proud to say it.

L-O-V-E

Pastor Jason Montano: I learned about the love of Christ from a pastor who never acted or even had the air of being a successful large church pastor. Jerry would have been the same man in a church of fifty people somewhere in Kentucky as he was at Grace. The top three things I learned from him all center around love:

People Over Programs: Even when the staff pushed the envelope with him on certain stances or events, Jerry always took us back to the care of people. He wanted us to note not just how our decisions would affect one element of ministry, but the people of the church as a whole. He would ask, "Is this going to be good for our church family?"

Shepherd Over CEO: Even though Jerry was technically the chief executive officer of Grace, he did not act like a CEO. He was a shepherd, which goes back to the high value he placed on loving people.

He was so countercultural on how to be successful in the American church. There is not one book out there that I have come across or read that outlines one of Jerry's models. He did not incorporate all the modern methodology on how to grow your church. He just loved people! The experts out there would buck this and say, "Well, that is not how you grow a church."

Love and Know Your Staff: Jerry loved his staff and knew his staff. He loved *me*. He knew *me*. Every day when he came into the building, he would do his tour through the staff offices to check on everyone. He would say, "All right guys. How are you doing today? Jay, how's Kristen?"

I was making peanuts as a junior high youth pastor, and we had lots of medical bills from our son's hospital stay. Jerry got that real serious face with the squinty eyes and said, "Hey, Jay. We're going to take care of all those medical bills with Caleb. All right man? We're going to take care of you. You don't need to worry about that."

And this is just one example of his love and care. From trivial things to big things to encouragement to thanking us—he would always say thank you—he personified love. If there was a thankless job at Grace, it was youth ministry. The only people who liked us and thanked us were the kids and the parents, unless they were mad at us, which is the other side of youth ministry. The rest of the church would wonder what we really did. Not Jerry. He valued young people. He valued us. And he told us this all the time. He really, really cared.

The other side of this was *how* he knew us. During my time at Grace, being a younger leader was not celebrated in a lot of ways. Jerry knew one of the things I would try to do was to get away from people because I did not want to hear their feedback or criticism. Jerry never shied away, and he taught me to not shy away but to be where the people are, to be among them and listen. This was part of loving them.

Ministry Marinated in Grace

Bob Magruder: Pastor Jerry wanted his ministry to be marinated in the gospel of grace. He rightly understood we could never exhaust the mystery of God's immeasurable grace. His own profound gratitude for God's grace motivated, captivated, and energized him for ministry. It filled his spiritual horizons. And because so many churches are regrettably graceless, he earnestly desired his ministry to be a tsunami of God's outlandish grace. This was a dominant force that motivated him. Pastor Jerry nurtured an incurable confidence in God's grace and sought to exemplify this reality by creating it in the lives of others.

Hang Onto God

Debbie Kultgen: My husband, Terry, and I were separated. I had been attending another church and switched to Grace to participate in a support group designed to help people in my situation.

Jerry and Jane hosted the group in their home. They were gentle, kind, and giving. They were so attentive and gave their whole selves. Our conversations weren't about them acquiring my story. They were just present, totally present. I had a trust issue, but I trusted them immediately. They loved me and it showed.

Jerry and Jane walked faithfully alongside of my husband and me. They prayed for us and supported us throughout our seven-year separation. When I needed them, they were there with their gentle and encouraging counsel to help me refocus. I lived with the thoughts, *I don't know where he is at or what he is doing.* And I lived with fear.

Jerry got me into different Bible studies. He always told me, "Hang on to God. He will see you through."

One time Terry called me at work and said he was going to file for divorce—he was drinking in those years. I remembered how Jerry told me to hang on to God, so I said, "If you want to divorce me, you go ahead."

I knew God would take care of me. It took me many years to get to this point, but I got there. When Terry and I got back together, I remember telling Jerry that I would rather be divorced than live like I was living. Terry would come home late, and for a while it seemed like he was making me pay for us getting back together.

"Deb, you are waiting for the other shoe to drop," Jerry said to me. "You have got to stop."

After Jerry said this, I decided to turn it all over to God, and I willfully choose to forgive Terry.

Jerry was one of the godliest men I have ever met because of how he loved and how he lived his life. It wasn't just what he said, it was what he did. His life spoke for itself. He had a light that could not be put under a basket. He was non-judgmental and someone I could always trust.

Agape Love

Terry Kultgen: One profound quality I saw in Jerry was his authentic love. My relationship with him started out with me waiting for him to judge me. I expected him to judge me and to ask me why I did what I did, but that never happened.

He did a lot of listening. I had not experienced anything like it. Along with his authentic love, there was patience and long-suffering. He knew it wasn't his job to change me; that was the Holy Spirit's role. When someone does that with you, walks that way with you, it makes you question how you should be conducting yourself. Jerry was serving the Lord and was an instrument in his hands.

After getting to know Jerry, I felt that he really, really loved me, and he was willing to say hard things to me. You can't just hammer lost people with truth, truth, truth. He never did that.

One of my favorite Scriptures, even though people say it was put in after the original manuscripts, comes from John 8:3–11. Jesus is talking to some self-righteous men and says to them, "Let any one of you who is without sin be the first to throw a stone at her." He then asked the woman they caught in adultery, "Woman, where are they? Has no one condemned you?…Go now and leave your life of sin."

In this account you sense the deep compassion Jesus had for that woman and this was the deep compassion I felt from Jerry. When we talked about agape[16] love, I felt it from him. I did not have that in my home life. My dad died when I was twenty-seven, and the night he died was the first and only time that I heard him say he loved me. I am not blaming him; that is the way he was raised.

I call Jerry my spiritual father. I could go to him, say things to him, talk to him, and he was listening.

---

[16] Agape is one of several Greek words for love. In the Bible, agape refers to a pure, willful, and sacrificial love. Agape is a love of choice versus a love due to obligation or attraction. It intentionally desires another person's highest good.

Loving People With the Gospel

Dr. Robert Gullberg: Jerry always fell on the side of grace. This is another gift he gave me. I have learned from him to fall on the side of grace. But don't get me wrong, he was a truth guy too. There is no one perfect in grace and truth but Jesus. Jesus gave the woman at the well great grace but also told her to straighten out her life.

I loved this "grace first" attribute of Jerry. He had such a gift, and it really kept people coming back to see him. If people aren't ready or don't want to hear the truth and you hit them with a hatchet first, they are going to leave and never come back.

Pastor Jerry was also an excellent counselor and he was masterful in one-to-one relationships. He was a good observer, could come to quick conclusions, and could accurately discern what was really happening with people.

With Me

Phil Adams: Our first son, Nathaniel, was born the day of the Space Shuttle Challenger disaster, January 28, 1986. He was not well and things were very touch and go. He was rushed to Children's Hospital of Wisconsin in Wauwatosa, and Pastor Jerry drove me up and stayed with me. He was a rock, and I really needed it.

He Gave Me His Time

Pastor Kent Carlson: Jerry would always have time for me. He did not have it to spare, but he always made it and would spend it lavishly. I never felt I was putting him off. As motivated and as busy as he was, he was never looking over his shoulder to what was next. He was there and present with me.

He Loved Instead of Judged

Maria Rosa Griffin: Pastor Jerry did not judge; he loved. He did not condemn people; he accepted them. Instead of pointing fingers, he favored people.

Available to Serve and Love

Jack Bell: Some of my closest friends were going through marital issues, and they could not get counseling at the church they were attending. I had heard of Pastor Jerry and knew that he had a degree in counseling, so I called him and we made an appointment to talk.

I told him about my friends and he said, "Jack, I would be more than happy to help."

I was not a member of Grace and neither were they. Pastor Jerry did not care. He made himself available to serve the Lord and love people.

Eyes Aglow With the Holy Spirit

Sheri Kobriger: I will always remember meeting Pastor Jerry. I came to Grace in 2003 after a friend had invited me several times over the course of a few months. I wanted to go in, sit in the back row, and not be seen. At this time there were about 1,400 people attending Grace on a Sunday, so I thought not being seen would be quite easy. Before church, an exceedingly kind man came up to me and asked me my name and thanked me for coming.

Next, this kind man got up to speak! I thought, *Oh my gosh! He is the pastor. The pastor of the church spoke to me.* It made me cry because I wanted to be invisible. I was coming from a place of shame, a divorced, single mom not living a very good life. I knew God placed Pastor Jerry there to meet me with love and kindness right where I was.

He was humble and so filled with joy. You could see the glow of the Holy Spirit in him. His eyes were light. And he was so wise. He opened his mouth and when he spoke, he spoke with meaning that hit hearts. It was *the* truth, not just *Jerry* truth. The Lord gifted him with just the right words to speak to people's hearts and to my heart. This helped me hear truth in a positive way even if it hurt.

A Recipe for Loving

Bryan Hesters: For as long as I can remember, the Hesterses [Jane's family of origin] have had a family reunion every two years. This was started for my grandparents during an anniversary celebration to ensure that regardless of what path each of their children found themselves walking and wherever they settled, they would have an opportunity to maintain closeness by reuniting for a week somewhere in the world to reconnect. It was at these reunions that I most remember getting to know Uncle Jerry, Aunt Jane, and their daughters, Janna and Jennifer.

The connections these reunions created among us are hard to put into words. The amazing love and unity our family has is immediately restored when we see each other again. Sure, we stay connected on social media and keep track of family developments to the best of our ability, but the choice to prioritize time to get together in person has been so foundational in our lives and has created a foundation I don't see in any other families I have met. We choose to be close. We collectively agree to see beyond individual challenges, choices, decisions, and perspectives that divide so many friends and families. We push topics like politics or divorce into the background and focus on the family. Uncle Jerry was a critical part of that recipe even though he married into the Hesterses.

It is not that there were never any disagreements, conflicts, or arguments. Uncle Jerry and Aunt Jane both lived with a spirit of patience and love that helped all of us see past the minutia and focus on the heart of what mattered.

I remember Uncle Jerry having an amazing way of bringing conversations around to Jesus without preaching. As a teenager, I remember engaging in a conversation with one of my uncles about religious topics. Jerry was there quietly listening to the conversation and smiling. My uncle mentioned that he was attending a congregation made up of people who came from different religious backgrounds. From them he had come to understand that God was in all of life, that love was real, that we shouldn't focus on any one belief or dogma, and that science and nature collectively made up their idea of who and what God was.

I thought that sounded great as a young man who wasn't raised in a religious household. I told him, "I think I agree with that view. Scientology sounds like the right way to go! That is what you are talking about, right? Science and love? That's Scientology!"

Jerry couldn't stop laughing for at least thirty minutes! I am certain that he walked away from that conversation praying for both of us, and I sure needed it.

I did not come to really know Jesus as my Lord and Savior until after I finished college. It was then that I found myself leading worship services at a Salvation Army church in Denton, Texas. I remember telling Jerry about our church at a reunion, and he asked if my wife, Valerie, and I would be willing to lead the family in a worship service on Sunday. I found my laptop and had several Christian songs on the hard drive, and our family was able to praise God that Sunday.

Jerry gave a brief sermon, and I don't remember a word of it, but that is why I need to share it. To me, this is the most telling memory of my Uncle Jerry. When he was there, he was fully present and fully engaged in whatever we were doing. When he spoke, you heard the truth of the Bible spoken in a loving and uplifting way that did not feel like a sermon. Whether you were a follower of Jesus Christ or not, you felt renewed by his presence and fully understood the wisdom and truth of what he said. You understood the message he was communicating without hanging on every word, and it was always a message of how much he loved you.

My Uncle Jerry was a follower of Jesus Christ, and one of the best worldly examples of him I have ever known.

Will the Community Weep?

Pastor Jason Montano: From Jerry I learned to teach the church to love in their community, and that if we must ever close our doors, we want the community to weep, not just the church attenders.

Genuine Care

Joe Kobriger: It is a gift to have genuine concern for and interest in others—Jerry had both. Working in sales, I discovered it is a learned skill to be able to ask people questions about themselves. Jerry learned the skill, but not out of selfishness. He genuinely asked questions because he cared about and wanted to know people.

Show and Tell

Debbie Palmer: One of the special things about Pastor Jerry was he knew the generations of my family—my grandparents, my parents, my cousins, my husband and me, and our kids.

My grandpa was told he could no longer be a member at another Racine church because he owned a bowling alley and the bowling alley had a bar that served liquor. It really hurt his feelings. Jerry went to his house and called him by name and talked with him.

I took my dad, Mac, to the Assembly of God Church and he saw *Heaven's Gates & Hell's Flames*[17] and accepted Christ. He was a cowboy

---

[17] *Heaven's Gates & Hell's Flames* is a touring evangelistic drama that has been performed worldwide. It is based on an evangelical interpretation of the gospel and presents the message that one must believe in Jesus to be saved and to go to Heaven or face eternal punishment in Hell. It is a production of Reality Outreach Ministries.

and would walk into Grace wearing his cowboy hat. Pastor Jerry would make a point to say, "Hey, Mac! How are you doing?"

Dad would take off his hat, smile, and talk with Jerry for a few minutes. Pastor Jerry made him feel so special. You can *tell* people they are special or you can *show* people they are special. Pastor Jerry went out of his way to do both.

He Put His Hand on My Shoulder

Larry DeRosier: Just my second time at Grace Church, I was sitting in the pew and was very emotional because I was going through the worst season of my life. Pastor Jerry and Jane were seated behind me during this Saturday night service. I had no clue who they were. After the sermon message, I was crying and Jerry put his hand on my shoulder and asked me if I was okay. He comforted me before I left.

The next day I came to my first Sunday service, and there preaching was the man who had comforted me and humbly cared for me the night before. I knew God put me in just the right place to encounter his faithful, loving, and caring servant.

Why Would You Marry Them?

Cindi Stewart: I remember a time when Pastor Jerry said he was marrying two non-Christians. I had come from a legalistic background, and I was appalled by this and thought, *How could he marry non-Christians?* So, I went up to him right in the church lobby and asked him.

I remember his answer clearly. He was calm and never defensive. He just smiled at me and said, "They are going to get married somewhere even if it is not here. This way, I at least get six weeks to counsel them and tell them about Jesus. And, maybe by the time I marry them, they will know Jesus."

This was new information to me and changed and softened my rough edges. I learned that day that maybe I would never be able to live outside the box of legalism that I was brought up with, but that I was free to think outside of the box. Pastor Jerry's love was life changing for me because he showed me that people always had to be the priority, not just following the people-imposed rules.

Playing the Long Game

Dave Arnone: Grace Church owned a home next to my parents' home in Racine. The Worshams became our neighbors when I was seventeen. Jerry was truly kind to me, nonjudgmental, and always available to talk and be neighborly. He was my neighbor first and a pastor second. That's another way of saying that he communicated with me about normal stuff, especially sports. He was patient, approachable, and a great listener. He never witnessed or evangelized. Our relationship was simple in my mind. He was much younger than my parents, yet he was older than me, and he was a friend. I was always able to be myself around him. Never in all my years of knowing him did I have to behave differently around "the pastor." He accepted me.

Our homes were remarkably close to one another. In the summer, I would have my bedroom window open, and twenty feet away were the Worsham's open kitchen and dining room windows. I would play my stereo as loud as the equipment could handle. There is zero doubt the Worshams heard enough of Fleetwood Mac, Cheap Trick, The Beatles, and other rock bands to last a lifetime! In hindsight, I was incredibly rude, but the Worshams never said a word to me or to my parents. In my early twenties, my parents would allow me to host parties for my softball team. Loud, obnoxious, and straight-up crazy stuff happened during these parties, and again, not one word from the Worshams. Because Jerry and Jane did not complain, they did not shut down the developing relationship I had with Jerry. They did not build walls; they were playing the long game. I moved from my parents' home in 1985 but always made a point of seeing Jerry and Jane when I visited my folks.

Life really changed for me during this season. I graduated from college, got married, bought a home, and had a baby all within two years. I had a whole new set of conversation topics to discuss with Jerry, and he was always interested in what I had going on in my adult life. He was a great listener and encourager.

When I proposed to Nan in 1986, neither of us were going to church, we were living together, and we did not have a pastor to marry us. My first thought was to ask Jerry to marry us because he was my friend. Nan readily agreed.

Looking back, asking a leading pastor to marry non-Christians who were living together ignored the marital process of the North American Baptists. Yet, Jerry married us anyway. I often wonder if Jerry would have declined if either Nan or I would have become Christians.

Shortly after we were married, Jane invited us to a Friendship Sunday[18] at Grace. Nan went, I did not; and Nan started attending Grace alone. After a couple of months, I realized that she was getting blessed by being part of Grace. We also had our only child at this time and I thought we should do church as a family. I wanted to be a good example to our son, so I decided to attend as well. Nan and I both eventually became believers, were baptized, and became members of Grace.

Need a Glove or Shoes?

Laura Kienzle: Pastor Jerry coached the Grace women's softball team one summer when I was a player. It was so fun!

I remember him compassionately asking me if I needed a glove and if I had the proper shoes to wear since we were on a furlough from the mission field. Even in trivial things like this, he made people feel very cared for and seen.

---

[18] Friendship Sunday was an outreach event created by Pastor Jerry where church members could invite friends to attend church with them, hear the gospel, and learn about Grace Baptist Church.

Cook and Bottle Washer

Dr. Robert Gullberg: Pastor Jerry set an example for me of how to interact with people and patients at the hospital bedside. He loved meeting with people when they were sick and looked at it as a call and a responsibility, never a burden.

Pastors have different gifts. Jerry was a cook and bottle washer; he could do it all. He helped me to interact with those I work with and minister to in a Christian manner. I received tons of good mentoring from him.

He Supported His Flock

Michelle Jenks: Pastor Jerry lived out his faith, and the biggest example of this came on the night my mom died.

I was only thirteen, with one younger brother and one older brother. My mom had gone shopping on a Saturday and my dad was working his shift at the fire station. We were old enough to be home alone, so we were going about our Saturday business. In the late morning, we got a phone call from my dad relaying that my mom had been hospitalized because she'd suffered a heart attack, and that he was at the hospital with her.

This was before the time of smartphones and instant updates, so we waited and heard from my dad only one more time that day. He told us things were looking okay, and that it was likely that after a certain procedure Mom was having, she would be okay. The day dragged on. We did not hear from our dad again, and we wondered what could be taking so long. Late in the evening, my brothers and I were sitting in the living room when my dad walked in. Pastor Jerry walked in right behind him. I knew before my dad could get the words out that my mom had passed away. Pastor Jerry must have been with my dad at the hospital and may have even driven him home. He was there for my dad and my family in one of our hardest moments, and he showed the love of Christ by staying with us and by being there in the hard and terrible moments that followed. And I know we are not the only family he did this for. Not only that, but Pastor Jerry knew my mom, and he would have been impacted by her death as well, but he never made it about what he felt. He supported his flock.

To this day, when I think about that day and remember the image of Pastor Jerry standing there and supporting my dad and all of us, I am overwhelmed. This is what it truly means to love one another.

God Will Take Care of Her

Jack and Julie Bell: There were times when we were struggling with our daughter, Jodi. She was often invisible and had a meek and mild temperament.

We talked to Pastor Jerry to get counsel because he had two daughters. He encouraged us to just love on Jodi and to remember that Jesus loves her more than we ever can or will. He assured us that God would take care of her whether she had a husband or not.

He Loved by Following the Bible

Jerry Morrison: When I teach the Bible, I tell my classes that church discipline is to be executed according to the Scriptures. While I was a member of Grace, there was a high-profile man in the church who was living in open sin. Jerry followed the Scripture to a tee. First, Pastor Jerry confronted him one on one, then he took a deacon with him, and when there was still no repentance, the man was brought before the church and asked to leave as he was continuing to live in non-repentance (Matt. 18:15–17).

Acknowledging sin is not popular in our day, but Pastor Jerry was always true to the Word of God.

Have You Done Everything to Restore Your Marriage?

Larry and Maggie White: "We have a unique story," Maggie said. "Larry and I were married for ten years and got divorced. I was dating someone who was going to church at Grace, and this man and I met with Pastor Jerry. In that meeting Jerry asked me, 'Have you done everything you can to restore your marriage?'

"Larry and I had been divorced for five or six years by this time, so I thought it was a strange question. Ironically, the relationship that put me in front of Pastor Jerry ended, but his words stuck with me. The next time we talked, I told him this, and he told me he wanted me and another woman to do a Bible study called *Operation Timothy*. He was going to pray about who I should study with. When I got back from vacation, he introduced me to Sue Kind. She became my best friend. We did *Operation Timothy* and many other studies together.

"When Larry and I were first married, my expectations for him as a dad were probably unrealistic," Maggie said. "He came from a family with a father who wasn't involved, and the way he disciplined was rough. I felt I knew how to fix his behavior. Fortunately, after we divorced, Larry became a really good dad. While we were divorced, our daughter would say she had the best of both worlds because Larry and I were always friends and both of us cared about our kids," Maggie said.

"We even bought a house together while we were divorced," Larry said.

"I told Pastor Jerry that Larry and I wanted to get back together most of the time we were divorced. Neither of us had remarried; we had two children, and so we went together to talk to Pastor Jerry," Maggie shared.

"Pastor Jerry was who I called for advice," Larry said. "When we were trying to get back together, I would call him and say, 'You would not believe what she did!' He would ask me, 'Well, what did you do Larry?'

"Then, when we had an argument at home and would go to church, the sermon would be about that very subject. I joked with Pastor Jerry many times saying, 'You can't come up with a sermon on your own. You're bugging my house!' We were having problems and at church Pastor Jerry would be talking about our exact issues," Larry shared.

"When we got remarried, the people of Grace Church opened their arms to us. Pastor Jerry remarried us here," Larry said. "As time went on, he and Jane invited us to events like a Christmas round robin. We thought, *Man, we have been to other churches and they barely even talked to us!*" Larry said.

"As Pastor Jerry got to know us, before and even after we got remarried, things were hard," Maggie said. "He said to Larry, 'You are like a lawyer. You like to argue.' When he said that, it really made sense to me. He helped us work things out."

"I got along with Pastor Jerry well," Larry said. "I think he saw me as a challenge. When I first met him, I would never pray out loud. I never did that. We went to church and it was just something to do. Jerry took me under his wing and I grew in obedience to the Lord through him. He showed me how I should be living, what I should be doing, why we go to church, why we pray, and why we serve. He made me see the direction I should be going. He helped me see things the correct way through Jesus' eyes.

"Jane called us one day and invited us to join their Bible study," Larry said. "There was no way I wanted to do that! It was with the Cohills and Booths—those I called the upper management people at Grace—who prayed like crazy," Larry said.

"At Bible study I would purposely ask Pastor Jerry questions to see if I could trap him. He would start to answer and then he would stop and tell me where I could find it in the Bible. He told me to go read about it and come back to him if I had questions. What a strategy!" Larry joked.

"As the study went on, we knew we had jumped into a whole deep well," Larry said. "Pastor Jerry would ask me to pray occasionally and I would say, 'No thanks.' Then he got me to pray once, and then again, and by the end, I was the Bible study leader. His mentoring helped push me.

"It was Jerry's goal to make me a serious Christian, and it was my goal to break him down," Larry joked. "That is why I tell stories about him jumping over the desk and choking me until I said Jesus was my Savior and other stuff. I was the actor, the jokester, I would throw Jerry's name in any story I could. He would get afraid at Bible study wondering what I was going to say!"

"Larry brought out a different side to Jerry," Maggie said. "It is hard to explain the impact Pastor Jerry had on us. Larry and I were not perfect people, not in a perfect marriage, not doing perfect things, yet that was not what he was looking for."

"That *was* what he was looking for," Larry said, "...people who weren't perfect."

"And he was accepting of us not being perfect," Maggie said. "That drew us in. We were his friends. This man who did so much and impacted so many lives wanted us as friends.

"If you ever feel like you are not worthy, all you need is for someone like Pastor Jerry to accept you. I know we have Jesus, which is like having parents who are totally accepting. Jerry added to this. He loved us *through* Jesus. He never said, 'You are not good enough.' Well, he may have said that to Larry," Maggie joked. "Seriously, Jerry filled a void in our lives."

Everyone Needs Compassion

Jim and Stephanie Kerkvliet: Having observed Pastor Jerry in a variety of settings, we were amazed by how compassionate he was with everyone. At one time or another we all have a situation in our lives when counsel and comfort is needed. We witnessed and experienced Pastor Jerry's compassion in our couples' small group many times.

Everything Changed When
My Lens Changed

Bob Stanwood: I met Pastor Jerry when I was dating Lori Richardson, who is now my wife. She was a member at Grace.

I was a practicing Catholic and had no personal relationship with Jesus Christ. While I was dating Lori, I attended a Catholic service first thing Sunday morning, then I headed to Racine to attend a Grace service with Lori.

When I would hear Pastor Jerry preach, I got answers to my questions. I had never heard preaching straight from the Bible.

When Lori and I wanted to marry, Jerry discussed what was necessary to be married. He had refused to marry Lori and I as she was a believer and I was not. Jerry did not leave me to flounder around on my own but offered a way out of my situation. He arranged to meet with me every week to give me personal instruction from the Bible.

Everything changed in my life when my lens changed; I became a believer in Jesus through Pastor Jerry's help. This is the most important thing in the face of eternity! Pastor Jerry also helped me grow in my personal relationship with Jesus by teaching me how to study the Bible, by demonstrating the importance of fellowship with other believers, by being an example of someone who humbly sought God's will, and by encouraging me to have an accountability partner to help me walk the Christian life. Pastor Jerry helped me identify my spiritual gifts and then recommended ministries to serve in. His support helped me step out in faith and serving. I eventually headed the Men at Work Team. We did home upkeep projects for those unable to do things themselves, mostly seniors, single moms, and widows.

Hug Your Child

Dr. Paul Durbin: My wife, Jen, and I took a course on parenting at Pastor Jerry's encouragement. He reminded us to discipline out of love and never out of anger. He also recommended that you should hug your child after disciplining.

Changed by One Gesture

Nancy and John Henkel: "Our daughter was disobedient and disrespectful. I called Jane, and she said we should come over," Nancy said. "Jerry must have been exhausted as this was a Sunday after church. It meant the world to us that they would invite us into their home and enter into our situation. It was this one, simple gesture that forever changed me. I saw up close what it meant to take someone in, nurture them, support them, not leave them, and persevere through something with them. Pastor Jerry and Jane's love to us is why I now open my home for studies and women. Their presence in our trial made all the difference. They helped us grow. We knew we could not stay where we were or the situation would affect our marriage and our lives."

"Sometime later we were still having problems with our daughter," John said. "Pastor Jerry and Jane brought us into the Welcome Room at church, closed the door, sat down with us, and just listened. They were a caring presence. They wanted us to know they were not done with our problem."

God Is in Control

Dave Arnone: One lesson I learned from Pastor Jerry is that God is in control. I was a thirty-two-year-old dad of a five-year-old boy when my wife had a kidney transplant. Jerry prayed with us, and he prayed for me. He would routinely say to me, "God is in control."

I look back at those times and wonder how I handled it all. I know Pastor Jerry's guidance convinced me to give the whole situation to God. By turning it all over to him, I released myself from the constant state of anxiety and fear.

We Can Show People Jesus by Our Lives

Cindi Stewart: Grace was much smaller in its early years so I could just call Pastor Jerry to ask questions. One day a situation arose about a lesbian couple I knew. This was in the early 1980s, so no one really knew who was or was not homosexual. I called to ask Jerry about what to do and how to interact with them. I did not know anyone like them at the time in my little world.

Joyful as usual and without missing a beat, Pastor Jerry said, "You can eliminate them from your life, but maybe you are just the people they need to be able to see Jesus. We can show people Jesus by our lives. We are not saying we agree with what they are doing, but we can say that Jesus loves them, and because he does, we can too."

Light Bulbs Went On

Geri Baumblatt: My husband, Don, was not a believer. He grew up Jewish, and his family did not really go to church. He clicked with Pastor Jerry right away, and that was a wonderful blessing. I know Pastor Jerry made him think about Christ, and I think he thought differently about Jesus because of how Jerry lived. It helped that Jerry always treated Don as if he was a member of the church, not an outsider.

A few times after church, Don and I went to get a bite to eat with Jane and Jerry. Don was a doctor, and he and Jerry liked to talk about medicine. Don always wanted to know what kind of medications Jerry was on; they connected that way.

Don would also come to church with me on Friendship Sunday. Pastor Jerry had clever ideas like this to make people comfortable visiting.

Through Pastor Jerry's preaching, light bulbs went on in Don, and he wanted us to pray together. If I would forget at a restaurant or other times, he would remind me that we had to pray. We always prayed at the table wherever we were. Pastor Jerry valued prayer and Don started to value prayer. Don was listening and changing through Jerry. In his sermons Pastor Jerry would say, "Hear me, now listen, or listen up." When he did, this would make Don and everyone perk up.

Don was sick for a long time before he died, and Pastor Jerry would call often to check on him. When we went to Mayo Clinic, Jerry called. When we got home, Jerry called. It meant so very much. I believe Don gave his life to Jesus at the end, and Jerry's love toward him played an enormous part in this.

He Loved Everyone the Same

Maggie White: One reason I liked Jerry so much is he loved people the way I loved people. He treated them the same no matter who they were. In my eyes, he was a leader and above me, but he never put himself on a pedestal nor expected to be treated differently.

I work with people with physical disabilities; like them we are all spiritually disabled. Pastor Jerry treated all people with love and care right where they were.

He Built a Church Infused With Love and Care

Peter and Heidi Jundt: "After we visited Grace, we stayed because there was something about Jerry's preaching; we were so engrossed," Peter said. "He had so much to say, and it was always gospel oriented, biblically solid. No matter the subject, there was always something to take away."

"We were just beginning to get plugged in at Grace and only knew a few people when our son, Jacob, got sick. That was December 2002," Heidi said. "He had a Wilms tumor which is childhood kidney cancer; 95 percent of Wilms tumors are now curable. Jacob was in the 5 percent of children with unfavorable pathology. His tumor was in his belly and was the size of a football. It weighed four pounds."

"He was four years old, just shy of five," Peter said. "His birthday was in January and his diagnosis came late in the day on the tenth of December. We went right from St. Catherine's Hospital in Kenosha to Children's Hospital of Wisconsin, and early the next morning I called church."

"When Peter said that he was going to call I was thinking, *Why call? Nobody really knows us there*," Heidi said.

"I did not talk to anyone," Peter said. "I just left a message, and the wheels at Grace started rolling."

"As soon as Peter made the call, we were flooded with love and support from people in the Care Ministry, from people in the Music Ministry, where Peter had just started to serve, and from so many church members. It was love and support like we had never experienced before—gas cards to go back and forth from the hospital, staff members praying with us over the phone, food being delivered to our home, steady hospital visits, one thing after another after another," Heidi said.

"Somewhere along the way we got introduced to Jane and Jerry. I remember Jerry speaking to us after Jacob's diagnosis. He sought us out and let us know the church was there for us. I don't remember Pastor Jerry coming to the hospital—Peter and I were talking about it—I don't think he ever did. He did what *he* was gifted to do. He had built a church infused with love and care and had all the people in the right places. He knew he could trust everyone to go and do what they were called to do," Heidi said. "The people of Grace met all our needs during Jacob's illness through the direction of Pastor Jerry."

"Carol Bullmore [Grace Church Care Ministry co-director] was a big part of the Hands and Feet Ministry at that time, and Pastor Jerry really released her to serve," Heidi said. "Often churches expect the lead pastor to be the one who shows up at every single thing—the funeral, the wedding, the hospital visit, whatever—and if he doesn't you hear, 'We are leaving this church. They don't care about us!'

"Pastor Jerry was good about keeping his focus on leading, preaching, and shepherding. The people who did ministry with him were excellent at their jobs. He did not have to do everything or have his name on everything. Yet, as the shepherd of Grace Church his fingerprints were on everything," Heidi said.

"The first Sunday after everything happened with Jacob, I needed to come to church," Peter said. "I think I was sitting close to the front. Pastor Jerry noticed me and prayed for our family from the pulpit.

"I started writing an email newsletter to quickly update everyone about what was going on with Jacob called *The Jacob Updates*," Peter said. "It started out small, but then we discovered that people were forwarding it to individuals all over the world to pray for Jacob.

"Pastor Jerry would make comments to me about what he was reading in the newsletter and would tell me he looked forward to reading them," Peter said. "It was validation that he was in tune with everything we were going through and he was praying."

"There are many parts to our story before Jacob's illness and after his illness; God used Grace Church and the leadership of Pastor Jerry to totally transform our spiritual walks," Heidi said. "Jerry would not want anyone to say it was *him*, but God working *through him* and all glory to God! He would never want anyone to draw attention to him as a man. He would want people to be eyes up and looking at Jesus."

"Yet, we can't ignore that through his obedience to God, the pieces were put in place for transformation to happen," Peter said. "As a manager, he had an amazing ability to build and empower a team. He put people in place and empowered them to do what they were gifted to do. And that is no small thing. Pastors in many churches we have attended want to micromanage everything and be in control of everything. Jerry did not seem to be like that. He put people in place, gave them the authority to act, and then backed them up."

"There was so much activity going on when Jacob was sick, that when he passed away, we landed in a very dry season. But even in our dry season—the slow down where it felt like everything in our lives came to a weird sort of halt—we would go to church and still get fed through Pastor Jerry's preaching," Heidi said. "I know we don't go to church just to get fed; we go to church to worship God, but that is the way our souls healed, through teaching and worship. It was a weird season. If it had not been for all the things that had happened prior and the ministry of Grace, we would not have been able to deal with that very dry season."

"Pastor Jerry's preaching was the consistency we could rely on in our mourning. Going through a battle like we did with our child was just spiritually, psychologically, emotionally, and physically so intense, and then it was just done. Over. It was like all the air got let out of the balloon," Peter said. "Grace Church was a place where we could go, and hear, and still see that God was right there with us."

"After Jacob died, people were still ministering to us," Heidi said. "We had just gotten to Grace when Jacob got sick. We went through that journey, but there was no time for anything. Jerry encouraged us to go to family camp, we went, and it was so life giving to us.

"I also remember Grace members coming over to help me paint our son Isaac's bedroom in weird sort of ways—pale blue, green dots, etcetera," Heidi said. "This all-encompassing love and help was part of the culture of Grace Church. Jerry taught his people to be the hands and feet of Christ and to be loving servants.

"The part of our story that many people may not know is that there were people outside of the church watching what was happening and saying to us, 'I have never seen a Christian church that acts like a Christian church.' And Grace really was loving us like Jesus intended," Heidi shared. "Our family members who were not close to the Lord or who had bad experiences with churches and found their reasons and excuses to stay away saw something at Grace under Jerry's leadership."

"It was so attractive that it blew them away," Peter said. "They could not believe it."

"To this day, we still have family members tell us how they remember watching everything that the church did and how miraculous it was," Heidi said. "People could not believe that a church would do what Grace Church did.

"Now, of course, Pastor Jerry did not say intentionally, 'Let's serve here, let's go there and minister to that group or family, or let's go to their unchurched family so they can hear. It was all just love in action—very unintentional mission work."

"Grace Church, through Pastor Jerry's leadership, was a beacon of light to us in that very dark time," Peter said. "And not just us, but everyone around us who was plugged into Jacob's story and what we were going through."

What's in a Name?

Kiyomi Bryson: At the time I came to Grace Church, I was afraid to talk to American people. When I first met Pastor Jerry, I did not know he was the pastor. He asked me my name and I told him, "I am Kiyomi." He repeated my name perfectly and never forgot it or mispronounced it.

My husband at the time, Neal, and I missed a few weeks of church. When we came back to church and Pastor Jerry saw us, he came right over and greeted us using our names. This was so important to me because it was hard being from Japan and not knowing English. Lots of people made fun of me because of my poor English.

Pastor Jerry loved and paid attention to me and individual people. He was approachable and wanted to know your story.

It Was Special to Me

Cindi Stewart: I think a great strength Pastor Jerry had was how he learned and knew everyone's names. Seriously, he really did! It was important to him to meet, greet, and welcome new people, and if they returned, he would remember their names.

My parents would visit Grace a couple times a year, and sure enough, Pastor Jerry would remember their names. My dad would be amazed every time and tell me how special that was to him. It was special to me, too, because they were my family. It also validated me as part of the family of Grace that Jerry would make a point to know them and greet them.

Perfect Words for a
Hurting Momma's Heart

Loreen Radke: While I was on staff at Grace Church, our nineteen-year-old daughter told my husband, Kurt, that she was pregnant. I was devastated and Kurt called Pastor Jerry to let him know.

The next morning, I was in my office and the very first person to walk in was Pastor Jerry. He sat across from me and offered me words of comfort and kindness that eased the shame that I was feeling. I will never forget this gesture of Christ-like love and concern to this momma's hurting heart.

A Living Devotional

Janine Carls: Pastor Jerry was unique. When you met him, you knew two things instantly. First, he was glad to meet you and wanted to know more about you. Second, he was worthy of respect. I don't know how else to say it. You knew he ran a tight ship but with a lot of grace. He really walked that line well.

Everyone jokes about how he often said, "Okay." But after talking to him, things always were *okay*. He would use this phrase just to let you know he was listening, engaged, ready to get started, all in, and ready to show grace.

He was always smiling. Always interested. Always wanting to know how God was at work in the lives of others. He liked stories—telling them, hearing them, seeing God in them. In a way, he was like a living devotional with every story pointing to God's love, sovereign will, grace, gentle correction, and even humor.

Pastor Jerry modeled family, but he was gracious in his understanding that not everyone had the same family experiences and sometimes things were tough.

I remember when I expressed frustration about the tasks I did in our home that my husband neglected to notice. His advice to me was straight forward, "Do everything you do as unto the Lord (Col. 3:23). God sees everything even if your spouse does not."

Please Come Pray!

Denise Pipol: Shortly after we started attending Grace, before my husband Jerry or I ever had a chance to personally meet Pastor Jerry, my dad ended up in the ICU (Intensive Care Unit). His condition was critical.

While I was sitting in the waiting room one evening, I spotted Pastor Jerry visiting with another family. I frantically ran up to him, blurted out that we had just started attending his church, and that my father who had just prayed to receive Christ a few days ago was now in the ICU. I asked Pastor Jerry to please, please, come pray with my dad.

As soon as I asked, I realized I had unintentionally pulled him away from the other family. Without even blinking an eye, he gave me a big smile and said that of course he would be happy to pray. He immediately came with us to see my dad.

I don't remember all the words he said, but I do remember feeling so comforted by his Christ-like presence and his prayer for my dad. I am still touched by his willingness to serve us like that—people he did not even know.

Love Administrator

Nancy Ganzel: Pastor Jerry became more than just the guy behind the pulpit to my family. He and Jane soon were a part of most of our family celebrations—graduations, birthdays, holidays, and even one Thanksgiving where Jerry's parents also joined us.

Through the years, Pastor Jerry stood with and administered love, wisdom, and encouragement to our family as we faced some tough years when our son was incarcerated and our daughter married at a young age. He was there to bring comfort when we buried my mother. He was there to share in the grief of burying a stillborn grandchild.

There was nothing he would not do for his flock, and we saw that expressed in so many ways. Like the time my granddaughter left her "piggy" at church and would not go to sleep without it. Jerry went over, unlocked the church, and made two parents and one little girl incredibly happy!

Pastor Jerry was always helping and loving. We had a foreign exchange student from Mexico. Jerry came and spoke with her in Spanish and made her feel welcome and at home.

Once at a roller-skating party, Jerry was my partner and he was having a tough time skating in time with the music. I jokingly said, "Hey, I thought Latinos had a built-in sense of rhythm!"

He laughed and said, "I must have been absent the day they passed out that gift."

But he had so many other gifts God had abundantly poured out on him that he, in turn, poured out for others.

My husband, Dick, and Pastor Jerry died just two weeks apart, and they are now buried side by side in Graceland Cemetery—a fitting end of Pastor Jerry's involvement with our family.

He Hugged Me

Maria Rosa Griffin: I am not a person who receives and remembers words, but I am a person who remembers how someone's words made me feel. Jerry's words were always encouraging and affirming.

I also remember how he hugged me. My own dad did not hug me, but the Lord used Pastor Jerry to hug me and meet me in my neediness. When I came to America from Bolivia, it was extremely hard for me because Americans did not hug too much. When Pastor Jerry preached about his daughters and how he would do things for them, I received his words as a blessing for me from the Lord. God used him to demonstrate Abba [Daddy] to me.

Meeting Hurting People

Yvonne Manning: I remember one woman I was counseling was so upset because her fiancé was not a Christian. They were living together, and I suggested that they make an appointment to meet with Pastor Jerry.

She called me in tears and told me that in one meeting with Jerry he had become a Christian. She was crying. I was crying. She told me how they had decided after meeting with Pastor Jerry that they were not going to live together anymore until after the wedding. This was *so* God and *so how* God worked through Pastor Jerry. This was not a one-time, unusual thing.

Jerry masterfully welcomed hurting people to Grace, met them in their hurt, gently pointed out when he saw things in their lives that were not of God, and watched God change them. He had the ability to be firm with people yet so soft, always steering them toward the gospel.

Are You Okay?

Karen Smith: At its peak membership, Grace Church was very large. I had emergency surgery and I should have died; I was so thankful to be alive. I remember being in the hospital, my phone rang, and on the line was Pastor Jerry calling me to see if I was okay.

There were so many pastors on the Grace staff at that time, and he did not have to call. I just remember being surprised. We knew Jerry and Jane well enough, but we were not good friends.

He said, "Karen, you've been through a lot. How are you doing?"

He was humble, authentic, and just took time to love people.

I'm Cindi's Pastor

Jeff Stewart: I started attending Grace Baptist in January 1992, when I started dating my wife, Cindi. I met Pastor Jerry a few times before we started to date, so he knew a little bit about me when I showed up at Grace with Cindi one Sunday. We got engaged in May that year, and we asked Pastor Jerry to do our pre-marital counseling.

I think it was during our initial counseling session when he told me very kindly but frankly that he was Cindi's pastor, that it was his responsibility to help protect her from making a wrong decision about marriage, and that he would be helping us to see any red flags in our relationship.

We both took the Myers–Briggs Type Indicator tests to use in the counseling sessions, and to this day we still laugh about how opposite we were in some of the characteristics. Pastor Jerry taught us to recognize the differences and work through problems in a healthy way to develop a strong marriage. He got to know us intimately during those counseling sessions, and he officiated at our wedding that November. Thinking back, it makes me tear up; he had a role in cementing our relationship and helping us build a life together in Christ.

Love Like Christ

Kim Kind-Bauer: Love like Christ. This is what Pastor Jerry displayed and lived through all the years I knew him.

I'm Talking to Luke

Juliana Toutant: After church one Sunday my son, Luke, and I ran into Pastor Jerry. I wished him a good morning. He replied with that big Pastor Jerry smile, "Hello Juli." (Because once you told him your name, he knew it and never forgot it!) He then introduced himself to Luke and vice versa. He asked Luke a series of questions to get to know him. In the process of their question-and-answer session, someone was seeking Luke's attention to have him take a student to the high school area.

Pastor Jerry, in a very kind manner, explained that he was talking to Luke and that they should ask someone else to tend to that.

I remember thinking, *Wow! Luke is important to Pastor Jerry.* He made everyone feel loved and important no matter their age.

Now Catch This

Jeff Hart: My wife, Ann, and I attended Grace Church for forty years. One of my favorite Pastor Jerry sayings was, "Now catch this." He said the phrase when he wanted to be sure he had your attention.

From Pastor Jerry, I caught more than preaching. When we first started attending Grace, my Christian faith was lukewarm at best. The example set by Jerry profoundly influenced me. He demonstrated that a relationship with Christ was not to be taken lightly or for granted. I really appreciated his sincerity. He genuinely loved God and loved his congregants. It is Jerry Worsham's honest, deep love of Jesus Christ and his love for others that has had the greatest effect on me.

He Helped Me Hold Onto My Childhood Faith

Kristen Pedersen (Pulda): Just weeks away from my twentieth birthday, I found out that I was pregnant with my oldest daughter, Kyah. To say I was terrified is an understatement! Even though I grew up in a Christian home and knew that I could go to my loving parents with anything, I still found myself very afraid, but mostly ashamed. I was raised believing that sexual intimacy outside of marriage was a sin, and I felt like a failure. *How could I have let so many people down?* When I went to my parents with the news, they were also flooded with emotions ranging from anger and shame to surprise and worry. The first thing my dad did was call Pastor Jerry and let him know what was happening, and he immediately scheduled a meeting with us.

Our meeting with Pastor Jerry was full of grace, truth, love, and compassion. At no point did I feel condemned or judged. He welcomed all of us with open arms. He had a lot of wisdom to offer us when we were full of questions and uncertainty. He reminded us that a baby is always a blessing and never a mistake. He also reminded us that God can make good things come out of our sin. He encouraged me to slow down, to pray, and to wait on God's timing. I will never forget the phrase he used. It was, "I am not in the business of marrying and burying." I felt relief and hope at that moment.

He and Jane promised to walk through the journey with us. He offered many hours of counseling, encouragement, and nothing but love and support as we continued to attend church at Grace.

My pregnancy was extremely hard. I was often sick and found it difficult to keep a job. I applied for a part-time position at Grace and did not get it. I was heartbroken and discouraged. Shortly after, Jane called me and asked if I would be willing to work with her mom who was suffering from dementia and needed a part-time caregiver. There I was single, pregnant, and Jane and Jerry were loving me by offering me a job!

As the months of my pregnancy went on and my due date grew closer, Jane, her siblings, and Pastor Jerry sat me down and asked if I would be interested in living full time with Jane's mom, Jo.

I was terrified and wondered, *How could I, as a single mother, take care of my newborn and an aging person with dementia?* I prayed hard about the decision and felt the Lord was giving me an opportunity to be able to stay home with my daughter and have housing and an income. I continued to live and care for Jo until the next summer when Kyah's dad, Jared, and I were married.

Jane and Jerry forever changed the life of my family. They showed undeserved grace to a sinner, walked out the love of Christ, never once made me feel judged, and embraced me and my family like family. They modeled Jesus for me at a time when I was vulnerable and lost. This allowed me to hold on to the faith I had discovered as a child. I had always had a deep love for Christ, and I wanted to honor and serve Jesus but instead found myself in sin. Jane and Jerry kindly discipled me in a way that allowed for and led to repentance. This strengthened my faith.

To me, Pastor Jerry was always kind. He had a gentle smile and made me feel like I was cared for and important. I can picture the way he would laugh. It was special. He practiced what he preached, and his love for Christ was evident in the way he lived and how he loved his family and others.

His sermons were full of hard truths but were spoken in a way that demonstrated God's love. I am grateful that I was under his leading and that both Jane and Jerry loved me. I will forever remember them as having a vital, redemptive role in my family's story.

He Exercised Tough Love

Paul and Laura Kienzle: At one point while we were on the mission field, we struggled in our marriage. When we came home on furlough, South America Mission entrusted us to Pastor Jerry's counsel. When we laid out our situation to him, he did not sugarcoat his reply but exercised tough love with us. Though he was compassionate, he gave us clear directives regarding what we needed to work on. He asked us to set goals and to return for our next meeting when we had worked toward some of those goals.

We tried to get him to admit that he had done some of the same unwise things we had done, and he gently told us that he had not done those things and that he had always prioritized his relationship with Jane.

While at first that felt non-transparent, inside we knew it to be true because we saw it in Jerry and Jane and in their relationship.

Overcoming

Suzanne Schackelman: I started attending Grace Church because a couple I knew was attending. My marriage was falling apart and their marriage had been repaired by the counsel and teaching of Pastor Jerry.

When I first counseled with him, he asked me, "Are you saved?"

I thought to myself, *His wording is a Baptist way of asking if I believe in Jesus.* I knew what to say or what I thought Jerry wanted to hear so I answered "yes." I was raised Catholic, married a Dutch Reformist, and attended a Presbyterian church; because my husband had got romantically involved with another woman there, I no longer wanted to attend. She had been a friend of ours, so it was torture for me to stay in that church when he wanted a divorce. Because I had counseled with Pastor Jerry, Grace was the natural choice for me and my two sons to attend.

After the divorce became final, Pastor Jerry continued to counsel me. He was a sound spiritual and biblical guide and teacher to me through my years as a single mother. He also encouraged me to seek counsel from wise women at Grace.

Pastor Jerry also helped me and my boys in practical ways. I had just purchased a home and we were moving into it from a rental house. This was the second time Jerry and men from church helped us move.

The night before I was to move, I was at the new house cleaning and found carpenter ants. The next morning, I had the exterminators come and give me an assessment of what to do. It was worse than I thought. I had carpet beetles as well. All the carpets and drapes had to be torn out. The exterminators began spraying the ants and beetles as the Grace men and Pastor Jerry were at the rental house loading our belongings. I cleaned the rental while the group was unloading at the new house. I got into the corner of the rental house and couldn't move. I was overwhelmed, angry, and fearful to the point of being paralyzed. Pastor Jerry came over and told me to get out of that corner because people needed me at the new house to show them where to put the furniture.

I was hoping and expecting him to be gentle, kind, sympathetic, and empathetic. This is not what I got. Instead, he firmly told me to get a move on! I did what he said because I knew that he knew best. I had grown to trust his pastoral wisdom. I knew he would not lead me to a place that was not for my protection.

Many Grace men, women, and families poured their love and energy into my life and the lives of my two boys. I have come to know Jesus better and deeper because of them and especially through the leadership and friendship of both Jerry and Jane. He demonstrated such sacrificial love—a shepherd's love. When I got remarried to Joe, Pastor Jerry officiated at our wedding ceremony.

Root Beer Floats on a Summer Day

Tim Rush: A couple of months before Jerry passed, Jane sent me an email on his behalf, wondering if I would like to come over to his house to talk. He said he had wanted to get together for some time.

Jane, in her calm and comforting manner, told me that it was okay if I did not feel comfortable or have time. I was compelled to go—this was Pastor Jerry and he was inviting me to his home. I was incredibly nervous and was not sure what we would talk about, but I prayed and I knew the Lord would guide our conversation.

It was a warm, sunny day when I went to visit. Jerry and Jane welcomed me into their home. We looked at pictures in their living room, and Jerry told stores about his children and grandchildren; Jane filled in details as needed as speech had become very difficult for Jerry.

Jane suggested we go outside to talk more and offered to bring root beer floats. As Jane prepared these, Jerry and I sat under the overhang attached to his garage and talked. I can't tell you the exact details, but he was kind, smiled, and I felt loved and honored to be with him. I am so grateful I had this opportunity.

The Gospel in the Last Hours

Debbie Arndt: Pastor Jerry led my daughter-in-law Sarah's dad to the Lord within hours of his death. Jerry was retired at the time, and he told Sarah that rarely does anyone accept the Lord when they are so close to death. Yet, Jerry lovingly shared the gospel and he came to Christ!

Sarah has Pastor Jerry in her heart forever because of this.

A Life Characterized by Love

George Gorton: I would say Pastor Jerry's life was characterized by one word: love. God says the greatest commandment is to love the Lord your God and the second is to love your neighbor as yourself

(Matt. 22:36–39). Pastor Jerry was a man who loved God, who loved his neighbor as himself, and who loved his congregation.

He met every single one of the attributes of love in 1 Corinthians [13:4–8a] and I want to mention them because they need to be mentioned; every successful church has got to love one another. "Love is patient, love is kind." And Jerry was both. "It does not envy, it does not boast, it is not proud. It does not dishonor others, it is not self-seeking, it is not easily angered, it keeps no record of wrongs. Love does not delight in evil but rejoices with the truth. It always protects, always trusts, always hopes, always perseveres. Love never fails."

Special-Needs Ministry Birthed

Nancy Henkel: I saw this bedraggled family sitting up front at church one Sunday morning, and I befriended the dad, Dick. He had two sons; one of them, Chuck, had special needs and his other son had borderline special needs.

At Pastor Jerry's encouragement, my husband, John, and I started to meet with Dick every-other-week for lunch. He was eighty-seven years old, had no one to help him, and no car; yet he loved the Lord. He was not in great health and ended up in the hospital and was dying. I was present with him when he passed.

When Dick died, Pastor Jerry sent John and me up to a lawyer by Mayfair Mall in Wauwatosa to make sure everything was in order for Chuck and his care. We ended up being his legal guardians. From this special-needs family, a ministry to special-needs people was birthed at Grace.

He Did Not Mind Her Orange Fingers

Reannyn Bickle: I became a single mom due to a very unexpected pregnancy. Thankfully, I had my dad [Joe Kobriger] and his wife, Sheri, and I went to church with them.

I took the child dedication class Pastor Jerry led. I was a young, single mother and felt quite out of place. Everyone else in the class was married, had likely planned their babies, and were "doing life the right way." Yet, no one in the class treated me differently.

I remember Pastor Jerry giving us all the same guidance. This was especially important for me as a single mom. I felt like I let down myself, my parents, God, and the church with my poor decisions and sin.

I think my life would have gone very differently if I would have had a different church experience. I never felt judged at Grace coming into church with my dad, Sheri, and my big belly. Everyone was super nice and welcoming, and people prayed with me. One day my dad had the elders and Pastor Jerry pray over me. This group of six men really encouraged me. I thought, *Wow! I made a big mistake, but that does not define the rest of my life. I can't go back in time, but I can control my decisions moving forward.*

I was never a bad kid, but, you know, you turn into a teenager, get your license and freedom, and sometimes there is fall out. Regardless, I was really supported at Grace.

At the child dedication service, everyone else was dedicating babies or older kids. I was the only one chasing around and dedicating a toddler. I had my daughter in the commons because she was so loud. Someone came and got me and told me they were getting things started. We were delayed coming into church so we were the last in line. My daughter was running around on the stage, and I was so embarrassed. She was eating her little Gerber cheese snacks and was getting her beautiful dress full of cheese dust. I was wearing a white sweater so I was covered in cheese dust too. I remember thinking, *What am I doing? I must look like a fool!*

Finally, it was our turn. Pastor Jerry whispered something like, "We'll see how she does, if she will let me hold her. If not, it is fine."

She was and still is a very friendly kid. She went right into Pastor Jerry's arms holding onto him tightly and grabbing him with her orange fingers. He laughed and did not think it was a big deal. He made me feel so much better about it all. Some pastors are stuffy and serious, not him. He was happy to have us there. He demonstrated to me that Christ loves us all, and if we are going to be like him, we need to reach out to everyone—even if it is messy.

A Special Discernment

Lisa Kincade: In middle school I started a new school and met some friends who went to Grace Church. They invited me to go to their youth group, I went, and I really liked it. At that time, my family attended another Racine church. I asked my parents if we could go to Grace and we started attending.

I continued going to the youth group and I wanted to be involved in everything. I remember asking Pam Saxton [one of the adult Worship Team members] if I could sing with her. I had such a desire to worship; I just did not have a relationship with God yet.

At the end of my senior year in high school, I got pregnant. I felt so much shame and instead of going to my family or Christian friends, I went to my non-Christian friends, and they told me to abort the baby. I was so afraid; I heard what I wanted to hear, and I had the abortion. I knew my decision was wrong. But at that time, I reasoned that if I just got out of the situation, I could start new again. I wasn't thinking of it as a baby.

About a week after the abortion, I was part of Middle School Madness.[19] At the event, we were dancing and I started hemorrhaging. I had not told anyone about the abortion. Thankfully, my sister was there. I told her, then we told my parents, and I went straight to the emergency room. My parents called the church and our youth pastor came, and later I met with Pastor Jerry and Pastor Cole. It was such trauma, but the weight was coming off me because now people knew.

My parents tried to keep everything as normal as possible for me going forward, so I still went to college that fall. I knew God forgave me, but I did not *feel* forgiven. I couldn't make friends, no one would call me, and I think I was depressed. Then I got pregnant again with my daughter, Jada, and I left college. I just wanted to go back home. It might sound strange, but Jada was a blessing. I never thought that God would give me a baby again after what I had done.

When I came back to Racine, I went back to Grace Church. It was my peaceful place. Pastor Jerry always knew my name; he talked to me as a person—someone he really knew and cared about—and he was easy to talk to. When it came time for me to dedicate Jada, I wanted her dad to be part of the dedication ceremony. I was so young and wanted us to look like a family. It seemed shameful to me to be up there by myself dedicating my daughter. Pastor Jerry came to talk to me and he said, "Lisa, this is what you are doing for Jada. Her dad does not come here, so I don't think he needs to be a part of it."

Another time, John Czerwinski [the director of worship arts] was doing an Easter event. I tried to be a part of any musical event at Grace I could because when I sang, I felt close to God. John wanted me to be part of the service but shared that Pastor Jerry asked him to find out where my heart was with God first.

---

[19] Middle School Madness (MSM) is a Youth For Christ event. It is an intense week of fun, games, and hearing about Jesus designed specifically for middle school students. For more information visit https://youthforchristwi.com/msm/.

I remember being very angry when Pastor Jerry talked to me about Jada's dedication and even angrier when he asked John to talk to me before I could be part of the Easter event. I had respect for Pastor Jerry, but I thought he was judging me when instead he was loving me. Through it all, I just kept coming to church and listening to his sermons. I did not get it all then, but I knew it was truth. He always spoke truth.

Years later when I got married, my husband was an unbeliever. I started to search for churches that might interest him, and I found a church that seemed on fire for God. During COVID when I was still attending this church, Jada and I were on the phone because she was watching the service from Illinois and I was watching from Racine. Out of the blue she casually said, "Remember that one pastor and how I would lay in your lap in the pews, and we would listen to him?"

"You mean Pastor Jerry?" I asked.

"Yes," she said. "I really liked him."

Her words brought back the comfort of Grace Church and growing up at Grace. That same day I saw on Facebook that Pastor Jerry had passed away. I texted Jane right away and told her Jada and I had just been talking about her and Jerry and how sorry I was for her great loss.

By this point, I had not been attending Grace for almost two years. When I stepped through the doors of Grace for Jerry's memorial service, I knew it was where I should be. It was home to me. I needed to plant my feet there, get involved, and start using my spiritual gifts.

Looking back, I know what an enormous impact Pastor Jerry had on me. I think he saw who I could be in Christ. Though angered by his earlier words, they caused me to not come forward to use my worship gifts until the right time. I always knew I would sing for the Lord, and I think he knew it too; he had a special discernment about him.

He Did Not Want to Hinder Anyone

Luke Binkley: My grandpa lived his life to further the kingdom of God. He made sure he led an upstanding life so he would never hinder people from receiving the gospel. For example, my grandpa chose not to drink alcohol. It wasn't that he did not believe in drinking, but if someone in the church had a drinking problem, Grandpa did not want to hinder their faith in any way. Drinking alcohol is something he could have done; it is not sinful to have a beer on a Saturday night, but he held back to make sure no one in his church would go astray because of him.

There were lots of little things like this that he did because he loved God, loved people, and cared about making an impact for the kingdom.

Not Worthy of a Pedestal

Terry Kultgen: Pastor Jerry set the bar high. I saw his life up close for many years, and it was so consistent. He genuinely considered others more important than himself. When you were with him alone, in an elder meeting, or with a group of people, he never dominated the conversation.

When I said things to him about how well a meeting went, he never wanted to receive attention. He would say, "Terry, that is not a pedestal that I am worthy of."

We know Jesus said the two greatest commands were to love the Lord your God with all your heart, soul, strength, and mind and to love your neighbor as yourself (Matt. 22:36–39). I don't know if there is one attribute to completely summarize Jerry except that he loved—he loved the Lord and he loved his neighbor as himself. He got those right, and if you get those right, everything else falls into place.

Chapter 6

THE MARK OF HUMILITY:
The Way Up Is the
Way Down

For all those who exalt themselves will be humbled,
and those who humble themselves will be exalted.

LUKE 14:11

One of Pastor Jerry's favorite books was *Humility: The Journey Toward Holiness* by Andrew Murray. In this book Murray deems humility "our true nobility" and "the distinguishing feature of discipleship."[20]

Pastor Jerry certainly had this "distinguishing feature of discipleship." When I asked interviewees to describe Jerry, nearly everyone used the word *humble*. Many of the men he mentored said he was big on giving out little books, and *Humility* was one of the little books he gave out often.

---

[20] Andrew Murray, *Humility: The Journey Toward Holiness* (Bloomington, MN: Bethany House Publishers, reprinted edition, 2001).

Jerry Took Himself Out of the Equation

Ralph "Easy" Worsham: One huge influence in Jerry's life was Johnnie Jenkins, a missionary who came to Panama. Jerry talked about him all the time and wanted to go places and do things with him. Johnnie was a great man, and Jerry was a lot like him.

Jerry had a hand in Johnnie talking to me about Christ. He was concerned about me, and with the attitude between us as brothers, I think he knew it may be hard for him to reach me. So, he humbly took himself out of the equation and put someone in place who he thought could better minister to my needs. Johnnie led me to Christ, he handled me, guided me, and was never pushy.

Servant Leadership

Pastor Mike Lueken: Jerry talked about servant leadership over and over and the word humility captures what servant leadership entails. He would talk often about the need for humility and burned that thought into the staff.

People who would clash or have trouble with Jerry were those who were overly flamboyant, thought they were gifted in some extraordinary way, or thought too highly of themselves. He would mentor these people and introduce them to reality by encouraging servant leadership.

Jerry taught me that part of humility was also helping people understand that I have a role to play as a pastor, but I am human. The role of pastor does not make me superhuman. For Jerry, humility always started with his deep dependance on God.

You Are Not That Special

Pastor Brian Petak: When I first joined Grace in 1990, there were only a few staff members; things were very organic and simple. The church started growing very quickly and operations became more complicated with the growth. Work went from organic, simple, and informal, to having lots of systems in place to try to keep up with everything. The church was experiencing a lot of success. Grace was the "it" church in Racine at this time.

I think there were one or two services early on with just a couple hundred people. Attendance exploded. We added a third service and then a fourth service on Saturday nights just to make room for people. It was like the wild west! We were trying to hang on as things grew and the church was bursting.

Jerry stayed steady and humble through all of this. I remember him saying things to the staff like, "I'm no one special. None of you are that special." He wanted to make sure we all stayed grounded and humble.

Not the *Jerry Show*

Pastor Greg Smith: Simple. That was Jerry. His preaching wasn't flashy or charismatic, but it changed peoples' lives. He did not try to be the biggest person in the room. He wasn't passive, but he also wasn't domineering. In a group of leaders, you get passionate people who are trying to push directions. Jerry was always humble.

If you are not humble, you don't release responsibility, and if you don't release responsibility, you burn out. Out of his prayer life came the recognition that this is not the *Jerry Show*.

Empowered by Humility

Chuck Dumars: Pastor Jerry was not above laughing at himself to promote good humor. He resembled the character Tatoo [played by Herve Villechaize on the television program *Fantasy Island*]. Sometimes he would see a paper airplane someone had thrown and would point to it and say, "The plane! The plane!"

Humility is one of the most difficult aspects of a Spirit-led life to display, and it is one trait of Christian character seen so rarely today.

Pastor Jerry was extremely humble, yet his humility did not negate the influence of his leadership: it empowered it.

On occasion at our elder meetings, he would cry over the sins of our church that damaged families and individuals. It makes me tear up picturing him.

I Must Decrease

Bob Magruder: I remember how genuinely humble Pastor Jerry was. He did not act humble. He did not work at choreographing humility. He was humble! He personified this verse: "Do nothing out of selfish ambition or vain conceit. Rather, in humility value others above yourselves" (Phil. 2:3). Humility was completely native to his being, like a reflex responding to stimuli.

His ministry was never about notoriety, accolades, or high-powered gimmicks. He was a man of impeccable character and unflagging integrity. Even though his ministry was indeed flourishing, he shunned the temptation to build a one-man empire. His interior life resembled John the Baptist's blazing motto, "He must increase; but I must decrease" (John 3:30 ESV). I never heard him talk about his accomplishments. He was all about exalting Jesus Christ.

He Did What Pleased God

Pastor Rusty Hayes: Jerry's greatest strength was his holiness. He walked remarkably close to Jesus. Everybody who worked with Jerry knew that he was a man of outstanding integrity and humility. He was the kind of guy that if he was stranded on a desert island with somebody and there was only one bottle of water, he would give that other person the bottle of water. He was going to do what was pleasing to God regardless of the cost.

This Is What I Would Do Differently

Phil Adams: Jerry Worsham was a humble, humble man. He entered into suffering with me and gave me the advice he thought was best at the time. But years later, he was humble enough to say, "If I had to do it over again, this is what I would do differently."

It Is a Mystery

Pastor Greg Smith: Jerry was willing to admit what he did not know. I can think of several times where I went into his office and told him what theological construct I was wrestling with. Most often his response to me would be, "It is a mystery."

I didn't like that, but I did like the reality in Jerry's statement. This was just another sign of his humility.

Flexed on His Family

Pastor Jason Montano: Greg Smith and I had a digital turntable, and one day we decided to remix Jerry's sermons. We took sound bites of him saying, "Okay, okay, hear me now Grace, okay." We were in the middle of the remix and in walks Jerry to our hysterical laughter. We froze.

Jerry started laughing saying, "You guys! Man, okay man. Remixing me? Okay, okay."

Jerry was humble, and he could laugh at himself. He would not talk about himself, his role, or his accomplishments. The only thing he talked about was his family and his grandkids; he always flexed on them, that was where he was not humble!

Ask Me the Tough Questions

Terry Kultgen: Pastor Jerry and I were accountability partners for about five years. When we started, I asked, "Jerry, how do I ask you the tough questions?"

"You ask me the tough questions," he said. "Show me no favoritism. Don't overlook things. Ask me what you would ask anyone else. If I am doing something wrong and I don't know it, it is a blind spot. We all have blind spots."

Open and Transparent

Craig Vaughn: Everybody knew Pastor Jerry and he was a friend to everyone, but there was a small group of men with whom he could be real with and be himself. In this group he was just *Jerry, a regular guy*. With us he laughed; he had fun; and he processed the struggles of men, husbands, and fathers.

During his last ten years at Grace Church, there were challenging times. When you go through those times together, the ups and downs, a bond is formed. We surrounded Jerry and iron sharpened iron (Prov. 27:17).

When Jerry's pastoral ministry was moving toward its end, I formed a team of guys to come around him and help him process what it would be like to transition from thirty-five years of ministry into retirement. Dr. Bob Gullberg, Terry Kultgen, and I met with Pastor Jerry regularly to walk through what retirement would look like. We gave him a space to share how he was feeling and what he was thinking. We supported him and prayed for him to finish well.

He was open and willing to be transparent with us. He shared his concerns and fears and was vulnerable.

Not Showy

Dr. Robert Gullberg: When Jerry retired from being head pastor, he sat up in the balcony. He felt comfortable there because he did not want to be too influential or be showy in any way. This was just another example of his humility.

Just a Sinner in Need of a Savior

Dr. Paul Durbin: Pastor Jerry was a very humble man. I never sensed pride in how he conducted himself. He admitted that anxiety was an issue for him, and I appreciated his honesty in sharing this with his church. He never made himself out to be perfect. Instead, he emphasized that he was a Christ follower, just a sinner in need of a Savior.

Last in Line

Debbie Kultgen: I watch behaviors and am into people's mannerisms. I noticed that at church functions Jerry and Jane always went through food lines last. It was something so simple that demonstrated humility. They lived to be last instead of first.

Seasoned in Humanity and Humility

Pastor Mike Lueken: I saw Jerry very clearly soften as he aged in the pastorate. He was always loving and soft and shepherded in a way that remembered souls were at stake, but as he grew older, he realized that issues recycle and come back around—another broken marriage, another addiction, another worship war, another wave of staff departures, whatever the issue.

When I talked to him years later about all the waves that hit the church, it was clear he realized it was just human sin nature. When he was younger, he might have gotten agitated by the situation and tried to clamp down on, control, or snuff out the sin. But later he started to go about it all in a different way. It was like he became seasoned in the rhythms of humanity and humility, and that created in him a little less dislike for things not being neat.

Where Does Your Importance Come From?

Pastor Rusty Hayes: Jerry's relationship with God was his joy. It brought a stability to him. He was one of those guys who had a fatherly quality about him. I am guessing that—even as a young man—he was always the adult in the room because he was content in the Lord.

He did not need money or want any fame. I would say, "Why don't you write a book? You have so much wisdom."

"I don't need that," he would say.

For him, I think he felt it would be pretentious, and now he has a book being written about him!

I pursued a doctorate and Jerry arranged for the church to give me a scholarship. Before I took my first class, he sat down with me and asked me, "Rusty, why are you doing this? Why are you getting a doctorate? What's that about?"

"You know, one day when I am an old man and I won't be able to be a pastor anymore, I would like to teach at the seminary level, and I would like to learn too," I told him.

"Okay, okay, Rusty," he said, "because if it is about you being important, that is not where you get your importance. You don't need a doctorate to be pleasing to God."

He Delegated With No Strings Attached

Pastor Greg Smith: Jerry was very approachable. Many pastors of churches the size of Grace become so busy that they are not available and approachable. Jerry focused on a few things, and he did them well so he would be available and approachable. One sign of his humility is just how much he delegated to his staff members, and another is how he delegated to us without a lot of strings attached. He emphasized, "This is yours to run with and the riverbanks are wide. Let me know if you need anything."

To me, that is releasing control, and that is a sign of humility.

He Was a Servant Leader

Pastor Brian Petak: Jerry lived out this passage: "In your relationships with one another, have the same mindset as Christ Jesus: Who, being in very nature God, did not consider equality with God something to be used to his own advantage; rather, he made himself nothing by taking the very nature of a servant…" (Phil. 2:5–7a).

Jerry lived like Jesus. There are so many examples, but one is seared into my memory. One Sunday morning, the Worship Team was busy rehearsing and working out our music and songs for the services. Pastor Jerry could have been praying or reading over his preaching message or sitting on some lofty perch as the lead pastor, but instead, he was walking the church hallway and mopping the floors. His servanthood was all there to see.

As a lead pastor, I consciously think about him mopping the floors because on Sundays, inevitably, there is always something that needs to be done to tidy up the worship center. For Jerry, it was mopping. For me, it is stacking Bibles. At our church we have Bibles available for people to take. It seems like every week they are dusty and unevenly stacked. So, every week, I dust them off, stack them evenly, and make things presentable. I cannot help but think of Jerry when I do that.

Ministry Longevity

Pastor Isaac Miller: Jerry's longevity in ministry at one church for so long is almost unheard of. I think it all came down to humility and his prayer life.

I Want To Be Like Jesus

Jeanne Ferraro: I remember Pastor Jerry preaching through Revelation and then studying the book in a small group with him. He said, "I want to be like Jesus." It was so beautiful to have your pastor tell a group this. He really wanted to die to his own ways. And he was so much like Jesus in his humility, his kindness, and his sensitivity. He lived for Christ and through Christ's enabling.

Humble About the Bigness

Jane Worsham: Jerry was always humble about the size of Grace as the church grew. He would mention it often in his sermons, and he would also mention his struggle with pride as well as worry.

He never shied away from talking about his weaknesses. He believed it was important to talk about and be open and vulnerable about the struggles he had as a pastor.

Singularly Focused on the Glory of God

Pastor Brian Petak: Jerry was singularly focused on the glory of God. He was so close to Jesus. You never saw pride. You never saw self-centeredness. You never saw inappropriate anger. He confronted me on my own sin issues. He had a heavy task to hold me accountable, and he was not happy, but he was full of grace even when he was frustrated or angry.

Humble is a word everyone used to describe Jerry. He was a man on his knees. Always praying. He embodied Paul's words "pray without ceasing" (1 Thess. 5:17 ESV) because his whole life was postured toward humble, prayerful dependence.

Just Grandpa

Levi Binkley: When I was growing up, people often came up to my family and told us what my grandpa meant to them, how he had saved their lives, or how he saved their marriages. These things really did not sink in when I was younger. Back then, my grandpa being a pastor meant that I got to go into the church building after hours and have NERF Gun wars!

As I've gotten older, I have realized the impact he had on so many people who viewed him in such a different way than I did. So many people had stories about him. One person saw my grandpa as the wise mentor who helped save his life, another person called him his trusted friend, another saw him as the teacher, and yet another as someone who was always listening and loyal. Even in my own family he was the father who my dad wanted to win over so he could marry my mom! Just who Grandpa really was to so many people came to a head for me at his memorial service. Whether people knew me or not, they wanted to share what a difference my grandpa had made to them and in their life in Christ.

The accolades were great, but to me he was just my wise, loving grandpa; a big family man with bad handwriting that my mom had to translate; someone who wanted to play chess with me, talk theology with me, spend time with me, and who loved me. I never thought of him in the way others did, but it was amazing to hear all the points of view that made up the portrait of who he was.

Knowing the impact my grandpa had on the kingdom of God is inspiring. He would always say, "I am no one special. I am just little old Jerry, a grandpa, a guy with a family."

He had such an amazing impact on the world as "no one special." I am certainly no one important, no celebrity, just a normal person—but I believe I can also have an impact on people's lives just like him. My grandpa changed lives with the gospel, and so can I.

God Called Them to Stay

Joe and Sheri Kobriger: "It takes a lot of humility to hand over the leadership of a church you have pastored for most of your adult life and even more humility to stay a member of that church, worship every week, and remain in the background. It was remarkable to watch Jerry do this," Sheri said. "People will always naturally gravitate to the old leader; but Pastor Jerry made it clear to the Grace congregation that *senior pastor* was no longer his role, and he encouraged members to follow the new pastor. He did everything he could to support and affirm the new pastor, his wife, and their family."

"This just shows that Jerry Worsham did not ever look at Grace Church as his church, but as God's church," Joe said. "He knew it was God who built Grace Church and God who blessed Grace Church with a building and finances and laborers. Pastor Jerry's attitude was, 'I was blessed to be the pastor here, and now I'm blessed to be a member here. I don't run Grace Church, and I never have. It is God's.'"

Chapter 7

THE MARK OF SHEPHERDING:
Follow Me as I Follow Christ

*Then I will give you shepherds after my own heart,
who will lead you with knowledge and understanding.*

JEREMIAH 3:15

Pastor Jerry faithfully followed Jesus, the Good Shepherd, who laid down his life for the sheep (John 10:14-15). From family members, to staff, to up-and-coming leaders, to his congregation, Jerry led, guided, and protected those God entrusted into his care.

As an under shepherd, Pastor Jerry was never afraid to say hard things that would bring people back into communion with God. He gave encouragement when encouragement was needed; warnings when warnings were needed; and words of rebuke when words of rebuke were needed. When I think of how he communicated with his flock, I think of Proverbs 25:11–12: "Like apples of gold in settings of silver is a ruling rightly given. Like an earring of gold or an ornament of fine gold is the rebuke of a wise judge to a listening ear."

Jerry Kept at It

Ralph "Easy" Worsham: Mom wanted us to get a bit of culture, so she had all four of us [Jerry, Lorain, Easy, Arvin] take lessons to learn to play a musical instrument. I did not take the lessons too seriously, and while I was waiting for my siblings to finish their lessons, I would throw rocks over the walls to try to hit someone. I encouraged our brother Arvin to do it too. Jerry grabbed us and said he would tell Mom if we did not stop. He was always trying to steer us onto the right path and point us in the right direction.

When I was growing up, I was on a different wavelength than Jerry. I did not like it if someone gave me directions, and when I was encouraged, it did not always stick. For some reason it was hard for me to receive it or enjoy it. Jerry just kept on encouraging me. He got me to go to church youth group, camps, and retreats. He was good at getting people involved.

Shepherding Janna and Jennifer

Jane Worsham: Our girls never liked me telling them that we would talk to Dad when he got home about what had happened. Discipline was always an event and meaningful. Whether it was a spanking or time out or grounding or drafting an essay when they got older, Jerry was all about making discipline a teaching time and a prayer time.

We learned early on that Janna and Jennifer were wired very differently and all our interactions with them would reflect that. Knowing them, studying them, loving them, and challenging them in their uniquenesses was our goal. In their teenage years, we talked and laughed about it; and we all took temperament tests to better understand and appreciate one other.

He Graciously and Lovingly Confronted Me

Pastor Brian Petak: When I was a full-time staff member, I was leading a duplicitous life. Publicly I was this on-stage worship leader. Privately, I was making poor choices.

On December 15 three decades ago, Pastor Jerry called me to his house to have a conversation. I thought he was finally going to give me the raise I deserved because the end of the fiscal year was coming up. Instead, he graciously and lovingly confronted me about areas of my life where I was not walking with Christ.

I had a choice. I could either accept accountability that was being afforded or reject it, protest it, and rebel against it. I chose to take it, and I went willingly into a restoration process. This is how God shows grace, even in church discipline. Many churches do not even follow biblical church discipline, but it is in the Bible, and it is there for a reason. It is there for the beauty and the purity of the church.

What I did not know was that day was Pastor Jerry's birthday. After I found out, every year on his birthday I would go into his office and thank him.

I would go into his office and say, "Hey, Jerry."

He would say, "Hey, Brian."

I would say, "Thank you for saving my life on December 15."

And when I moved to Nashville, I would get on the phone, call him, and do this same thing.

Jerry was committed to being as holy as one person can be, but not in his own self-righteousness. In the strength of Jesus and with the power of God to help him, he overcame sin and temptation. He embodied that as a leader.

Jerry extended such amazing grace to me and to so many individuals. He walked with so many church members through personal sins, failing marriages, things falling apart, and continued to lead Grace Church. I saw him heartbroken over my sin and the sins of others, and because he walked so dependently and so closely with his Savior, he was able to walk faithfully and graciously with me and with others.

A Stolen Picture Is Worth a Thousand Words

Larry and Maggie White: "I took, okay, I kind of stole, a picture from Pastor Jerry's memorial service—the big picture by his casket. I told Jane I was taking that one home," Larry said.

"She asked, 'Why do you want that, Larry?'"

"I said, 'Because I want to put it up above my desk so I see Jerry's smile.'

"It's in my office now," Larry said. "I go in there and look at Jerry smiling. He was a good mentor to me. He pointed me in the right direction. He was a friend and someone I want to remember daily. I don't ever want to forget about him. Jerry's leadership changed my life."

"He did so much for us," Maggie said. "And when you have someone like him who has been so very important in your life, you want to display a picture."

Among His Sheep

Jerry Morrison: Pastor Jerry is my example when I teach how a pastor can be a shepherd among his sheep yet still hold authority over them. He did not lord his authority over anyone, but his quiet, affirming way made it evident that he was your shepherd. He managed his position with so much grace and love.

I know we are all sinners saved by grace, but I never saw a glimpse of conceit, selfishness, or ungodliness in him. Jerry was Christ-like and simple. By simple, I mean so down-to-earth that he could be understood by anyone of any age. He made the Christian life so understandable that it seemed so simple. He was an outstanding example of what a Christ follower should be.

A Personal Touch With People

Dr. Robert Gullberg: I came to Racine in 1986, and before I moved here from Chicago, I asked people about the good evangelical churches in the city. I got a standard reply of six church names and Grace Baptist was one of them.

The first time I went to Grace in the old church, there were 350 to 400 people attending two services. Pastor Jerry and I had an enjoyable conversation after the service.

I came back a couple of weeks later and was impressed with his memory of who I was. A remarkable thing to me about Pastor Jerry was the individualized touch he had with people. He was a true shepherd. He had a great memory for names. He said, "Hey, Bob, how are you doing? Glad you came back."

He was friendly, amiable, just a warm guy. It was his warmth that really shined brightly that day. Jerry was a kind, caring, compassionate leader—which you do not get all the time.

When I met my wife, Jan, shortly thereafter, I was regularly attending Grace Baptist Church. She started to go to Grace with me and got to know Pastor Jerry too. He did our marital counseling and married us at another Racine church.

I know Janet feels the same way I do; we have an overwhelming love for that man. He is dear to our hearts. Pastor Jerry was always steady for us, always there for us as a couple, and always encouraging. As we started having children, he would always ask about our kids by name and what they were doing.

Theology of Suffering

Pastor Kent Carlson: Jerry, in his uncomplicated way, had a theology of suffering. He had enough counseling chops and psychology chops to simply be with people who are suffering without having to give advice. He knew his stuff but would not be an advice giver.

My mother-in-law would say her time and training with Jerry, and the love she received from him, saved her life.

Present With People

Pastor Greg Smith: Jerry was very present with people. One thing I wrestle with as a pastor is when I am with someone, I sometimes think of other people or other places where I need to be. I never got this sense from Jerry. When you were with Jerry, Jerry was with you.

He Took Time

Pastor Cole Griffin: Jerry zealously loved Grace Church. It was his chief priority next to God and his family. He would literally do anything for his sheep.

Jerry and I were in many challenging and crazy situations and conversations with people, and he always pointed them back to the Lord. He wanted God's best for his sheep, and he always let them know how much he loved them and cared about them. And he really did. Those were not just words he threw out. The reason I knew this is because he took the time. Pastors, you know, we're all so busy, and it's really a huge statement when somebody takes time for you. Even with the incredible pressures and the substantial number of things he had on his plate, he would prioritize his sheep and especially his staff. He would always, always prioritize staff and do anything for us from financial help and personal counseling, to just being there in a life moment. He was a pastor who showed up in people's lives.

The Greatest Reunion

Lorain Worsham Evans: I had the privilege of having Jerry as my older brother, and I ran to him for support. He was always there for me. When I worried or had a crisis in my life, I called him. He never turned me down, no matter how busy he was. He was truly a shepherd for everyone. Jerry had such a deep love for Jesus, he poured into people, and he was a giver.

The Holy Spirit was extremely powerful in Jerry. He was a mighty warrior for God. I cannot wait to see him again. It will be the greatest reunion.

God's Shepherd for a Season of Explosive Growth

Scott Demarest: I do not remember the first time I met Pastor Jerry, but I recall watching the way God used this humble, often quiet, servant-leader to accomplish his will. When my wife, Cynthia, and I first started attending Grace Baptist in the early 1990s, it quickly became evident that Pastor Jerry loved the Word and knew it well. He preached the truth unapologetically.

Grace was still a small congregation but was growing rapidly. Pastor Jerry expressed gratitude to God for all the blessings. He did not seem proud or astonished at the rapid growth of this little church of about three hundred attendees. Even after moving to three Sunday morning services, sanctuary aisles still had to be filled with folding chairs to fit people. With great humility and steadfastness, he took it all in stride.

I've often wondered why God chose the 1990s to dramatically grow this congregation that was founded in 1854. All I know is that God determines how and when his sovereign plans will come to be, and he chose Pastor Jerry to shepherd the church through this season of explosive spiritual growth and physical expansion. Pastor Jerry handled this as he handled everything: He prayerfully sought God's will and gave his all to share the gospel message.

He Imitated Christ

Craig Vaughn: Our connection to Pastor Jerry and Jane began around 1986 shortly after Lori and I got married. We visited the church on Northwestern Avenue a few times, and Jerry and Jane arranged to come to our Racine upper flat to connect with us, get to know us, welcome us to the church, and to answer any questions we had. This was our first, up-close encounter with them. It was the beginning of my relationship with Jerry that grew deeper and deeper and lasted thirty-four years until he died.

Shortly after he and Jane came to our door in 1986, they hosted a series of Bible studies in their home for newer folks at Grace. It was called *Operation Timothy*. They invited us, and we began to do life together.

Jerry was such an instrumental pastor for our whole family. We have three girls, and he was at the hospital the day each of them were born to pray with us. He was also present at various events throughout their church journeys and their high school graduations. When our daughter Kristen got married, he was there even though he was in the hospital emergency room just days before.

Not only was he there for important things in our lives, but he knew my parents well. When they would visit from Illinois and come to church with us, they would talk with Jerry. My parents knew how influential he was in my life.

A few years ago, when my dad passed away, Jerry heard about it and texted me for details. I told him that I did not expect him to come and that it was a three-hour drive one way. I tried to talk him out of it, and Jane likely did too.

"I'll be there," he said.

He drove three hours by himself, came to the visitation, gathered my family together, shared briefly from the Word, prayed, and then drove back three hours! That speaks to being a true shepherd. He was more spiritually influential for our family than any other person we knew. It is a combination of things that made Jerry stand out above and beyond others. Certainly, among them were his authenticity, consistency, and genuineness.

The Apostle Paul instructed believers: "Be imitators of me, as I am of Christ" (1 Cor. 11:1 ESV). This was how I saw Jerry living his life; I could imitate him because he was constantly imitating Christ.

He Left the Ninety-Nine

Terry Kultgen: One of the strongest attributes I saw in Pastor Jerry was his shepherding ability. Everything he did with me was shepherding, and it was instrumental in my spiritual formation.

One day my wife, Deb, came home and said, "Pastor Jerry wants to know if you want to go to Promise Keepers."[21]

I thought, *I am calling his bluff and saying "yes."* I was totally thinking it would not happen. Jerry called me to give me the details, and I said, "I am not staying overnight in Chicago." He said, "Okay, then you will have to drive back and forth."

He could have gone to Promise Keepers and sat with all the other guys from Grace Church, but he did not. Jerry left the ninety-nine sheep to go after me, the one lost sheep (Matt.18:12–13). He drove down to Chicago with me. He drove back home to Racine with me. He sat with me. He ate a box lunch with me. He invested in me more than I was worth. And I needed that. God gave Jerry the grace to put up with me.

This is shepherding. He did more than talk about shepherding; he invested in people.

Learning on Bumpy Roads

Yvonne Manning: Pastor Jerry knew how to gather good, gifted people and place them around him in every part of the church. He could

---

[21] Promise Keepers was founded in 1990 by Coach Bill McCartney and originally focused on helping men live with integrity. For more information visit www.promisekeepers.org.

have just kept things the same year after year, but instead, according to the times, he moved the church forward.

He trusted his team so much. There was a season when I think he even trusted us too much. Massive things were happening at Grace Baptist Church. We had the most fruitful, powerful worship music; we were doing many things that had never been done before. Pride slipped into this team, and Satan used this to get into our hearts and cause us to lose focus. We were thinking, *We were all that and a bag of chips*, and some of us fell into sin. To see the look on Pastor Jerry's face during all of it...that look. I think at some level he took all the responsibility for our choices. I left the church not because of the discipline—it needed to be done—but looking back, I think it could have been done better.

Later when I came back to the church, I remember Pastor Jerry doing a sermon and confessing how he struggled with worry and control and how he needed to give that up. I think the church really learned something.

When I returned to Grace and I was allowed to sing a song, all the elders were up front and Pastor Jerry was right there. I remember singing, and it was pure like Holy Spirit redemption words. Afterwards Pastor Jerry and I embraced, and it felt like a soul connection. You can't go through everything we went through including the restoration and not feel like family. Pastor Jerry and Jane felt like my family.

All I know is that everything I am today as a therapist has been informed by what I went through during those bumpy roads that I walked at Grace. Pastor Jerry was a true shepherd, always saying God is going to be faithful and is worthy of glory.

Just Part of the Group

Patti Booth: We were in Pastor Jerry and Jane's small group for more than twenty years. It was easy being in a group with them. Jerry was just such a natural shepherd.

We loved the in-depth Bible study he would lead. We used to say, "Jerry, just give us the answer!" But he never would and he never took over the conversation. He was just always part of the group.

A Shepherd Who Unified

Pastor Greg Smith: One of the conversations Jerry and I had was about the dynamic between man's free will and God's sovereignty. Pastor Jerry held to God's sovereignty, but he recognized the mystery of how man's part could obviously be under God's sovereignty.

Jerry connected with people who were theologically different from him. When I was at Grace, it wasn't a reformed church, per se. Jerry had very strong convictions, but I appreciated how he clung to them without making things divisive.

We used to sing a song at Grace based on Psalm 133:1 about dwelling together in unity. At that time, Grace was a very unified church. Jerry did not ever compromise his positions, and he was dedicated to unity.

Stay Calm and Bring in Christ

Jon Nelson: Jerry had great gentleness, compassion, and calmness. I saw him in many situations and he knew how to stay calm when the wheels were coming off. He was especially remarkable when someone received bad or sad news. He brought the presence of Christ in and had a steady hand on the rudder when the storms were raging.

Modeling Integrity

Jeff Stewart: I remember a question someone asked when I attended my membership class back in 1992. He asked if church members were allowed to drink alcohol. Pastor Jerry shared a Scripture or two about moderation and stated that drinking is seen as a matter of individual conscience at Grace.

He stated that he chose to not drink alcohol as his strongest witness since there would never be any question about it in his life. He shared it was easiest for him to model integrity by not drinking and he could never be a stumbling block to others on that issue.

The Lamb's Book of Life

Pastor Chris Amundson: Pastor Jerry had a Bible study with third and fourth graders in his office that went a month or two. Thinking about it now, it was such an interesting thing that Jerry took time to do Sunday school for nine-, ten-, and eleven-year-old kids. But I am very thankful he did it. He was very purposeful in making disciples.

I remember the morning he shared the very classic gospel bridge presentation with us. On one side of the bridge was us and our sin, and on the other side of the bridge was God. He explained how we were separated from God by our sin and the big chasm of death and hell, and that Christ is our bridge back to God.

He gave a classic gospel call, Billy Grahamish, pray along with me, raise your hands, that type of thing. I know we do not do that much anymore, but I know in that moment I believed.

I remember Jerry talking to us about what raising our hands meant. His words specifically were about the Lamb's book of life and that your name is now written in that book in inerasable ink (Rev. 20:12–15). I remember feeling relieved and secure because I had struggled with feelings of not being good enough. Learning that it was not about being good enough but trusting that Christ was good enough was comforting.

Jerry was one of the early influences that God used to help me see Christ in his fullness. When we look at conversion, it is a process. There are things I know now, but my memories of that time were a lot about feelings. I remember feeling worried about where I was going when I died and wondering, *Does God love me? Do I have a relationship with God? Am I good enough?*

Jerry was there at the point when the light switched on. No doubt his gospel presentation flipped the light switch, opened my eyes, and melted away all the worries and anxieties. I remember feeling happy, relieved, and joyful because I knew I was saved.

I've Got This Grandpa

Luke Binkley: Grandpa and Grandma planned special days with all the grandkids individually, all six of us. On one of my days when I was about five, Grandpa was taking me fishing and I was super excited. Because we went one other time and I caught a fish, I thought I knew how to fish and didn't need any help.

Grandpa started to teach me how to fish again, and I said, "I've got this, Grandpa."

I held the fishing pole, threw the line back behind me with my whole body, and I fell into the water. I knew how to swim so they were not worried, and they were dying laughing. This showed just how stubborn I was!

Grandpa grabbed the back of my shirt and pulled me out of the water, and it turned into a teaching moment. Grandpa could turn anything into a teaching moment. I learned the importance of listening and respecting authority and not being so stubborn.

Not Just Our Parents' Shepherd

Michelle Jenks: We started attending Grace Church when I was nine years old. I knew Pastor Jerry as the man who stood up front each week and spoke to us about this God that I was just beginning to learn about.

I did not really interact with Pastor Jerry until I entered a class he held in his office. This class was an introduction to faith for kids who grew up in the church. It was the first time that we took ownership of our faith or started to think about faith as our own, not just something our families did. For a few weeks we met with Pastor Jerry and talked about what it meant to believe in God and what living faith looked like. He gave us an overview of the Bible, and we memorized the books of the Bible. At the end of the class, we had the chance to get baptized. I remember at the time thinking it was cool to be in Pastor Jerry's office because it seemed so "off limits" before that time. But those classes were Pastor Jerry's way of showing us that he was not "off limits." We were just as much a part of his flock as our parents and the other adults in the church.

Opposites Attract

Cindi Stewart: Pastor Jerry married Jeff and me in 1992. Going through marriage counseling with him was a learning experience for us! We learned a lot, but what we learned mostly was that our personalities were off the charts in opposite directions. This could have been a huge problem for us if Pastor Jerry had not recognized it and explained what it meant.

He told us that Jeff thinks before he speaks and that I think while I speak. This means Jeff must be patient with me while I'm talking and thinking and wait for me to make my point. Pastor Jerry pointed out that I was totally different than Jeff who says exactly what he intends to say.

Twenty-nine years later we laugh when we are not tracking with one another as we communicate. Pastor Jerry's explanations were necessary for the survival of our marriage. He told us up front that if we did not know this information, we would not make it; and he was right!

Gentle and Kind

Pastor Isaac Miller: Pastor Jerry's gentleness with people and his challenge to the staff to be gentle with people really impacted me. Pastors shepherd people through good and bad seasons, through the highs and lows in life, and through sins and temptations. Jerry's gentle spirit was something to emulate.

He was really respected throughout the church and in the community, and I think this had to do with his genuine love for people. No matter whom he interacted with, he showed love and concern. Even his focus on remembering names and stories demonstrated love. In outreach he knew people needed to be seen and cared for to hear the gospel. He was never too busy to care, even in a large church, where people could be invisible. Sometimes attention can come to a church just because it is large, and then it can become marred if the staff does not love. Jerry loved.

I Have Called You Friends

Chuck Dumars: "Good to see you, my friend."

Pastor Jerry always said this to me and to hundreds of others. He truly loved the Grace Church family and was sincere in his friendship to us.

For Your Good and God's Glory

Nan Arnone: I was intrigued the very second Pastor Jerry opened his Bible during our pre-marital counseling. Many gospel seeds had been planted in my life before Jerry counseled and married Dave and me. Jerry watered those seeds.

I vividly remember sitting in the back row of the church on a Friendship Sunday. Jane invited me and I loved the sermon. It reinforced my early impressions of Pastor Jerry's wisdom, kindness, and grace.

From Pastor Jerry I learned many lessons, but two are huge ones. First, the mark of true integrity is how you are when you are alone (as opposed to adapting your behavior while you are with others). Second, when I faced a kidney transplant, Jerry counseled me through this very difficult season. He said, "Nan, I don't know how well your transplant may work, but I do know that what you are walking through is for your good and for God's glory."

His words were applicable time and time again through various situations.

May I Marry Bob?

Lori Stanwood: When I first met Jane, it was because I dropped my son off at church only to find out the kid's event he was attending was at a different location. Jane took him there and went out of her way to be kind to my son and me. We felt like we belonged at Grace. Both of us instantly found Christian fellowship, solid teaching from Pastor Jerry, and awesome Sunday school classes.

Pastor Jerry had a wonderful way of prodding people on to personal growth and then encouraging us to spur others on to growth. I was struggling as a single, and under Jerry's guidance, I stopped making poor choices and waited instead on God for my given husband.

After I met Bob and went to Pastor Jerry to ask if I had his permission to marry him, he expressed reservations. Instead of a flat "no," he gave his time to discipling Bob one morning every week. This led to Bob accepting Christ as Savior, which brought me a husband, my son a father, and all of us into new positions and places of service for God.

After Bob and I were married, we joined Jerry and Jane's small group and had the blessing of living life alongside them for about ten years.

A Faithful Shepherd

Craig Vaughn: Pastor Jerry was a creature of habit; he did things a certain way and had a certain routine. He was a disciplined guy who led a disciplined life.

When he was preparing his sermons, he sat down with paper and his Bible and would write them out by hand. He would underline and highlight things to stress. Then he would go to church on Saturdays and rehearse.

Often, I would go check in on him on Saturdays. Several times I walked into church and found him in a corner of his office by himself. He was on his knees or prostrate on the floor praying. He did not know I was there. Praying alone when no one was watching was his authenticity, his character, who he was. God chose to bless Grace Church through his leadership. He was a faithful shepherd.

Wholly Devoted to Following Christ

Matthew Hagemann: We started attending Grace when I was about six years old. My earliest memory of Pastor Jerry was he and Jane coming over to our house for dinner which became a yearly tradition. I was always struck with how interested in our lives he and Jane were. Jerry was always very encouraging. Even as a kid, I loved being at the dinner table and talking with him. I always got the sense that he was behind me, supporting me, and wanting me to succeed.

Pastor Jerry lived a life that was wholly devoted to following Christ and enjoying Christ. I think about it quite often; it is the quality of his I most want to emulate and the example that I chase.

I learned the most about following Christ through Jerry's examples of consistency, humility, and genuineness. I learned that who I am is more important than who people think I am, and that what goes on in secret in my life is more important than what people can see. He also taught me that following Christ and growing in godliness is more important than status or perceived spirituality. Finally, I learned from him that all ministry service must come from an overflow of what God is doing inside of me.

(Author's Note: Matthew Hagemann is now a Grace Church elder.)

Walk Through the Open Doors

Cindi Stewart: We have one son, Samuel. I miscarried after he was born, and I never got pregnant again. My husband, Jeff, and I were considering adoption and had lots of ideas and thoughts to sort out.

We met with Pastor Jerry and he was full of wisdom. He never gave advice, but he gave us the godly, biblical way of thinking about or looking at things. The decision was for us to make. I found his shepherding one of the most awesome ways of counseling and receiving help.

Pastor Jerry talked about he and Jane's experience with adoption, which was helpful, and we ended up considering adoption. His advice was simple: "Pray. Move forward. Go through every open door until the door closes. Then, you will know God's leading and answer."

The answers to our questions were not always so hard when put in the simple terms Pastor Jerry put them. Jeff had no doubt in his mind that we should move forward and adopt, but the idea was new to our extended family and me. Pastor Jerry gave his thoughts so confidently and with such passion that it moved me to have the confidence to go forward through those open doors. And now, we cannot imagine life without our daughter, Abigail!

Our Earthly Shepherd

Patti Booth: Pastor Jerry was the one we went to for counseling. He helped Chris and me in our marriage and our children, Kristin and Patrick, when they were growing up. We knew he would direct us God's way and we all trusted him.

I do not know if anyone could match the way Jerry shepherded the church. He took on everything and he did so much: marriages, funerals, hospital visits, preaching, counseling, youth classes.

In fact, when Chris was an elder and the church was growing and growing, he told Jerry that he needed to have some of the other pastors and staff members help with counseling. Jerry wanted to hold on to this because he loved his sheep and wanted to know what was going on with them. He just cared so much for his people and had such personal connections with everyone. Chris was very up front with Jerry, and he let him know there were things he needed to give up for his well-being.

Jerry was there to guide us. He was our pastor, but he was so much more than that. He was our friend and the main earthly shepherd for Chris and me. If you look at what a good shepherd does and looks like, you'll see Jerry. He was a man full of integrity and humility. He was a God-loving, God-fearing man, and it came across no matter what he was doing.

A Shepherd Who Made Shepherds

Nancy Henkel: It was through Pastor Jerry that my husband, John, and I were asked to do marriage seminars at the Racine Correctional Institution in Sturtevant, Wisconsin. We went into the prison sharing the love of Christ once a month for three or four years with ten couples. We met with the inmates and their wives who came in just for these seminars.

Since this time, we have been involved with prison fellowship, inmate aftercare, inmate support groups, and Bible studies for females at Robert E. Ellsworth Correctional Center in Union Grove, Wisconsin.

Through Jerry's invitation to serve, the Lord really opened our eyes and hearts to the many inmates who needed the Lord. One inmate we met, Hammer, was an enormous African American man. When I asked him why he was in prison, he said, "Bank robbery."

Then I asked him what he did before prison.

He said, "Bank robber."

I said, "No, before prison."

He again said, "Bank robber." That was who he said he was, his identity.

Many inmates have pen pals, and he started a pen pal relationship with a gal. She would come in for the marriage seminars. When he got out of prison, they got married.

Hammer became a believer, got a new identity, and we still exchange Christmas cards.

Permission to Steal Tootsie Roll Pops

Caleb Adams: My parents were on staff at Grace Baptist Church, and I grew up running through the church halls with my brother, sister, cousins, and friends. I have several clear memories of that time, but one stands out as integral in my walk with Christ.

Just one negative interaction with a pastor can sometimes stunt the growth of a young person's walk with Christ or immediately cut it off at the root entirely. My childhood interactions with Pastor Jerry did the opposite: they formed in me, at age seven or younger, a picture of what a true shepherd of God's people looks like.

Jesus Christ is the one who said, "Let the little children come to me, and do not hinder them..." (Matt. 19:14a). And so, when I would regularly sneak into Pastor Jerry's office to "steal" the Tootsie Roll Pops that were in a jar on his desk, he would meet me with a smile and the kind words, "Hey, Caleb. Go ahead."

Also, sometimes my brother, sister, cousins, and I would walk in and interrupt pre-service prayer meetings and Pastor Jerry would still meet all of us with kind words and a smile. He was a tender, loving, and caring shepherd who embodied the humility and love Christ showed to children. His example taught my family and me to show this same love to "the least of these" (Matt. 25:40).

A Sacrificial Husband and Father

Dave Arnone: Jerry's pastorship through the years taught me how to be the best sacrificial husband and father I could be. He helped me understand that life is full of seasons, and God will reveal those seasons to each of us in his timing. When you are a young husband and father, everything revolves around the home. From Pastor Jerry I learned that godly men should set aside things of the flesh that consume too much of a limited resource, time. All men have something they just love to do. It could be golfing, fishing, playing in softball tournaments, crafting beer, you name it. A man cannot do everything, let alone do everything well.

Jerry taught me that investing in your wife and children is by far the best way to honor God and lead a content household. I have passed along the truth I learned from him to several young dads.

A Consistent Shepherd

Pastor Chris Amundson: When a church doubles in size, it can change a person. Jerry never changed as a shepherd. He was always consistent even though the church went from 250 to more than 1,000 attendees and then back down again to a smaller size.

Even through all the struggles as a congregation, he was never a different person. He was always the same and that is a credit to him as a leader.

What a Regular Guy Would Do

Jim Arndt: To me, Pastor Jerry was a regular guy. You could talk to him about anything: sports, work, family, or sit around and have some food. People related to Pastor Jerry. They saw him as the pastor and had all the respect for him, yet they related to him on an ordinary level. He never put himself above anyone, and he kept his role in perspective.

I will never forget once when he stood up to start the service. He said, "I just want to do one thing. Now Jane, will you stand up please?"

Jane pops up with this big smile, and she has no clue what is going on. You can see it right away. They are both wearing a dark blue shirt and black pants. The colors matched identically. It was perfect!

Jerry said, "I just want everyone to know, I got dressed first today. Jane, you can sit down now."

This is what a regular guy would do. He would want everyone to know he wasn't matching clothes with his wife!

A Christmas Miracle

Jon and Deb Hilker: "Pastor Jerry married Deb and me. He was a shepherd-teacher beyond anyone I have ever met. He just knew people. He told me that Deb was always going to say just what she thinks and process things out loud. This is so true of her. He also told me I was going to have to give her time with her friends," Jon said.

To me Pastor Jerry said, "You are going to have to put Jon first and really respect him," Deb shared.

"I know Jane and Jerry were praying for us while we were dating," Deb said. "Pastor Jerry thought Jon was dragging his feet with his marriage proposal and when we finally got engaged on Christmas Eve, he said enthusiastically, 'It's a Christmas miracle!'

"Our wedding message was so personal; he really took time to know and shepherd us. Pastor Jerry talked about Jon as a carpenter with me as the helper coming alongside him," Deb said. "He said our marriage was to be built on the foundation of Christ."

A Mark to Shoot For

Phil Adams: Have you ever met someone who wasn't a visually formidable person? Have you ever met someone whom you thought you could intimidate until five minutes into the conversation when you realized you were dealing with someone very formidable? Have you ever had someone like that in your life who becomes someone you were forever trying to first impress, and then emulate, though you always felt like you never fully arrived? For me, this person was Pastor Jerry. He gave me a mark to shoot for. He was the best leader I've ever served under because of his unwavering choice to follow God through spiritual disciplines.

Without exception, the other pastors I have served under found it very important to just *convey truth*—they told us how we as the church needed to be a trained people, to be a fasting people, to be a people who hunger for the Word of God. Pastor Jerry made it his life calling to *do these things*, to live them out. And by living them out, he led people to follow Christ.

Under His Wing

Kim Kind-Bauer: Joe and I were going through pre-marital counseling with Pastor Jerry, and at the time Joe was not saved. Both Pastor Jerry and Jane had strong biblical opinions about being unequally yoked in a marriage relationship. Joe and I broke up because of some concerns they shared.

After we counseled with Pastor Jerry, Joe became a believer in Christ and started his spiritual journey. Pastor Jerry took Joe under his wing and went through the *Operation Timothy* discipling program with him. As Jerry discipled Joe, he began to grow as a believer.

We have now been married for more than thirty-seven years and are still going strong. Pastor Jerry warned us of potential issues we might face in our marriage based on what he learned about us in our sessions. I have to say he was 100 percent right, and I frequently remind Joe that he was warned!

10/70/5 and *Win, Build, Equip*

Chuck Dumars: Pastor Jerry was a man of purpose, and Grace became a church of goals. One of the most well-known goals during his pastorate was *10/70/5,* and it was printed on the worship guide. We believed, trusted God, and prayed for 10 percent growth of new believers based upon membership numbers, that 70 percent of members would be involved in discipleship, and that 5 percent of the congregation would be in leadership training. This was later replaced by *Win, Build, Equip.*

Bring People In

Don Amundson: Pastor Jerry was very approachable. You could talk to him about anything. He had an interesting approach to getting his way. He knew what he wanted and he was clear about the way he wanted things done, yet he always did it in a kind and gentle way as opposed to a hardliner who demanded, "I want it done this way." Therefore, people followed him.

I was not a Christian when I came to Grace Church. I absolutely became a believer there. My faith is totally, 100 percent different than when I was attending our old church.

I was at a Sunday night service and the sermon was on Malachi. I could not tell you one thing that was talked about, but in the car ride home, the Holy Spirit led me to accept Christ. I remember it like it happened yesterday. I am guessing it was six months or a year into our family's time at Grace.

Soon after, Pastor Jerry challenged me to consider doing a construction mission trip to Bolivia, and surprisingly he asked me to lead it! He often discerned peoples' skills and abilities and how God could use them. Part of what Pastor Jerry wanted me to learn on this trip was the significant difference between leading a group of people on mission versus doing a job somewhere else, like at Johnson Wax where I worked. I learned there is a great amount of prayer and trust involved. And this is exactly what Jerry wanted me to gain.

Pastor Jerry also hooked me up with Don Cohill [a physician and longtime elder at Grace Church]. Every Saturday morning Don would do a Bible study at the hospital where he worked, and then he would come and disciple me. He spent a long, long time doing that. Pastor Jerry poured into Don, and Don pouring into me really changed me. I even started a Bible study at Johnson Wax with a friend.

He Fully Understood Grace and Truth

Pastor Danny D'Acquisto: When I think about grace and truth and I think about Jerry, it was clear that he saw the connection between the two. He realized it's not just balancing the two, but the grace of God is entirely true and the truth of God is saturated with grace.

I saw he fully understood grace and fully understood truth and tried to live in both to the glory of God. It is easy for someone to know grace and to know truth in theory, but I think what was special about Jerry was his ability to discern when grace or truth was needed. He exemplified that as he shepherded.

The Care Captain

Michele Gipp: The Care Ministry office was located in one of the cubicles within the main church staff office when I began my position. Pastor Jerry lovingly stopped by what I personally called "his troops" every morning to greet each staff member. It was reassuring to have him quietly confer with each of us like the captain of a ship. When a staff bulletin came out, the administrative assistant always titled it "From Captain Jerry." From then on, even after he retired, personally and professionally I addressed him as "Captain" or "The Captain." He would humbly smile when I addressed him as such.

I came from a medical background steeped in charting and procedure manuals. In one of my early weeks on staff, I asked Jerry if there was a procedure manual that I could follow for my job. I don't remember his exact words, but he just laughed and assured me there was not such a thing. He told me to trust in the Lord. Looking back, I realize he must have thought my request was hilarious!

Most of my direct supervision came from other pastors on staff so I only directly reported to Pastor Jerry for a brief time early in my tenure. During one of our meetings, as we discussed my ministry, he came out with this: "Michele, you're a good leader." No one had said that to me before nor did I know I had a leadership gift. It was a great compliment, which made me really want to fulfill his declaration. I felt so blessed to have his appreciation and affirmation for my work.

Often in our Care Ministry office we would have a large measure of laughter. It was a healthy means of caring for our own souls. More than once, Pastor Jerry popped his head in, marveling at our exuberance, trying to discern why he could hear us all the way down to his office. I can see his face even now. He wanted in! Despite not knowing the whole scoop, he would laugh with us, quietly smile, shake his head, and return to his office. He probably wondered how he could have such crazy gals working on his team, but we always felt his support.

Being on staff at Grace Church was the greatest time of my life. I grew so very much during my tenure under Pastor Jerry. From him I learned to listen to the Lord for each step ahead. I always told new staffers that it is not about what you bring to the table; it is about what God is going to do in and through you.

In difficult situations I observed Pastor Jerry always conducting himself and leading the church in accordance with Scripture. He brought the staff and the congregation through many church struggles in the years Grace employed me. From him I gained a greater understanding of the life of the church: all the good, bad, and ugly; the beauty; and the high calling of it. He was always available to answer questions, and he backed me up when I had to make tough decisions.

At a particularly tough time where individual staff disappointments, needs, and other things were heavy on his heart, he turned to me and jokingly and confidently said, "You better not leave me too!"

I had the privilege of visiting congregants with him at the hospital, in the emergency room, and in homes. Pastor Jerry was gentle and kind as he ministered to people in great need and pain. People always welcomed him, and I welcomed his mentorship. Most times we had no answers for people. Our role was to listen, love, and point our brothers and sisters to Jesus. It was so wonderful to be entrusted with people's lives in this way.

Attention to the "Small Things"

Pastor Chris Amundson: Pastor Jerry memorized names of new congregants. With a congregation of more than 1,000 at one point, even if I was really committed or disciplined, I couldn't do it like he did. He remembered your name and the things you talked with him about. That is the kind of thing that is seemingly small, but it made people feel valued.

Even as the church got large, there was humility about him and great attention to the "small things"—and in the Grace bubble Pastor Jerry can be made larger than life, but he was not like that, he never took that on. And I say "small things" with quotes around them because they're not "small things." They are very important and valuing things.

Even now with Blaze [the Grace Church junior high and high school ministry] and new kids coming in, I think about how Jerry memorized names. I have all these new kids and I want to get to know their names so I can call them by name like Jerry did. There is just something special when you are called by name.

He Knew His People

Geri Baumblatt: One Sunday a woman came up front to our team for prayer. Her daughter was totally paralyzed. We prayed with her, and afterward I told Pastor Jerry about her. He already knew all about her situation. He knew his people and their stories and cared about them. I just could not get over that. I had been at Grace Church for so very long and had no idea of the cross this woman carried. But he did, and he helped her shoulder her burden.

Fostering Staff Community

Loreen Radke: In my role as the Family Life Ministry assistant, Pastor Jerry was my boss, and I scheduled a meeting to talk to him about my job. During the meeting, he said to me, "You are wired for ministry." Those words stuck with me and gave this typically insecure, self-doubting, stay-at-home mom of nineteen years courage to keep following Christ and serving Grace.

I was impacted attending all-staff meetings, which fostered a sense of community. Additionally, instead of each department becoming a silo, we were also expected to attend staff prayer and staff fun. In busy seasons we would grumble to ourselves about attending, but Pastor Jerry knew that we needed to meet to discuss ministry, to give our ministries and our hearts to the Lord in prayer, and to step away from ministry for a few hours and have fun with each other.

Once after staff prayer, I received an email from Pastor Jerry saying that he was sorry for just sharing his concerns about his mom's health and not asking about my mom who was going through treatment for cancer. His sensitivity and humility blessed me more than if he would have asked me about Mom during staff prayer.

Pastor Jerry continued to foster a sense of community by having a staff retreat each fall. He showed his commitment to family by inviting the staff spouses to join us. Once again, all staff was invited—not just the leaders. I remember rich times of sitting in a big circle listening to people's hearts as they shared from their times alone with the Lord; times of laughter as we played silly games; and opportunities to get to know each other better as we shared meals together.

Jerry also encouraged our spiritual growth by giving us books as Christmas gifts. That is how I developed an appreciation for Andrew Murray. He also required each staff member to have an accountability partner. It did not matter what staff position we held; he was concerned enough about each one of us to impress the importance of accountability. My accountability partner and I still meet, even though I have moved to Michigan. What Jerry gave to the staff as a requirement was, in fact, a deep and lasting gift.

Ask and Listen

Jessica Schultz: I learned significant lessons from Pastor Jerry about building personal relationships with people. I felt his pastoral love and care when he came into my office and directly and genuinely asked how I was and what was happening in the children's ministry.

I try to use what he modeled for me about relationship building when I talk to people and simply listen to them. Most people want to tell you about themselves, and when you ask questions, you show you care.

Anything to Help the Flock

Yvonne Manning: Pastor Jerry brought me on staff as a female counselor to help lead support groups. Grace was on the forefront of the Christian counseling ministry. He said that the church should be a hospital. That was what my heart bled. I wanted to help struggling people because I was a struggling person. He was open to starting any group he thought would help his flock.

He taught me so much about how to do biblical counseling. I remember thinking, *I have never met someone so gifted to just be able to speak life into people.* I lost count of how many times I told Pastor Jerry and Jane, "I don't know if I can teach this group." He would shake his head, encourage me, and tell me I was doing great and that these groups were God's will. We had every group imaginable from post-abortion groups to Overeaters Anonymous, to miscarriage groups, to substance abuse groups.

If I ever had to pick someone to go into the trenches with, I would pick Pastor Jerry.

God's Shepherd

Tim Rush: I am sure many people will mention how Pastor Jerry remembered names. When he was the head pastor, he would walk down the sanctuary aisles to make a point of getting to know us. When he retired, he sat in the balcony near Stacie and me. If there was a new face in the area, Pastor Jerry would make a point to make a connection with the new person or family. Retired or not, he was God's shepherd.

Pastor Flash

Jim and Debbie Arndt: "Jerry and Jane gave so much time to our son and daughter-in-law, Gary and Sarah. They really had a relationship that built over time. Their nickname for Jerry was Pastor Flash," Debbie said.

"They got that from when Jerry was on the softball team," Jim added. "He told them, 'I'm not a great fielder. I'm a not a great hitter. But I sure can run!'"

"The love they had for Jerry was immense. During the early months of COVID, they were very afraid of their kids getting sick; so, they did not go out anywhere, but they came to Pastor Jerry's memorial service. Nothing else would have brought them out during COVID," Debbie said.

He Wanted to Meet

Larry White: Our Bible study group had been together for thirty years, and we were all aging; many in the group were dealing with serious health issues. Jerry still wanted to meet and was the driving force to get us all together.

I would say, "Jerry, this guy is sick. This gal can't." He would not accept that. He would have Jane call again to have me get us together. As a pastor, he knew we needed one another.

Pain Written in the Plot; Victory in the End

Kelsey Kottke (Vaughn): For those who attend, college is an exciting experience. Students are presented with many metaphorical doors, each representing a potential career path. Slowly, but surely, through trial, error, and much self-reflection, students commit to a door, open it, and walk through.

Upon graduation, I was overwhelmed by the number of doors I was presented, and I was terrified that I would walk through the wrong door, with no turning back. I was under the misconception that God had one plan for my life and that I, with one decision, had the power to derail that plan.

During this transitional season of my life, Pastor Jerry, who was retired by this time, patiently listened as I desperately and creatively attempted to crack the code of God's plan for my life. I had thoroughly analyzed the potential outcomes of all options; wrestled with contradictory thoughts and feelings; verbally processed all the what-if-this and what-if-that's; and weighed pros and cons. Then Pastor Jerry began to teach me about God's providence, which he defined as God's purposeful and intentional intervention in the lives of his children.

Although I was familiar with the term, the gentle passion with which he spoke conveyed that God's providence was not simply something he acquired knowledge about through study but something he had wisdom with through personal experience. With a face filled with wonder, his hands pulled apart as he said the word *providence* as if the word itself would materialize between them in expanding bubble letters.

"Do you know why I enjoy reading biographies and autobiographies?" he asked me.

He then shared that every biography and autobiography he had read or listened to pointed to God's providence. That while different, they contained themes so consistent that they became expected. As he listened to the audio-book version of my story, a smile of recognition crossed his face as familiar themes emerged; his conclusion confirmed. Although every story ended in a victory, that victory was never won before repeated defeat and its accompanying discouragement and doubt. Pastor Jerry was confident that, although there was pain written into our plots, there was a profound purpose for the pain. He encouraged me that victory would surely come if I remained steadfast, trusting in the goodness of God. Until then, I could rest in the real, everlasting victory that was already won by Jesus Christ.

I cannot think of a better way to honor the life and ministry of Pastor Jerry than with a book of his own. Pastor Jerry's story reached its victorious climax when he, after remaining faithful during the plot, stood before the Author of Life, and was crowned with many crowns.

He Asked Me About Me

Pastor Danny D'Acquisto: I learned something about shepherding from Jerry when I sat down with him and talked about our next steps for the church plant that we were undergoing.

I tend to be very excitable, and Jerry was this way too. We are passionate about what we are doing, and we want to share that passion with everybody. It can lead to a disproportionate focus on what is right in front of us.

We were deep into the church plant transition process, and Jerry was helping us with strategies and next steps. When we met, I sat down with him and immediately wanted to talk about what to do next. He let me share a little bit and then stonewalled me, not in a condescending way, but he disregarded what I had asked him about the church plant and asked me directly about me.

I was at least intuitive enough to pick up what he was doing. I heard, *Okay Danny, you are running ahead and worried too much about what you need to do. I am more concerned about how you are doing and what God is doing in you.* I don't think he said that was what I was doing, but it was clear to me when I left, that I was running ahead.

I learned from him in that shepherding moment that I needed to discern the difference between what people are saying or asking and feeling, and what God is doing in them. I needed eyes to see with true spiritual discernment.

Stop People Pleasing

Luke Binkley: Grandpa and Grandma were visiting us in North Carolina and Grandpa wanted to get coffee to have one-on-one time with me and catch up. He always cared so much about what was going on in my life. Sitting down with him I could see in his eyes how much he really cared about me. When you are talking with people, you can tell if they are really interested in what you are saying, and my grandpa was always interested.

First, he let me know how much he appreciated how I was a kind, nice, and positive Christian, but then he encouraged me not to do things to please people. Instead of avoiding conflict and not dealing with issues, he wanted me to be careful about pleasing people because there are issues that can come from this.

At the time I was listening, but I did not take his words to heart. Later, there were times when my mind went back to that conversation, as I really needed to heed his advice. Now I really try to add his counsel to my life and be more up front with people when I need to be.

Great Because He Followed Jesus

Caleb Augustyn: My brother, sisters, and cousins talk about how we wish we would have gotten to spend a few more years with Grandpa because he wanted to mentor us. When I got to high school, I was too immature to soak in everything Grandpa was telling me for what it was.

I remember one time he and I met to hang out halfway between Racine and Gurnee, Illinois. When we sat down to talk, he wanted to know all about my life: what was going on, what struggles I was going through, and what he could do to help. Grandpa gave me advice and shared his wisdom.

I am convinced that I will never meet a man as good as him. I talked with my grandma about this and how I could follow Grandpa as an example because he exemplified the characteristics of Jesus. Obviously, he was not perfect and was not Jesus, but the way he conducted himself was a good example for everyone. It was always so encouraging to be in his presence. Every time he spoke, the grandkids would listen up. He was so wise and we knew it. One day, I will tell my wife and my kids about my grandpa who was the greatest man I ever met because of how he followed Jesus.

Chapter 8

THE MARK OF LEADERSHIP:
Show, Develop, Send

And how can anyone preach unless they are sent? As it is written:
"How beautiful are the feet of those who bring good news!"

ROMANS 10:15

Throughout his thirty-five years of ministry at Grace Church, Pastor Jerry discipled and mentored many individuals who would go on to be pastors, worship leaders, and missionaries. He also poured into the Grace staff, elders, and congregation so they would be prepared to lead in the cause of Christ in their families, in their neighborhoods, in their schools, at their workplaces, and anywhere God might place them.

Leading by showing, developing, and sending was not, in Jerry's mind, just for a select group of people. He included the entire congregation. He discerned, prayed, and then called people into positions and trusted God to equip them and use them for his plans, purposes, and glory.

Jerry had a "hands-off" leadership style. He wanted his staff and the congregation to pray first and then jump in to do as the Holy Spirit led.

He Led Us

Ralph "Easy" Worsham: Jerry was always organizing and leading us in something. He wanted us to be involved in sports, baseball, everything. He would say, "Try this. Try that. Take your mind off that and put it on this."

In the Canal Zone things were very military like. The American flag was raised at the beginning of our school day and taken down at the end. Jerry started Reserve Officer's Training Corps (ROTC) in his senior year, and he encouraged me to play "Taps" on my trumpet for the raising and lowering of the flag. The only thing I liked about it was that I could stop traffic! All military personnel stopped and saluted the flag.

We lived in the tropics, but we still had Christmas trees. When the decorations came down, the military base wanted all the trees collected. They organized groups in different areas to gather trees for a bonfire. It was a competition, and if your team won, you got a bunch of parties, desserts, free pop, and coupons for the commissary. So, Jerry organized us and sent us all out according to his plan.

He Mentored Me in Everything

Pastor Kent Carlson: It was 1976 and Jerry was brand new at Grace Baptist Church; he was twenty-nine and I was twenty-two. I was attending New Tribes in Waukesha, Wisconsin, intending on becoming a missionary. Jerry had a relationship with some New Tribes missionaries from Panama, and he called the school and asked if there was anyone graduating who might be interested in being a youth pastor. I had some college debt that I wanted to pay off before going onto the mission field, so I was interested in the job.

The thing that struck me when I first met Jerry was how young the guy looked. He looked younger than I did! I remember being impressed with an older church hiring a young guy to be its pastor. Jerry and I hit it off right away and he hired me.

Jerry gave me an extraordinary amount of freedom. I was a new Christian and had a dramatic conversion in college. I had a ton of energy and even more ideas. He was incredibly supportive of everything I wanted to do, and he let me put programs in place. Of course, I was also Grace's choir director and the janitor for a while—the worst janitor in the history of the church; I would get high schoolers to clean up for me!

In the four years I was at Grace Baptist Church, I do not ever remember being taken to task, complained about, or being told I was screwing up. I knew I did not know what I was doing. My skill set and my organizational abilities were not at the top of the charts. But Jerry's attitude was positive, supportive, and he believed in me. I would propose silly, ineffective, naïve things. I asked to do plays or musicals or skits and he said, "Sure." He never pushed back or was unsupportive.

One of the things I had to do at Bible school was create a chart of the end times. I was proud of my poster-board creation with its various dragons, arrows going up and down, pre-tribulation, pre-rapture perspective.

I was unpacking and settling in my office, and I showed it to Jerry. He said, "Oh, that is good, but I don't actually believe any of that." It was my first encounter with someone saying in so many words, "How you have been trained is not *all* there is to Christianity."

He opened the window to questioning things, and I never stopped opening it after that. I had the sense that I had been brainwashed—*is that too strong a word*—that I had been trained about the Bible by people who did not let me know that there were others who disagreed with their teaching. Jerry was the first person to help me see that Christianity was bigger than the training that I had received. I am very, very thankful for that. We can easily get stuck in our little tribe, thinking that what we know and how we have been trained is all there is.

I grew up in the Lutheran Church, was a confirmed atheist in high school, went to college, and had lots of fun. I had an encounter toward the end of my college career with a guy who had just become a Christian. I prayed the sinner's prayer late at night. I woke up and knew something was different. I had believed. I was still doing all the other stuff, but I knew somehow God contacted me or I had made contact with him.

This was at the tail end of the Jesus people[22] time, and the guy who led me to Christ and I traveled like bums, hoping people would take care of us. We were singers, I had a guitar, and we would go into these coffee houses and share our testimonies. People would put us up in their homes, that kind of stuff.

So, I come out of this zealousness, but no one is training me, pouring into me. I thought we had discovered Christianity, like it had not been around before.

Next, I went to this Bible school, got this training, was zealous for the entire world of missions, international missions, and reaching unreached groups. But there was no real figure in my life who had an influential role yet. Then came Pastor Jerry Worsham, this guy who hired me, believed in me, created a space for me.

He mentored me in everything from planning to dealing with people. He had some psychology chops and had done some training in that area. I sat and watched him and learned. There was never, "Come

---

[22] The Jesus people movement was an evangelical Christian movement which began on the West Coast of the United States in the late 1960s and early 1970s. Members of the movement were called *Jesus people* or *Jesus freaks*.

on in my office. I'm going to train you now." No formal mentoring. I was the only other staff guy plus our secretary. It was Jerry and me doing everything. We went on a mission trip to Panama and had fun times together.

I did not really comb my hair for four years; I grew it long. I did not have a belt; I used a rope as my belt. I was not making a statement; it just was who I was. And Jerry, he was always immaculately dressed. He drank decaf coffee; I drank regular. He would go about cleaning up papers; I would make a mess. This one individual, so different from me, who spent four years pouring out himself and mentoring me in the details of church life, changed my life. I became a church geek out of that process. I love the church because of my involvement with Pastor Jerry.

This Guy Believes This Stuff

Pastor Mike Lueken: When my brother and I got to junior high school, my mom got a little antsy about continuing to attend the Lutheran Church. She knew Dr. Don Cohill (who is now my father-in-law) because he and his family went to our church. At some point they left and started attending Grace. Don told my mom about Grace, so we started going there. I was in ninth grade at the time.

Shortly after we started attending Grace, Jerry came to our house for a pastoral visit. He used to do that when people were new to the church. He would visit with them in their home and answer questions. I will never forget the night he came to our house. I was fifteen and sitting with some pastor and my parents would be one of the last things I wanted to spend my time doing. For reasons I can't explain, I told my parents I wanted to meet this guy. We sat in our living room. I remember where we all sat. He started to talk about Grace, and he started to talk about faith and what church is. I sat listening to him and the predominant thought in my mind was, *This guy is different than any person of faith I have ever met.* I was intrigued and I felt myself being drawn in by him. It was not anything in particular he said, but I immediately saw the congruency between what he was saying and how he lived. I do not know why. I would not have even had such words for it then. The more street level to put it was this: This guy believes this stuff.

For some reason, I could tell Jerry was for real, that he believed the stuff he was saying, and that it was not just a job to him. He was not just reciting things or trying to get us to believe something. I knew he was encouraging us to live a certain way and that he lived that way. That stood out about him and made him so different to me.

When we started going to Grace, I would have said I had faith in God and that I believed in God. I had probably asked Jesus into my life about seventeen times at that point!

I attended church on Sundays and got invited to come to youth group by other students, including Julie Cohill, who is now my wife. I was not really interested. I was active in sports; playing football and baseball was my life.

When Jerry would see me, he would ask me about the game I had just played. We had those kinds of exchanges. Throughout high school, I continued to have the same feelings about Jerry that I had when I first met him.

It was very hard to figure out *if* and *where* I wanted to play college football, and my life really began to intersect with Jerry's. He would talk to me about Wheaton College. Yet, I was not saved so I didn't even consider it. I ended up attending the University of Wisconsin–Madison and chose not to play football. My second semester freshman year, I was living in the dorm, partying regularly and hard, and my buddies and I were in an air band. Our air band name was "The Rolling Stones" and we were in a contest. For five or six weeks, we would pack the bar with people from our dorms who would scream and yell at our performance. My buddies and I would be drunk so we could get up on stage and act like idiots. Easter break came and I went home to see my family.

At that time in my life, I would get on these kicks where I would read large chunks of the Bible. I don't know why, but that Easter break was one of those times. I would read for four hours and go back and read longer and pore through book after book. I was reading Revelation, and my mom had some cassette tapes from some guy who was preaching from it. I got them, and I listened to them in my bedroom. The guy talked about a verse in Revelation 3 about lukewarm people not making a commitment to Jesus and how there comes a time in our lives, multiple times in our lives, where we must choose to be with God or not. It was like God or Jesus was in the room with me. I felt overwhelmed and so convicted by that statement. I decided that night that I wanted to follow Jesus, and the next day, a series of dramatic changes began taking place in my life at warp speed.

I went back to college and I told my roommate, "Look, I had an encounter with God in my bedroom, and I'm not going to be doing this air band thing anymore." My buddies all thought I was out of my mind.

During a six-week period from after Easter break until the semester ended, one thing after another after another happened, and it was wild. I took a lot of heat in that dorm because of my decision and became very alone extremely fast.

When I came home after freshman year ended, I made an appointment to meet with Jerry. I sat in his office and I told him what happened, the whole story. That started a series of conversations he and I had that lasted for decades. I would come home for visits, see him at church, we would get together, and I would pepper him with questions. Somewhere during my sophomore year of college, I was having a discussion with him and I said, "Jerry, I don't know what this is, but for some reason I have this feeling deep inside of me that I can't shake that someday I am going to be in vocational ministry."

He looked right at me and said, "I have that same feeling about you."

All this was part of his mentoring: having open conversations, answering questions, and giving me his time. We would talk about dating; I was dating Julie at this point. We would talk about ministry and how I did not know what that would even look like.

"You know, Jerry," I would say, "I do not *feel* like a pastor should. I like sports. I do not like dressing up." He would listen to all my crazy thoughts and give me his insight.

He would also just let me watch him interact with others. Jerry and Dr. Cohill met together for more than twenty years on Wednesday mornings to pray. Don had a different approach and totally different style from Jerry, but he was also a mentor to me as someone of faith. Every now and then, they would ask me to go to a conference or other event with them. I would sit in the back seat of the car and would listen to them go back and forth on theology, preaching, R. C. Sproul's reformed doctrine, Calvinism, Arminianism, and a host of other topics. I ate it all up.

Julie and I broke up my senior year of college, and that was a gut-wrenching time. Jerry was a counselor to me. He helped me, listened to me, and prayed for me. He knew I was hurting, and he carried me along in that.

I finished college with an accounting degree and was living and working for a firm in Milwaukee and started going to a different church. Even though I was going to a different church, I stayed connected to Jerry and to Grace, and we would still meet.

Julie and I had got back together, and after three years of working for an accounting firm, I thought it was time to pursue ministry. I knew this meant going to seminary. So, I quit the accounting firm, enrolled in Trinity Seminary, moved back to Racine, began attending Grace again, and got married.

I started seminary in September 1989, and in January 1991, I came on staff at Grace as a part-time intern. I worked mostly with the youth group until I graduated in 1994.

I think before I became an intern, there was some period where I worked as the janitor. At Grace, somehow everyone is the janitor at some point! I am sure I needed the money and others who served as janitor probably did too. But perhaps, in a subconscious way, we all had a desire to just be around Jerry. And if sweeping the floor put us in that environment, so be it. Somehow, we would get a ten-minute conversation with Jerry in his office, and that would make cleaning toilets all worth it.

Grace had offered me a full-time position as the adult discipleship pastor when I finished seminary. When I graduated, it was during the era of seeker churches. Willow Creek in Illinois was in full form. Saddleback in California was doing its thing. Grace decided to start a Saturday night, seeker-oriented service where people from Grace could bring non-Christians. Jerry was instrumental in the conversations about this service and part of my role was to be the main preacher at that service.

I was beginning to wonder if I would be staying at Grace forever or if God had different plans for me.

It was 1994 and Jerry, believe it or not, was beginning to talk with me about his long-term plans including stepping out of his head pastor role. He knew it would happen someday, and at the time, he had a desire to see if I would be interested in stepping into his position. We would talk about that and all the feelings I was having.

There were things in Jerry's style I knew I could not, nor would not want to perpetuate. They were not bad; they were just not true to me. Jerry did not want me to leave, but he understood what was churning.

Julie and I moved to California in October 1995 to start a church, and ultimately became part of Oak Hills Church in Folsom.

My departure was difficult for Jerry. He felt some degree of rejection from me, and it hurt him a little bit—not our friendship—but I think it made him think in some way he was not enough. He used to say to me "You know, Mike," and then he would give me some truly kind remarks about my ability with this or that program, and then he would reference himself and say, "I'm just a simple man."

I would say, "Jerry. Stop. We are not going to do this again, are we?"

He wanted me to come back to Wisconsin and lead Grace when he retired, and this was his desire long after I had been in California.

God used my relationship with Jerry to fuel his passion for mentoring and pouring into young leaders. He found an incredible amount of satisfaction watching the light bulbs go on in young people, and he loved the work of leading and mentoring. God used my departure to help Jerry realize how good it was to send out leaders. He discovered this was one of his kingdom roles, and Grace had a period where it became a sending church.

He knew a lot of yards were being gained for the sake of the kingdom of God by investing in young people and turning them loose to follow God vocationally and serve the church.

I realized as time went on that Jerry was the reason I am a pastor. There is no one from a human standpoint who has had more influence on my life and my choice to be in ministry than Jerry Worsham. There is not even a close second. Jerry was and is in the top three men who have influenced me in general, not just in ministry. He influenced me with his character; he influenced me with the way he would direct his family; he influenced me with his passion for prayer; and he influenced me with his passion for Jane.

I had an incredibly significant, important, and emotional relationship with Jerry. He represented so much to me. He knew my story, my pain, what it was from, and he just filled up the space, and he knew he was filling the space, and I told him he was filling the space, and he so graciously took that space. He said things to me that I needed to hear and encouraged me in ways I wasn't going to get in other places.

Jerry saw things in me that I did not know were there. Jerry was aware of my frailties and flaws and one of those was a struggle with anger, probably partly why I was decent in football. You got rewarded for anger in football, but not in life. He knew I had issues and he walked with me in all of it.

I get so emotional when I talk about Jerry because he was so much more to me than just a ministry mentor and so much more than someone who taught me to be a pastor and do the mechanics of ministry. All that was such a distant second to his primary influence in my life: a man who saw into me; called things out of me; saw God's hand on me; and articulated belief in me and grace toward me over a long, steady time period when he encountered all my rough edges. There were and still are plenty of them. He would just create a space to soften these—he did this for a lot of us. He created a space where we could slowly discover who we were, who God was, and how we were to walk together with God. And there was a lot of tripping, falling, cuts, and scrapes along the way.

Jerry had a side to him that, as Kent Carlson [another former Grace Baptist pastor] put it "would motivate him to keep things neat." If you were part of what was making things messy, Jerry would sometimes get a little too motivated to straighten out the behavior instead of deal with the core of the behavior. I felt he could see past the brokenness and messiness of me through to the goodness intermingling there. This was the thing that sent such a message to me. Who doesn't long to have important eyes seeing you even though there is brokenness and messiness?

In many ways what I saw in Jerry was what I always wanted to believe God was like. If you do not have examples in authority to demonstrate what Jerry did, you are left to wonder, is God really like that?

I have not met too many authority figures who lived like Jerry, and it met a deep longing within me. I could tell by how he interacted with me that he deeply loved me. He knew I was not everything that I would hopefully be one day, but I knew he deeply, deeply loved me.

I do not know what my relationship meant to him, but I know what he meant to me. In some ways that "goodness in the midst of brokenness and messiness" is a theme of my thirty years of being a pastor. Jerry saw it first and helped me see it, and it was a gift I desperately needed then and still need now.

Bigger Plans

Joe Kobriger: I remember Jerry telling me that when he and Jane were in college, they thought for sure they were going to become missionaries, but after Jerry spoke somewhere, he was asked to come and pastor a church.

When he told me this, I looked at him and said, "God obviously had bigger plans for you!"

God used Jerry to develop, support, and launch missionaries all over the world instead of calling him to that role. Pastor Jerry was all about growing disciple makers and kingdom builders wherever God might send them, across the world or across town. Great leaders produce great leaders, and Jerry produced great leaders.

You see this in the business world all the time. In business and in the church, you must have a level of confidence to become a great leader. I can't think of a better way to have confidence in what God is calling you to do than to have a great leader like Jerry look at you and say, "God has this for you to do and he is with you. You can do this!"

Obviously, our strength needs to come from the Lord, but we are human and we need to have self-confidence and feel good about ourselves to face challenges. Pastor Jerry was the type of man who made people feel confident in themselves and in the Lord. He edified people and was particularly good at this.

When Pastor of Children's Ministries Isaac Miller was leaving, someone came up to me and said, "Now Isaac is leaving. Why does everyone just keep leaving? What is wrong with these guys?"

"It is awesome he is leaving," I responded. "He is going to go lead a church or be a part of pastoring another church. It was our job at Grace to raise him up to go and make disciples."

Jerry poured into Isaac and so many other men and women to go and make disciples.

I Was Not Going to Be a Pastor

Pastor Jason Esposito: I went to college at Anderson University in Indiana with Jerry's daughter Jen. She told me that her dad was a pastor in Racine, Wisconsin, and that his church was looking for a youth director. When she asked if I was interested, I told her I might be, although

I didn't plan to be a pastor but a professor and to do camping ministry. Jen gave my name to her dad and Mike Lueken, who was also working there at the time. Mike and I talked. It was the end of my senior year. I did not want to commit and pulled the plug on it.

Then, while I was going to Trinity full time, working in residential care, and working at Gurnee Mills, I ran into a guy named Brian Petak who was working at Grace. He shared that they were still looking for a youth director.

After our conversation, I decided to go to a service to check out the place. When I first saw Jerry, he looked like a combination of a famous television personality [Herve Villechaize] and the televangelist Jim Bakker, which I thought was interesting. After the service I thought: *This seems like a solid, biblically based church. They love Jesus. Why not take the job?* So, I did.

Both Brian Petak and Mike Lueken were filling multiple roles when I came on staff at Grace. I took over the whole youth program, which let Mike focus more on the Light Side service [a Saturday night service for seekers], while Brian moved into the music ministry. I still did not plan to be a pastor, but Jerry is part of the story of why I am.

I was actually trying to leave the whole time I was at Grace. I was disillusioned with the church. I had some pain in my growing up years due to a pastor who encouraged me and then walked away from the Lord. This was why I wanted to be a professor, teach church history and philosophy, and instruct people who do ministry. I wanted to be part of a church but never be a pastor of a church.

I remember talking to Jerry once and telling him, "Hey, I'm only going to be here for a few years as a youth pastor, and then I'm gone. I'm going to go get my doctorate degree."

He listened to me, said "okay" and "we will see." He saw something in me that I did not see in myself. He was very informally encouraging, meaning that there is a formal way to encourage, like by having regular meetings or being closely managed. That was not Jerry. He would walk into my office and say, "How's it going, Jason?"

We had a close relationship. He was one of the most significant men in my life. I saw in him the faithfulness of a regular person, a regular guy. And he had integrity. Because of his example, I thought, *Maybe there is something to being a pastor. Not all pastors go sideways.* This is an important message we need to be reminded of today.

Jerry was not a typical strategic leader. He was willing to take risks on young, inexperienced people. I was young, just out of college. Mike Lueken was just a few years older than me. Julie Bell, Karen Peterson, and Brian Petak were all young leaders. I could name names and go down the leadership line of Grace in the early years, and most of the staff members were wet behind the ears. Some men like Warren Wetherbee and Rusty Hayes had a bit of experience, but most of us did not. Jerry threw us in the deep end of the pool, and it was a little bit of sink or swim. Not everyone thrives in that environment. By God's grace, thankfully I did. He was good at seeing the best in people who were risky hires; I was a risky hire.

Jerry was a living example of faithful leadership. It was more caught than taught leadership at times, but that is what I needed. It was through Jerry's example and what God was doing through him and at Grace Church at the time that I decided I was going to be a pastor.

I do not know if or how God would have used somebody else to move me in that direction. All I know was before I met Jerry, I was not going to be a pastor. And now I am a pastor and have been for a while because I saw the example of a guy who was real and genuine. Through Jerry, I saw what God could do through the local church when the pastor and the people and the staff are yielded to Jesus and open to the Holy Spirit.

Things were really happening at Grace in those days. They were very incredible and powerful years for the church. There was tremendous growth. I remember there were some weekends when people were sitting in the hallways just to be there and worship. The Spirit was moving and was using Jerry and the staff. It was fun and it was a privilege to be part of that at Grace Baptist Church.

I was also there during some hard years when hard things went down. I got to see Jerry in those settings too. He was faithful and walked through it. He was a very even personality. I never really saw Jerry down when I was on staff.

Some of the toughest situations were staff situations. Jerry started staff fun days to let us be ourselves. This was Jerry trying to figure things out, trying to be strategic, and trying to create community.

He really loved Jesus, he really loved the people in the church, and he really loved his staff. I would be nervous about any pastor who found it easy to go through a hard season when firing staff, disciplining people, or asking people to leave was needed. That is not a person I would want to follow. I think part of what made Jerry great was things did hurt him, but he knew the church was not building widgets. We were in the people business. I learned that from Jerry.

Jerry is the best example of anyone I've interacted with—and I've been in ministry twenty-eight years now—of being a regular guy who God really did use in incredible ways. He was a solid leader. He was a solid preacher. He had solid people skills. He was just solid all the way around. But more importantly, he was a man of prayer, spiritual disciplines, and he truly, truly loved Jesus.

When people say, "I cannot preach like Andy Stanley," or whomever they think is the best preacher or, "I cannot lead like..." fill in the blank, I always think of Jerry. It does not matter. What matters is that you are fully submitted to Jesus, that you are humble, that you are tuned into the Holy Spirit, and that you are a person of prayer and the Word. And that was Jerry Worsham. His impact for the kingdom of God was amazing.

I stand on the shoulders of Jerry just as he stood on the shoulders of those who went before him, and we all stand on the shoulders of Christ.

A Stewardship

Pastor Rusty Hayes: My wife, Judi, and I were visiting her mom and dad during Christmas in 1994 and went to the Grace Baptist Christmas services. At the service Pastor Jerry, Jane, Janna, and Jen were interviewed in front of the church. I was able to see the dynamic of the family. They clearly loved one another and the church, and the girls really loved their dad.

I was graduating from Dallas Seminary that spring with a master's degree in theology. I was looking for a job and was open to opportunities. My mother-in-law, Gale Sunder, was Pastor Jerry's assistant, and she introduced us. He called me briefly that December to talk about staffing, and when I returned to Dallas, he pursued me. He said, "We are going to be hiring a small group pastor, and I am wondering if you might be interested in this position?" That started my process with Grace.

Jerry had a passion to develop younger men to know and serve God. It is something he passed down to me. Investing in young men is a big deal to me. At two of my previous churches, the men who are now the senior pastors are young men I mentored. That is a direct influence and impact from Jerry.

He believed that there was a stewardship we had to the next generation, and that the next generation was the legacy we leave behind. He taught that there was a responsibility of the older generation to pass down biblical values to the younger generation because one day they would be in charge. And here we are in charge. I am about the age now that Jerry was when I met him.

This stewardship was one reason he was always leaning toward contemporary worship and ministries: things like a Saturday night service, wearing more casual clothes, and adopting a different musical language. He wanted things that spoke to the younger generation.

Jerry Saw Me

Pastor Jason Montano: As God works, my employer started to go a direction I did not like or believe in. It was money over people, and I saw my head turning toward pastoring. At this time, I was volunteering, helping, and leading the Grace junior high ministry because Greg Smith was pastoring the youth by himself. I applied and interviewed for the open Grace director of junior high ministries position.

After the Youth Ministry Team affirmed my call, I interviewed with Jerry and the Elder Board. Jerry asked, "Why do you think you want to be in youth ministry?"

"I don't know," I said. "I don't know if I want to do it, but something is tugging at my heart; and I think I am supposed to do this."

It was a terrible interview, but I got called to ministry at Grace. Jerry saw the call to ministry for me that I could not see myself. I had no idea what I was doing, but he recognized the Holy Spirit element.

There were so many men who I went to school with at Trinity who aspired to be pastors. It was their dream. It was not my dream. My dream was pro football or baseball. I wanted to be on the sidelines as part of the medical staff. And so, my entire posture at that point was, *I do not know what I am doing. I do not even know what this call is,* but Jerry recognized it. As time went on, I learned that was part of his heartbeat: finding, identifying, training and equipping leaders.

Jerry furthered my development by sending me back to college to get my master's degree, which took me a long time because I took one class at a time. I had little kids. He also put me on the Grace Senior Leadership Team (SLT), which is still one of the things that most influenced my leadership style.

When he invited me onto SLT, we had a conversation and he told me, "I want you to know that there is push back about my decision to put you on SLT, but I believe in you."

He got a lot of flak for his decision because of who I was, who I still am. I am Gen X, always bucking the system, doing things outside of the box, pushing envelopes. Jerry looked past all of that to invest in my leadership development. He shut down the naysayers.

I did not say much in SLT; I got to sit back and watch the other leaders in action. It is where I learned the most ministry the fastest. It was raw. It was real. It was working through staffing issues. I could bring my questions to SLT and we could team think. This was so influential because I had a direct line to Jerry every week.

I grew so much from reading books he told me to read, by watching him interact with the leadership, and through prayer. I got to see what made Jerry really tick as a leader: where he was strong and where he was weak. In SLT I got to see the dark side of leadership too. Jerry never concealed anything. He would say leadership is hard. There were hard things we had to talk through and walk through. It was formative for me.

Sometimes I found myself frustrated with how things operated because I was young. Looking back, I think, *Oh my gosh, I was so dumb!*

I was frustrated because I always wanted to take the mountain. Jerry was like: "Okay, all right, let's think through that, okay."

He always gave us his sandbox analogy. He would say, "Okay, here's our sandbox, okay. You can play inside of this box. We have wide banks on theology, methodology, ministry."

He would fan the creative flames. I never heard him say, "No. That's a terrible idea! We will never do that in my church."

Now I take twenty-year-old men and bring them into leadership just like Jerry did with me. At Mosaic Church, we have what we call Lead Team, which is essentially the SLT of Grace. I took so many of our models from what Jerry developed. I want to see young leaders and identify who they are like Jerry did.

He took a huge chance on me and put his name on the line in so many ways. Grace Church was a large church in Racine when I was there. It would not have been good if the youth pastor was a knuckle-head; youth there were so valued. Now that I see it from this chair [lead pastor], I get what a huge risk I was.

Today, I am doing the best I can to lead like Jerry led, to emulate him. I am me and I will never be him, but I want to be like him.

Who is the pastor of my life? It is Jerry Worsham. He made me believe in church again, he called me to ministry, he invested in me, and he helped shape me as a husband, father, and leader.

Entrust

Pastor Danny D'Acquisto: Preaching and developing leaders would certainly be two of the top priorities of Jerry's life. He poured into young leaders because he had a real commitment to the continuing work of the

New Testament. That is what we see in 2 Timothy (2:2b ESV): "...entrust to faithful men, who will be able to teach others also."

I appreciated that he was not just a guy performing a role. Anyone who wanted could get to know him, and he intentionally poured into young pastors. I now have this desire because of him. I hope to take his example and do what he did over the course of my life.

I Imitated Jerry Like He Imitated Christ

Pastor Brian Petak: I cry thinking about this: here I am almost done with my doctorate. Yet, I would not have taken my first seminary class in 1993 if it were not for Jerry Worsham. I did not even know what seminary was; I never really heard about it, and I was not thinking about it. I got an undergraduate business degree. But Jerry brought me on staff, and I think in my first few weeks there he said something like, "Brian, you should take a seminary class or two."

So, I drove down to Trinity in Illinois to take a class. That turned into a certificate, which turned into a master's degree, and then a second master's degree. None of this would have happened if it were not for Pastor Jerry wanting to pour into a young leader.

He didn't have an intentional leadership training program; it was more like Paul said, "Be imitators of me, as I am of Christ" (1 Cor. 11:1 ESV). So, I imitated Jerry like Jerry imitated Christ and did the things he asked me to do: shape up my personal life, take seminary classes, and spend time in prayer.

I have become a lifelong student of the Bible. Here I am, fifty-one years old and still in school learning because of Jerry. He believed in young leaders that did not deserve to be believed in. I did not deserve to be believed in. I did not deserve the grace I was shown—which is the definition of grace, unmerited favor. I did not deserve to be given the leadership position I was given. In fact, I did more to violate the position; I was nineteen when Jerry hired me. I did not deserve to be leading publicly at that youthful age, and I certainly did not have the private life to back it up. But Jerry believed in young leaders and he always wanted to pour into young leaders. That is something I do to this day.

A Visionary

Pastor Cole Griffin: Jerry definitely had the spiritual gift of leadership. With this gift comes the ability to woo and persuade and, if need be, tell people what the next steps in a project should be. He was also a visionary, and there are few pastors who are both leaders and visionaries. But because Jerry was both, he would have a vision for what he would want to see happen or what he thought needed to happen and he could lead people toward that vision.

Masterful Leadership

Phil Adams: Jerry knew where he wanted to go. He involved the elders and other church members to get done what he had already prayerfully predetermined the church needed. He was good at strategy, talking to people beforehand, getting their thoughts and feelings, and gently moving people in the direction he knew things needed to go. It was masterful leadership, remarkable, very special. There were no blow-ups in the elder meetings, no grievous conversations. He did not demand things. Were there challenges? Yes. But there was a powerful sense of unity. Jerry was a unifying leader.

My Baseline

Pastor Kent Carlson: Jerry would always have the phrase "My Personal Response to God's Word" printed on the worship bulletin sermon note-taking section.

For years I put that same statement on the Oak Hills worship bulletins. Mike Lueken [a pastor at Grace Baptist and then at Oak Hills] made fun of this, and we would both tease each other about our styles at the pulpit and how we got a little like Jerry, rocking on the balls of our feet, doing the karate chop arms, saying, "Are you listening now?"

Jerry shaped me in my understanding of being a pastor in almost every way. I didn't keep all those ways with me throughout the years; I created my own style, but no one influenced me more on how to be a pastor, ways to do it, and how to approach it than Jerry Worsham. He was my baseline, the beginning of my understanding. He was a man of integrity and a man committed to God's calling.

The Messiness of Irritation

Pastor Mike Lueken: Jerry married a Grace couple at another church in Racine, and this church had a rule where their pastor had to have a role in the wedding if a pastor from outside the church was marrying the couple. At the end of the ceremony, the pastor of the church gives a prayer which turned out to have three points all starting with a P. I thought, *This guy is not praying; he's preaching. He is going to get his sermon in and do it through a prayer!* That drove me nuts.

"Didn't that drive you crazy?" I asked Jerry later when I was in his office. "You do your thing, and then he gets up and acts like he is praying, but he is not, he is preaching! Didn't that bug you?"

"You know, Mike," he said, "it used to, but I've let go of those things."

I was thinking, *No you haven't.*

In situations like this, I was learning from a guy who took ministry seriously, a guy who had to deal with all these crazy dynamics of being a church leader. I realized that Jerry was a guy who grappled with all these things and liked them sorted out and fixed.

When I left Grace and went out to California to pastor, I quickly realized that Jerry had a massive effect on me. I had picked up things from him that I did not even realize I was picking up. When Jerry told me about how that pastor's prayer did not bother him, I was learning about the difference between how Jerry was wired and how I was wired.

Jerry did not like the messiness of feeling irritated with a pastor who prayed on top of his sermon and preached a sermon in his prayer. He did not want that mess, so he wanted to clean that up quicker than I would. One way he cleaned it up was by saying, "It does not bother me."

My instinct was, *It is great if it does not bother you, Jerry, but are you sure it does not bother you?* How do you get to the point where those things do not bother you? Just saying something does not bother you, does not mean it doesn't bother you. I liked to dive under the surface with Jerry.

Let's Still Meet

Pastor Greg Smith: I remember it like it was yesterday when I was offered the job at Grace. I was to the point in the interview process where I had already met with Jerry and the elders, and I was now set to meet with Jerry at the Chancery restaurant in Kenosha for him to offer me the job. It happened to be on the day of the 9/11 terrorist attacks. I called him that morning and asked if we were still on because I was driving forty minutes and he was driving thirty minutes. He said, "Yes, let's still meet."

Two of the things that stood out to me that day were his steadiness and his calmness. A lot of people were like, "The end of the world is here!" I am sure the phones at Grace were ringing off the hook. Yet, he was calm, steady, wanting to meet when he was leading a church of 1,500. With a lot of people, the urgent would take them from the long term. Not Jerry.

THE MARK OF LEADERSHIP: Show, Develop, Send

His Approach to Golfing and Leading

Dr. Robert Gullberg: Dr. Don Cohill, Dick Ganzel, Pastor Jerry, and I golfed together in the early 1990s. Jerry liked golf, but he was just okay.

Dr. Cohill was a jokester and especially on the golf course. He would make noises, clap his hands, and mess around so much in the middle of Jerry's backswing that Jerry got ticked. It was the one time you would see him get out of sorts.

I can hear him say, "Come on, Don. I have got to swing this club correctly. You are doing these antics, and I cannot even concentrate!"

We had a lot of fun and laughed because his approach to golf was like his approach to leadership: He was organized in his swing and simply meticulous.

Fly!

Debbie Kultgen: Jerry was always behind his people. I knew nothing and there I was leading a Bible study. I thought, *Who am I to do this?*

And that was exactly it! Jerry and Jane encouraged me and others because they knew I could not do it, but God could take nobodies and make something out of them. They knew God could work through me by the Spirit. There was never, "Do you think you can do this?" from Jerry. It was simply, "Fly!"

I learned to minister to and lead people because Jerry and Jane ministered to and led me.

Reverence for Worship

Pastor Rusty Hayes: Jerry was very disciplined, he prayed a great deal, and he had a reverence for worship. One time we had a special communion service, and I was kidding around with the people next to me during communion.

The next week Jerry called me into his office and gave me a lecture on the reverence of the Lord's Supper and how it was no joking matter. And he was right. I was out of line.

He was serious about his walk with God, and he ran a tight ship. At the same time, he was very joyful and laughed a lot with the staff. He was very patient with the young guys as he taught us to lead.

Mentoring Another Shepherd

Jon Nelson: While I was still on staff at the Community Church of the Nazarene in Racine, the head pastor left and I lost my mentor. A week later, a member of our congregation passed away and the family asked me to officiate the funeral. I had never officiated a funeral before, so I made a beeline for Pastor Jerry.

From this point on, Jerry became my mentor in pastoral ministries. I would watch him in action and bounce things off him. He helped me enormously. When I worked on my ordination process, Jerry's mentoring was more important than the education piece. He humbly showed me what it was like to be a shepherd. He embodied patience and perseverance in ministry. He was a small man physically, but very much a giant in his faith and leadership.

A Leader Who Wanted to Be Prepared

Dr. Robert Gullberg: Pastor Jerry's leadership was infectious, and he had the ability to get people to unite and go the direction he felt the Lord wanted. In Elder Board meetings in the early 1990s, Pastor Jerry set a vision for the church to be gospel-oriented, yet seeker sensitive. This was the core of what Jerry was about.

His kindness and his ability to direct and lead people to the Lord were fantastic. His prayers were very authentic and he intensely desired God to be first in everything we did as elders.

He was a leader who really wanted to get out of the way. He fought the control issue like we all do, and he often preached about this. He had a CEO mentality at times and desired to be on top of things. He was very organized and his meetings always followed an agenda. He had charm and persuasiveness.

There is a famous Christian coach, John Wooden, who often said what Benjamin Franklin originally stated: "By failing to prepare, you are preparing to fail." Jerry would always be prepared. He never flew by the seat of his pants. He was a perfectionist and had a system for doing everything.

He met with the elders on a regular basis and had a strong staff. He mentored and launched dozens of young assistant pastors and youth pastors. In his leadership he was also very gifted in mentoring and had a strong influence on the lives of so many lay leaders, pastors, and missionaries. Even though I became a Christian at age thirteen, my life as a Christian would not be the same without him. He had an enormous influence on me.

Permission to Savor

Pastor Brian Petak: Jerry emphasized that the most important thing we could do as a staff person at Grace every day was to spend time with Jesus in the morning. He encouraged us to have an intimate relationship with the Lord. I remember him giving us all permission to come into work late if we needed to spend more time with Jesus.

Jerry gave us permission to have extended communion with the Lord and to savor moments with Jesus. I did not have to feel guilty if I came in late. He gave us permission to be less productive if it meant we were closer to Jesus. I remember having these sweet times of fellowship with the Lord, my Bible, my guitar, and my journal.

Staff

Pastor Jason Esposito: My wife and I planted a North American Baptist church. When I asked Jerry what the hardest thing about being a head pastor was, he told me, "Staff." And when I asked what the second hardest thing was, he told me, "Staff." So, at least at that time in his life, managing the staff was hard.

The people closest to you truly see the best and the worst of you. Who sees the best and the worst of me at this church? The staff. I have had good days and I have had bad days. I have made poor decisions and I have made good decisions. I am a flawed man and Jerry was too. You are with your staff more than anyone else except your family.

A Loving Older Brother

Eric Ernst: One impression of Pastor Jerry that sticks with me is that he never made me feel like he was talking down to me. He always felt like a loving older brother who came alongside me.

Step Back and Let God Work

Pastor Greg Smith: A major thing I learned from watching Jerry lead was to step back more, pray about life and ministry, and to let God do what only God can do.

Stephanie and I have been at this church [West Evangelical Free Church in Wichita, Kansas] for more than sixteen years now. For part of my time here, I was in a role that was not a good fit for me and I tried to be someone that I was not.

As I was reflecting on things about Jerry's leadership, I recalled that he was just always comfortable being who he was.

Mediocrity Was Not in His Vocabulary

Paul and Laura Kienzle: Pastor Jerry believed in the chain of command. He led a church that cared for its missionaries, and he led South America Mission well. If missionaries asked him a question that we should ask our field leaders, he directed us back to those on the field better able to answer.

Pastor Jerry taught us early on to do things with excellence and held us to that standard, as he did things with excellence.

"At first this was intimidating to me," Laura said. "I sometimes feared that I would not do things well enough, but this did lead me to work harder, plan more, know that I could always be more intentional, ask God for more strength and wisdom, and attempt things for God that I could never attempt on my own."

Mediocrity was not a word in Jerry's vocabulary, at least not for us.

He Delighted in God

Pastor Rusty Hayes: Jerry introduced me to John Piper's writings and the whole concept that strength in the Christian life comes from delighting in God. That "God is most glorified in us when we are most satisfied in him."[23] This had a profound impact on my life.

I grew up in the Deep South as a Southern Baptist where everything was guilt. Even to this day I struggle with guilt. It is my default posture toward God, but God wants us to know he comes with grace. You start to find victory and power in the Christian life once you realize God only always wants the best for you, that he truly is not holding anything back from you, and when you start to walk in that truth. There is a feast in the Lord that is better than anything the world can offer when you learn to walk in this truth. The battle is believing that. Jerry introduced that concept to me because he delighted in God and it was real.

---

[23] John Piper, *Desiring God: Meditations of a Christian Hedonist* (Colorado Springs, CO: Multnomah, revised edition, 2011).

Abide

Pastor Brian Petak: About twenty years ago, I stopped doing New Year's resolutions and started praying about a word for the year as a spiritual focus. I did not want to fail on my New Year's resolutions anymore; I wanted to focus on a word that could be spiritually enriching. The Lord had me land on the word *abide* for 2022. It comes from John 15, Psalm 91, and all kinds of places in Scripture.

I guarantee the first time I ever paid attention to the word *abide* was because of Jerry. He stressed abiding in God, meditating on the Word, and journaling—I still journal because of him. At one point he said, "While you are in the Word, it is helpful to have a notebook nearby and start jotting down your thoughts."

I put the book, *Abide in Christ* by Andrew Murray in my book bag a couple of days ago. It is just a little paperback, with the subtitle, *The Joy of Being in God's Presence*. It is a book Jerry gave everyone on staff thirty years ago. I did not expect to feel emotional about this, but here I am every day this year thinking about the word *abide* and praying about it. And I've got this book in my hand right now because of Jerry. He led us and taught us in so many ways.

Always Last to Speak

Jack Bell: Pastor Jerry led the Grace Church Council [a group composed of all the leaders of individual church ministries such as evangelism, adult ministries, children's ministries].

In these meetings Pastor Jerry would allow everyone to speak and would carefully listen while the group leaders talked through and dealt with all the issues facing the church ministry teams. He was open to hear whatever anyone had to say. He was always the last to speak and share how he saw the issues.

Later when I was on the Elder Council, I noticed that Jerry was an authoritative leader but in a noticeably quiet way. Some pastors would say, "This is not the way we are going to do things." And they would push their agenda. Jerry was just the opposite. He was always very calm and got consensus. He was very intense, not relaxed, but he was open to ideas.

Prayer and Praise Was a Priority

Craig Vaughn: Most of the time for Elder Council meetings, we would gather at Jane and Jerry's home. They opened it up to us to have our meetings because Jerry felt it was more comfortable and relaxing than being at church all the time.

We would sit in a circle around the room. Depending on how many guys were on the Council, there could be up to twelve men. We always started with prayer, hands joined, praying for one another, praying for the church, worshiping, and singing praise songs. Prayer and praise would go on for an hour before we would even discuss any agenda items. Most of that time we were kneeling on the floor. Praying was a huge priority that Jerry stressed to leaders.

At our meetings Jerry wanted to be just one voice. He stressed that everyone was there for a reason, everyone had a voice, and God would work through all of us. He wanted us to know we all had equal weight, it was never, "I'm the senior pastor, and I will take charge here." Most times he would defer to us. If he felt strongly or passionately about something, he was not afraid to speak out.

Those were some of the best times with Jerry. There was great humility and harmony among the staff and elders. Even when we saw things differently, there was still harmony. Most of this was due to the respect and regard everyone on the Council had for Jerry.

My wife, Lori, reminded me that I would get home long after she had gone to bed. We would stay talking because no one wanted to leave.

Elevating Women in the Church

Dr. Robert Gullberg: I liked Pastor Jerry's philosophy on women leadership in the church. He elevated them to do what they could do, uplifted them, and strived to understand their incredible giftedness and abilities for Christ. He recognized they could lead, teach, and minister. Perhaps this originated from his respect for his wife's giftedness or from interacting with missionaries so closely. I never asked.

We used to have something at Grace called a Church Council with meetings held once a month; about twenty-five people attended and twenty of them were women.

Jerry was still complementarian[24] from the standpoint of preaching from the pulpit, but he did have women speak on Sundays on occasion. He was a little more progressive than most churches in Racine in the 1990s and gave more weight to women in ministry.

Major on the Majors

Pastor Jason Esposito: Jerry was a great innovator, not because he invented something, but because he allowed for things. In a healthy way, he was an early adopter. For instance, he would take us to leadership conferences to help us learn when they were not popular yet. And he let his staff go and try new things, and God used this. At one point we started a Saturday night church service for those who were far from God, and Grace got a formal letter from a Christian radio station. They called us out for having popcorn at church and for being "church light." That was not the heart of Jerry at all. He was so orthodox and such a man of integrity, but he was willing to be an innovator and progressive in the non-majors.

---

[24] The historic, biblical idea that male and female are equal in their essential dignity and human personhood, but different and complementary in function with male leadership in the home and in the church.

One of the things that has really shaped the culture at CrossWay Church, where I am the lead pastor, is to major in the majors, and minor in the minors. Our tagline is that we are "a community for the curious." That is really something I learned from Jerry.

He prioritized the main things like the Apostle's Creed and the inerrancy of Scripture. But, if the word *Baptist* in the church name could hold the church back, he was for dropping it. If more space was needed for people to worship because the building was bursting at the seams, then he was for building a bigger church. If we need to reach the young people, he was for going ahead and incorporating modern, contemporary music and slides into worship services.

We all make mistakes, but Jerry had a heart for lost people and seeing people grow in Christ, and he would try many things for this.

Dependent on the Holy Spirit and Prayer

Pastor Brian Petak: The biggest and most obvious thing I learned from Jerry is the importance of prayer. I have not adopted the same system he had with preaching a prayer series in the beginning of the year, but my church has seasons of prayer and fasting every spring leading up to Easter. That was birthed through Jerry's influence.

His leadership did not really influence my preaching rhythms because I never thought I would be preaching. I was under him when my focus was worship and music. I was able to watch him from the front row of Grace Baptist Church for eight years. The rhythms in which I see his influence are my lifestyle of prayer and dependence on the Holy Spirit. I am confident that I am walking how God called me to walk as a leader because of that influence.

A Role Model and Spiritual Giant

John Binkley: To me Jerry was a mentor, father, pastor, and friend. Even though I was a foot taller than him, he was a spiritual and moral giant. He personified a 1 Timothy 3 leader and struck the perfect balance of grace and truth. My father-in-law was one of the few men I have encountered who truly lived a well-ordered, perfectly balanced, and rightly prioritized life.

Jerry modeled what it means to be a godly man, husband, and father during the peaks and valleys of life. He never wavered. He was always consistent. He demonstrated the subtle art of servant leadership to me in his marriage, with his family, in the church, and in the organizations he led.

He coached, mentored, and modeled unmatched humility, unwavering integrity, and the passionate pursuit of personal holiness.

Radiant Optimism: A Man of Velvet and Steel

Bob Magruder: Pastor Jerry felt it was an incontestable fact that character and integrity superseded giftedness when leading or performing ministry. In a day and age where toxic narcissism has run amok in evangelicalism, Pastor Jerry was ahead of the times.

I had the distinct privilege of serving with him on several Elder Boards. His faith was undaunted and undeterred by the fluctuations of church life. Adverse circumstances did not rattle him or cause him to lose his spiritual equilibrium. And throughout my tenure, there were many volatile issues that arose. I always marveled at the radiant optimism Pastor Jerry manifested as the elders would navigate through these rough waters. No matter how severe in scope or delicate the situation, he demonstrated an unfaltering confidence in God's power to remedy the situation. He nurtured a placid trust in God's presence in the situation no matter how bleak or desolate it appeared.

Even if a congregant were living a double lifestyle and the short-comings were monumental, Jerry believed God's grace could reach him or her and gently woo them back. He believed healing and restoration was for everyone, and he taught us to believe this. This does not mean he was a spiritual pushover or a pansy mindlessly overlooking serious offenses. On the contrary, he confronted sin head on. He was a man of steel and velvet, hard on sin and soft and compassionate to the sinner.

At times as a pastor or elder you are personally maligned or sec-ond-guessed by confused or disgruntled congregants regarding your decisions. Sometimes the sheep bite! Pastor Jerry taught us how to deal gracefully with criticism no matter how unfounded it was. We learned from him to not lash out. He would remind us that we are the examples to the flock, and we are the ones who must emulate Christ's love, com-passion, and mercy. He set the bar high for leaders.

Start With Integrity

Pastor Rusty Hayes: One of Jerry's general philosophies in min-istry is that ministry should always be an overflow of your inner life. When hiring our staff, Jerry said that talent is valuable, but start with integrity. Jerry said to pay attention to a candidate's relationship with God.

Jerry was not the most talented person on his staff. There were numerous others who came that were more talented than him. They had better musical skills, preaching skills, things like that. What Jerry impressed upon me was, *So what*. When it comes to the Lord, God does not measure a person by talents. He measures a person by their walk with him. God is not impressed by talent and neither was Jerry. He did not put people on pedestals, he just wanted the real deal. He used to say, "None of us in this room are that special."

Grace had one of the most talented staffs that I have seen in more than thirty years of ministry. And he would tell this very talented staff,

"You are not that special." At the time we were all young and it bugged us. We thought, *What do you mean we are not special?* But Jerry was right. He was absolutely right. The longer I am in ministry, the more I realize it. There is nobody special. Only God is special. Jesus is special. So, that was something very important I learned from Jerry. He is a very present voice in my head when I am dealing with people.

From Racine to Winston-Salem

Jerry Morrison: We have recounted many times how God directed us to Grace Church. We moved to the area and my wife, Jan, spoke with Pastor Jerry on the telephone and was immediately drawn to his warm, caring, and endearing personality. They spoke about the doctrine of the North American Baptist Church, and they spoke about the programs Grace offered for young families and children. There was something for everyone at Grace, and Pastor Jerry took a good amount of time to answer every question Jan had, never rushing through the conversation.

His unbelievably magnetic personality made such an impression on her that she advised me that we must visit Grace. In February 1981, we visited and never worshipped anywhere else until I lost my job at Jockey and we were forced to move in 1985.

I had been teaching the Bible for several years, but Pastor Jerry laid the foundation for a fruitful teaching ministry. I did not know what I did not know!

I team-taught with Pastor Jerry in a Sunday school class. This was his way of grooming me and honing my Bible teaching. We taught an overview of the entire Bible in a year's time. As I look back, I always tell my classes today that I only earnestly started studying the Bible when I was thirty-two years old and began attending Grace. Pastor Jerry planted a seed that is still growing.

Here's the fruit of what Jerry planted: we moved to Winston-Salem, North Carolina, in 1985, and I have been teaching the Bible since. I began on Sunday mornings, and I now teach Sunday mornings, Sunday evenings, and Wednesday evenings. In addition, my lessons were recorded on CDs, and anywhere from 15,000 to 25,000 copies have been sold and distributed in the United States and around the world. Today I have a YouTube channel where I post lessons to make the truth of the Bible available to anyone on the Internet.

The impact Pastor Jerry made on my wife was equally dynamic. She was a housewife, and he saw skills and gifts in her she did not know she had. He cultivated her gifts and, in addition to organizing the church social activities, she became a part-time volunteer receptionist. Collaborating with Pastor Jerry gave her confidence she did not previously have, and he nurtured her people gifts to bear fruit at Grace and at our next church.

When we moved to Winston, Jan volunteered at our church and soon became the pastoral care coordinator. She held that position (actually created it), for twenty-seven years. She directed the pastors' visits to hospitals, nursing homes, and congregants' homes and outlined how to best care for the needs of the church body. She managed the benevolence for the church, hearing people's needs and responding to them accordingly. One of her loves was to coordinate and execute funeral services for church members. This church had 6,000 members and a heavy load, and the foundation that Pastor Jerry laid helped her to minister to hundreds of people throughout the years. Even though she had to retire due to physical issues eight years ago, people still comment to us that she was the absolute best pastoral care person they had ever encountered. She attributes this to how Pastor Jerry gave her a ministry opportunity at Grace and nurtured its growth.

Plodders, Not Quitters

Pastor Rusty Hayes: Jerry always told me that he and Jane were plodders. They just plodded along. I saw Jerry betrayed. I saw Jerry slandered. I saw someone threaten Jerry's life. I saw people assume the worst about Jerry. Yet, I saw Jerry always do the right thing; he kept loving people, he protected people, he kept things confidential, and he kept running to the Lord.

He just did not quit. He knew he was right with the Lord and he was going to keep going. Jerry modeled for me how you get through the tough times of the calling: You go to the Lord over and over again. He shared that we win the battle in our quiet times with the Lord.

When I went through tough times, like every pastor does, I had his example, his experience, and his road map to get through the enemy attacks. I am forever indebted to him.

The God Road

Debbie Arndt: I worked for about one year at Grace Church in the children's program. We would have regular meetings with Pastor Jerry. He had profound respect for and high expectations of us. He would tell us that nothing is harder than to work in the non-secular world with secular people and honor God. And it was true. We would call people to help with the kids and would get a whole different person on the phone than we saw on Sundays. We did not expect that, but Pastor Jerry did.

He would remind us that we were a church with lofty standards, God's standards, and that we needed to treat people with respect no matter what. He never wanted us to fall into behaviors that can take place in businesses. He wanted the staff to be different. We had no fear of him, just respect. This was another beautiful part of his leadership. He always took the right road, the God road.

I pray for my grandchildren that only kind, gentle, loving hearts and minds will touch them at school and wherever they go, and that they will feel safe and comfortable. And Pastor Jerry was like this. He was trustworthy, and you were safe with him. The church was safe under his leadership.

You do not realize just how amazing his leadership was until you compare it to other people's leadership. There are very few people who just got it like Pastor Jerry. Pastors can be taught and trained, but Jerry had unique gifts and was a natural leader.

Leadership Should Not Be
Heavy Handed

Kirk Ogden: As the South America Mission (SAM) Chairman of the Board, Jerry was very deferential to others and did not do much hands-on work. Instead, he led by sitting in the place of authority as a reference point for workers.

I have a low-key perspective on leadership in general. If you look at my email signature, I do not have my title on there. I try not to dress to impress; Jerry did not either.

When we had SAM board meetings, however, he would always be seated at the head of the table, and I would be beside him. He communicated that there was a right authority and appropriate deference to leadership. The way he wanted the room set allowed for this. He did not believe leadership needed to be heavy handed. I recall how he would use "okay" to underscore a point, make sure his idea hit home, and get affirmation.

Pray and Stay Put

Pastor Mike Matheson: From Pastor Jerry I learned to pray more; pray as a first response, not a last resort; and to stay put if God will let me. I want to pray, preach, love, shepherd, and care for people right here at Grace Church for as long as God will allow.

I think as people talk about Jerry's impact and legacy, often they will tie it to things he said, but the power of those words is infused by three decades of care. The three decades of care is the difference between a shepherd and a hired hand. (I am using this by way of analogy; this is not exegesis.) The average length of a pastor's career used to be seven years. The rate at which pastors are leaving their ministries in the last two years is dramatically driving down that seven-year average. In two years, it has gone from seven to substantially less. Part of that is because when things get hard, the shepherd wants to move on. And, thankfully, throughout Jerry's shepherding days things were not hard for the most part. It was a glorious time for churches in America. It was the time we know of as the church growth era. That time is no more. However, I think Jerry would have stuck through right here regardless of the era of church history because he loved this church.

Mark Dever, a theologian and the senior pastor of the Capitol Hill Baptist Church in Washington, D.C., said, "Young men tend to overestimate what they can do in one or two years, and underestimate what they can do in ten."

Jerry did not say that, but he lived that. It would be my hope to emulate his prayer life and his pastoral longevity.

Heroic Endurance

Pastor Brian Petak: I am preaching a six-week series on contagious joy using the book of Philippians, and I am almost positive that Jerry taught an entire series on joy in Philippians. Here I am thirty years later doing the same thing. This is the thing; We are all a product of our entire life story. I do not know that I always overtly think, *This is from Jerry.* Some things I do or say are obviously influenced by him, but this series is evidence of something heavily influenced by Jerry, and I did not even know it.

The definition I have been using of biblical joy is *heroic endurance*. It comes from James 1:1–4 and Romans 5:3. *Heroic endurance* encapsulates Jerry. Grace Church experienced a lot of difficulty in his last years as its pastor, South America Mission required his leadership through many difficult years, and of course the last ten to fifteen years of his life were plagued with extreme health issues. He embodied *heroic endurance*, and we learned what that means watching him lead.

Pastor Jerry's Favorite

Michelle Jenks: Watching Pastor Jerry live out his faith and the way he included the youth in his flock was part of the reason I decided to make a career in ministry. There were other people who influenced me along the way as well, but Pastor Jerry's deliberate teaching of kids and his loving support of his flock were the earliest influences in my career choice.

I worked at Grace Church for about ten years when Pastor Jerry was lead pastor. There was a running joke among the staff that I was "Jerry's favorite" and received special consideration because of this. Of course, it did not help that at one staff retreat Pastor Jerry announced that I was indeed his favorite!

He was a part of my whole journey from childhood to adulthood. This man was a pillar of faith and a constant example of what it means to love Jesus and serve others.

Compelled by God

Phil Adams: The staff would go to Pastor Jerry with ideas and he gave us permission to try pretty much everything. I don't think he was a natural risk taker, but he did not believe that following what God was telling him to do was a risk. If he knew something was of God, he moved. Sometimes for the sake of wisdom, he would take things slowly still knowing he would get from A to Z but that the process would take longer.

He Pulled Us Along

Lee Smith: My wife, Karen, and I got involved at Grace because Pastor Jerry pulled us along with him. We heard what he said, watched how he lived, and he gently pulled us into ministry.

I never really saw myself as a leader in the church. I was someone who just did stuff. One of coolest things was when Pastor Jerry asked me to come on staff. That floored me! I would have never thought I could do a staff position, but he very clearly saw something in me. He was very affirming. God used him to show me what is possible with God.

It was interesting to see how Jane worked with Pastor Jerry in this. He had mentioned it to me on multiple occasions, and once she just put her hands on his shoulders and said, "Let's just give him some time to think about it, Jerry." She was a balancing force.

He was very insightful and a good teacher at the same time. One Sunday I went to tell him how I really enjoyed what he had preached. He did that thing where he smiled, nodded, and patted me on the back. Then he said, "You are such the encourager."

I thought, *He's got that all wrong! I am not an encourager. I don't encourage people. That is not what I do in any way, shape, form.*

A few weeks after Pastor Jerry called me an encourager, I was giving Sunday announcements. After I finished, a lady from the congregation said to me, "Man, you have not been up there in a while and I miss you. Every time you give announcements I feel so encouraged."

Her words took me right back to what Pastor Jerry had said. I learned it is not about me encouraging people, but that encouragement is a spiritual gift God gives. It was the Spirit encouraging through me. Pastor Jerry saw the gift, I never did. Pastor Jerry saw things like this. He lived life and he taught life at the very same time.

I Looked for Recruits Like Jerry

John Henkel: I got saved at Grace Church. Pastor Jerry was genuine, down to earth, and always told it like it was. God used him to soften my heart. I was always going one hundred miles an hour trying to build a business. He was steady and had a calming effect on me with just one word.

I was in the recruiting business and Jerry influenced who I started to recruit for companies. Most of my work involved talking. From Jerry I learned to ask good questions and determine hidden agendas.

Humility and Patience

Jack Bell: During one of my terms on the Elder Board, we were faced with some extremely critical issues and had to make decisions that were very unpopular with the church. Part of the problem was due to the nature of the issue; we were not free to share all the details of our decision with the congregation. Some congregants shared with Pastor Jerry that they did not like the way I communicated with them when they asked me questions.

Pastor Jerry shared this with me and told me to go make things right, to humble myself, even if I had said nothing wrong. I got back with the members, apologized, and asked them for forgiveness. I told them I was sorry if I had communicated with them in a way that had hurt them.

Later I found out that Pastor Jerry was taking a royal beating for his stance on this issue, far more than any of the elders knew or imagined. He never said anything or complained but instead just took it all patiently and humbly.

Through his leadership I realized that often elders must make unpopular decisions. When we got into tight situations, he wanted us to take care of things with humility and patience like he did. I can't even count the number of times I have reflected on his leadership and thought about what he would do in a tough situation.

Godly Leadership

Nancy Ganzel: When it came time for Grace to build a new church in the late 1990s, my husband Dick was asked to serve on the Building Committee.

Dick witnessed firsthand how Pastor Jerry's godly leadership led a committee composed of many opinions down the path of harmony. Constructing a new church building is a difficult endeavor and many churches do not survive it. During this time, Pastor Jerry's vast leadership qualities were on full display.

No Guile in Him

Pastor Chris Amundson: When Jesus was calling his disciples and saw Nathanael approaching, he said about him, "Behold an Israelite indeed, in whom is no guile!" (John 1:47b KJV). When we talk about the number of leaders Pastor Jerry influenced, it was surely partly because of this.

Guys were affected because Jerry was the real deal. I have been in church ministry for twenty years and there are only a handful of guys who have not stumbled or fallen. I have seen leaders fall behind the curtain because of sin, not that they are not Christians or do not belong in ministry. Jerry was not sinless by any stretch, but he was someone you listened to because he faithfully lived out his calling for thirty-five years with no wavering. I say he was unwavering because none of the church's successes or struggles shook him from what he was doing. He was never different because of any situation. The church changed. Staff changed. Situations changed. But he was the same man and pastor. This is why he made such an impact.

I also think he may have had some discernment about leaving a legacy. This was a big deal for him and he poured himself out for young leaders. I never worked directly underneath him in a vocational setting, but he took seriously the idea of pouring into people underneath him and discipling leaders. He never had an issue with not being "the guy." Thinking, *If this guy becomes too big, he will overshadow me* can be a stumbling block for pastors. I never got that impression from Pastor Jerry. He was never a jealous leader. He was just a faithful, consistent, unwavering leader.

A Voice Among the Influential and the Non-influential

Kirk Ogden: On a long, international flight to Brazil, one of the last trips that Jerry took with the South America Mission (SAM) board, he and several young board members ended up with seats in various spots on the plane. Folks onboard were talking about the ease of relationship that Jerry had with some young Brazilians on the plane. People were just drawn to Jerry; he was a natural leader.

He had a voice among the influential and the non-influential that was impressive. He had a certain ability that comes only from the confidence and authority of the Holy Spirit.

Some of our trips, while they were largely about SAM governance, had a ministry element to them; there were opportunities for Jerry to preach or to share the gospel. Preaching was certainly one of his gifts, but I saw his giftedness even more in how he related to, interacted with, and laughed with people.

More Than Filling Pews

Don Amundson: Pastor Jerry had a natural ability to develop and help people and move them forward. I think this was a passion for him, part of who he was. Jerry wasn't interested in just filling the pews and having people be at church for an hour on a Sunday. He wanted people to be involved, to serve, and to be part of bringing the gospel to the world. This was important to him. The number of missionaries, pastors, and people who he helped develop and disciple was incredible.

Everyone talks about him with honor and respect because he earned that honor and respect.

When I turned sixty, things were changing at Johnson Wax where I worked. Jack Bell [a Grace Church elder] suggested that I should think about taking over Grace's property management. There was quite a bit of turnover in the position the first few years in the new building. I sat down with Pastor Jerry to discuss things. At that point Ted Hinkle was managing the property, and Pastor Jerry suggested that we could do it as co-leaders. I told him I did not think that would work and that the buck must stop somewhere.

He said to me, "Why don't you work it out with Ted."

I thought that was interesting. It was Jerry's style: "You two work it out." Often this works better than someone else stepping in. And we did work it out. Ted stayed on as an associate, and I was in charge.

Focus on God

Janine Carls: One crucial aspect of how Jerry led was his focus on God, specifically asking, "What is God doing in your life? What is a recent God story you can share? How have you seen God working in your prayer life? How have you seen God working in the life of someone you are mentoring?"

We did staff studies from time to time. I remember working through Randy Alcorn's books *Heaven* and *The Grace and Truth Paradox*. I loved these. It was one way that Pastor Jerry set exact expectations for the staff. He modeled much when he taught us in small group settings. It drew us closer to Christ and one another.

Seeing Movers

Phil Adams: Pastor Jerry could identify if someone was a mover. It was never about who he liked or did not like, he invested in people who he saw had the gifts and strengths to propel the gospel and the church forward. And Jesus set the example. He had twelve disciples, but he invested more time in three.

Pastor Jerry had a presence about him, and it was a humble yet powerful thing. I remember knowing I would have the floor at an elder meeting and would have to persuade the group to move in a direction. I would practice, rehearse, and get it down to where I did not see any flaws in my presentation. I would then talk to Jerry and I would be so confident that I got it and he would say, "You know, Phil, it is really much more than that." He did that so many times when I thought I had gotten something right! Invariably he would find that one thing I missed. I thought I got a triple, but he was telling me how I could get a home run. It was not out of vanity. I can read that a mile away. He wanted it right; he wanted it to be as close to the pearl of God's wisdom as possible. I never took affront to it. I took it as I needed to step up my game, to improve, to get better as a leader.

If anyone else would have done this it would have been out of a root need to be important. I know it wasn't this way with Jerry. It never felt that way. And you know, we all did step up our game.

Apart from my own family, Jerry Worsham is the most influential person in my life. We had a lot of amazing years together, and I owe a great debt to him. He was an incredible man and leader.

Throw Them In

Scott Demarest: Pastor Jerry was always seeking potential leaders to mentor. I and many others at Grace before and after me chose to emulate this example.

We sometimes respectfully joked about one of Pastor Jerry's leadership characteristics. Through prayer he would select someone for a task or job. In many cases this was someone who did not yet have a lot of experience or seemed to be an unlikely candidate, although Jerry saw potential in them. He would give them the assignment, and then, as we would describe it, "throw the person into the deep end of the pool."

I know there were exceptions, but he generally did not give the individual a lot of direction. Instead, he trusted that they would seek the Lord, follow the counsel of others, and figure things out themselves. Nine times out of ten, this autonomy allowed the person to grow immensely more than if their every step was directed and protected.

Pastor Jerry would step in if the person was sinking, but his goal was for them to swim. I learned through Jerry that I needed to hone my mentoring skills to be more hands off and to encourage budding leaders to try new things and fully engage themselves in the task.

Ministry Is Like Swimming

John Czerwinski: We came to Grace just a few months before the new building was ready. I had interviewed for nearly a week, and it was grueling. After thirty years of ministry now, I can still say my interview with Grace was the most difficult I have ever endured. At the end of countless elder interviews, staff interviews, team meetings, rehearsals, ministry events, and an exhausting Sunday morning, we went out to eat with Pastor Jerry and Jane. He had met with leadership at Grace separately and was just wrapping up with us before we flew home. We truly had no clue if we were a fit for Grace. As he directed the conversation toward what seemed like it might be an offer to come on staff, rather than say, "We would like to offer you the job," Jerry instead said, "So, do you think you can do it?" I had no clue how to answer that.

From day one, Jerry told me that he did not hire me to do the job [of director of worship and music]. He hired me to give it away. Building a ministry with that principle at the core, created a team like no other. He would say, "If you get hit by a bus, the ministry needs to be able to go on." So, when a car did quite literally hit me, we watched the Worship Team at Grace lead well without me. He taught that effective leadership encourages others to serve fully.

Pastor Jerry's leadership became the absolute playbook for ministry. He identified and raised up leaders, coached, and corrected. He worked diligently to grow us all deep in the Word and in leadership skills. One staff quote that reflected Pastor Jerry's attitude toward staff development was, "It is very hard to get hired at Grace and even harder to get fired." By his own admission he made mistakes in leadership. Then he demonstrated how to work through those mistakes, those misspoken words, and humbly lead again. He said, "Ministry is like swimming: jump in, panic a bit, tread water, then swim."

Listen to His Voice

Pastor Dan Petersen: Pastor Jerry had a huge influence on my life. I went from a lukewarm Christian to an on-fire guy wanting to allow the Holy Spirit to work in and through me for God's glory.

Pastor Jerry was my mentor and the reason I got into ministry in the first place. I was riding home with him from a men's retreat, and ministry work came up in a discussion among those in the car. Jerry turned around from the front seat, looked directly at me, and said, "Dan, God is calling you. Listen to his voice. Go, prepare yourself for the work he is calling you to do."

He helped me prepare, encouraged me through all the academics and the ordination process, and prayed for me when I got discouraged.

As a result, I became a pastor and worked with the senior ministry at Grace.

As a staff member under Pastor Jerry's direction, I grew in my understanding of what doing ministry was all about. From him I learned what it meant to lead in a godly way, and that ministry was never about me but about God working in me and through me for his glory. Jerry was a prime example of godly leadership through his devotion to prayer, his gentle guiding manner, his support and encouragement, his instruction when correction was needed, and his integrity.

I had been a police officer for thirty years and thought my retirement would bring golf, fishing, and travel. Little did I know that God was going to put me in Jerry Worsham's path and change my life.

Little Steps

Chuck Dumars: God places some individuals in our lives who are essential for our spiritual growth and leadership development. Pastor Jerry was one of these individuals for me. I was fresh out of Bible college with lots of knowledge and ambition but with little wisdom regarding how to harness my energy to effectively serve God. Pastor Jerry had the ability to see a person for what he or she could be in their service to the Lord. He taught me with little steps at a time. From the beginning when I was asked to serve on the Elder Board, I was challenged by these remarks of Pastor Jerry:

- No organization can rise above the level of its leadership.

- Serving as an elder brings with it an expectation of sacrifice of time and energy. You may be asked to neglect some of your hobbies and free time to accomplish tasks, but never neglect your family.

- Elders must be men of God's Word, prayer, and a love of the congregation.

- Practice gentle tenacity.

Pastor Jerry set the example of all of these. He showed many others and me that accountability to the Holy Spirit's leading in our lives created a passion for prayer and obedience to the Word of God.

Always Developing Leaders

Tony Ferraro: When Pastor Jerry retired, he was at church every week. After services you would see him down front encouraging the young pastors like Mike Matheson and Danny D'Acquisto who were giving the sermons. He just cared. He always cared.

Who He Was

Cathie McGuire: Investing in and developing leaders was part of who Pastor Jerry was. I grew up at Grace Church and attended my whole life. There have been so many people who have come through Grace Church and who have gone out to lead amazing ministries.

Pastor Jerry impacted the gospel in such a fantastic way by training and by sending people.

An Invitation to Serve

Glenn Schultz: When my wife, Jessica, and I moved to Racine in early 2001, we did not really know anyone and wanted a church our young family could call home.

Once we started to attend Grace regularly, we were all in. Jessica and I started volunteering in the children's ministry within our first few months at the church. Pastor Jerry and Jane encouraged us as we began to serve. Five years later, Jessica joined the children's ministry staff. Shortly after, while we were at family camp at Village Creek Bible

Camp, we got called into the camp office to take a telephone call. Much to our surprise, it was Pastor Jerry. He told us that the director of children's ministry was leaving and asked if we would consider stepping into that role. Jerry did not want an answer right away but wanted us to pray about it. He told us that as a couple we would be a perfect fit to lead the ministry. He prayed for us, the children of Grace, and for God's will to be done in the situation.

We have now been faithfully serving in Grace's children's ministry for the past twenty years because of the dedication of Pastor Jerry and Jane to invite, encourage, grow, and make disciples of ordinary people like Jessica and me.

The Perfect Sounding Board

Dave Arnone: I believed Jerry would have been a great businessman. He enjoyed our conversation about business the most, and he appreciated the organizational and people aspects of business. It was pleasurable to engage a pastor about work and all the challenges. Being Jerry's neighbor was an absolute blessing because it brought a sense of casualness to our relationship. And through that relaxed, structureless relationship, I was able to be more candid and open about what I was thinking. I never had to make an appointment to talk to the pastor!

In 2014, a few years after Pastor Jerry retired, God led my wife, Nan, and me to an urban church in Milwaukee. It was small, under-resourced, diverse, and highly relational. I had no intention of being a leader in this church, but I'm convinced God placed us there for a season. The elders approached me to serve as the volunteer chief operating officer. The church was on the verge of bankruptcy and had no organizational processes in place, no budget, and no practical way to manage the church finances. I accepted the appointment and quickly learned that I was dealing with a group of people who did not understand or value my spiritual gifts.

Jerry would routinely spend time with me in his home and coach, affirm, encourage, and pray for our new church and me. The disciplines and processes I was putting in place as chief operating officer seemed obvious to anyone who operated in the business world, but progress was slow. Jerry was the perfect sounding board for me. I would review the concern of the day (there were many) and he would affirm my position. He kept me sane doing God's work as a volunteer. This was a season when Jerry's health had declined significantly and communication was difficult for him.

Jerry and I met numerous times to talk about my church issues, but in hindsight, I valued spending time with Jerry as his health declined more than having him endorse my decision-making. As we met, Jerry was able to see firsthand yet another person who was building God's kingdom because of his pastoral leadership and this made me happy. After thirty years of knowing me, Jerry probably thought I'd never feed the church as a senior leader!

Jerry Was a Vehicle God Used

Terry Kultgen: After Jerry retired, a group of former elders and leaders went on a mission trip with him to Cuba. Here is a paraphrase of something Pastor Terry Faulks who joined us said: I wish all pastors could have men around them who revere them like you revere Jerry.

The reason we followed Jerry Worsham's lead was because he truly was a man of God. He was the human vehicle God used to help us do what he intended in our lives.

Pastor Faulks saw that Jerry's life was genuine and authentic and that he was surrounded by men who loved him. The reciprocal nature of this was amazing. He was our leader first, but we were brothers. He had a desire to raise up men and prepare them to do what God had for them. He was an instrument in God's hands.

He Softened Over Time

Pastor Danny D'Acquisto: I got to know and watch Jerry lead in his later years. Looking back, he said there were things in his life and ministry early on that he wished he could have done a little bit differently.

When he was a young pastor, he was quite different from the seventy-year-old Pastor Jerry I knew. He went through a refining process as he faced the challenges of ministry. God softened him over time, and this gave me a lot of encouragement for what I will become years down the line.

He Trusted Me

Pastor Isaac Miller: My wife, Alyssa's, family grew up knowing the Worsham family. I was working at Racine Bible Church from 2004 to 2006 and I heard about an open position at Grace from Jason Montano [the Grace minister of student ministries] at a softball game.

"You have to come to Grace," he said. "We've got a position open in Fifty-Six [a Grace group for fifth- and sixth-grade students]."

I prayed and God clearly led us to Grace.

When I met Jerry, I remember him being very gentle and kind and clear.

Even my first interaction with him was telling.

"You know, I am not going to micromanage you," he said. "I trust you to lead."

I came in as a young pastor, and I was looking for a mentor. I thought I needed someone to interact with, shadow, and watch. He assured me that we would interact but reinforced that he trusted me to lead. He told me his door was always open if I wanted to talk with him, but he challenged me to take steps on my own.

I was expecting a father/son thing, someone holding my hand as I did things and took ministry steps. But Jerry told me I was beyond that and needed to start doing things on my own. It was hard at first, but looking back, I see the wisdom in it.

Jerry was a good leader, a strong leader, but his strength was never iron fisted or heavy handed. His style was to pray about it, talk about it, engage about it. And it was never in a passive way.

If a young pastor comes to me, I will lean toward doing things the way Jerry did them. Having an open-door policy allowed for conversations because I did not know what to do in every situation. He let me bounce things off him.

He told me he trusted me to lead, and he really trusted me; it had an enormous impact on me at the time. It was a huge stepping-stone for me since I had just started in ministry a few years before. Looking back, that position was integral for me. I was very encouraged to realize that a senior pastor who had been in ministry more than three decades trusted me and what the Lord would do through me.

Jerry led the staff well and the church well, but it was the way he led his family that impacted me most. He made his family a high priority and this really challenged me. I heard stories about their family Christmases and how he would set a theme for his family for the entire year. I also heard about how he met with his grandkids to encourage and build them up.

His example caused me to deliberately engage in conversations with my kids about things of the Lord.

I Count It a Privilege

Pastor Brian Petak: There is no other person, other than my dad, who had the kind of influence in my life that Jerry Worsham had. I know he influenced hundreds maybe thousands of people, but I count it such a privilege to have been a young, nineteen-year-old man whom he took under his wing, showed grace to, and gave tough love. He set me on a path and released me.

I was leaving Grace to go to Fellowship Bible in Nashville, Tennessee, and he ordained me the weekend I was moving. The pastor from Nashville flew to Racine, and in that ordination service, Jerry brought a runner's baton, the kind used in a relay race. He handed the baton to the pastor of Fellowship Bible and said, "We want to be about releasing great leaders. Here is a great leader." He handed him the baton and added, "You are in charge now of Brian's life and ministry. I am handing it off to you; steward it well."

I ended up handing that same baton to my own son, years later when I did a ceremony when he turned thirteen. That baton is in our family. Jerry thought of things like that, thoughtful and symbolic.

He Was Transparent

Pastor Mike Matheson: Jerry, Danny D'Acquisto [Grace mission director], Josh Poore [Grace worship director], and I went to a Monday night Packers game. Sadly, it was during the season Aaron Rogers was injured so it wasn't a great game, but it was a great experience.

It was fun to just hang out with Jerry. On the car ride up, he was transparent with us about his pastoral decisions:

- things he wished he hadn't done;

- things he wished he had done but didn't do;

- things he had done and did not regret doing,
  but which would be good for us to undo.

We saw a fun side of Jerry where he was free, willing to share, a little less guarded, and humorous. We were all very happy to have him around. He wasn't imposing. He wasn't overbearing. He was encouraging. I think it also helped him to hang out with some of the primary young guys who were leading things at Grace. It helped bridge old Grace and new Grace.

It was no longer about "Jerry's guys" telling us who he was; I appreciated the direct connection to him and seeing him on his own terms. Jerry was very aware some of those guys tended to mischaracterize him. Certain stories about him got tall, and he would laugh and say, "That is not how it happened at all! Let me tell you what really happened."

It was very helpful, too, because he would give us wisdom and insight into those people so we could love them in the way he did.

An Apt Word

Pastor Danny D'Acquisto: Jerry wanted prayer to be first and foremost. He gave me the book *A Call to Prayer* by J. C. Ryle, and I remember him reiterating to me that my ministry had to flow from my walk with Christ. It was a very powerful thing for him to say and meant a lot to me. How could I do what I did without prayer? The reason it was so impactful to me is because it was an apt word. It was. I think Jerry sensed my temptation to try to *just do it*. I am grateful for his insight and the wisdom he shared which would have been hard for me to get on my own.

The temptation to *just do it* isn't gone but having his words to draw back on is helpful.

Navigating Through Tough Situations

Pastor Mike Lueken: I watched Jerry go through the worship wars at Grace Baptist Church and older people saying extraordinarily unkind things. (I am not sure how you reconcile saying things like people said with their claims to be Christians, but that is not for me to sort out.) I watched him navigate everything with great strength and often-necessary tolerance for all the silliness.

One of the most painful things Jerry had to deal with was a staff situation. He cared deeply about each of these staff members and was hurt by the situation in incredible ways. He had mentored and poured into them, and I don't know how you ever get over something like that. It was painful to witness.

When Jerry realized something needed to be done in a situation, he was fearless about acting. He brought a tremendous amount of intentionality to the process to sort out what was going on, and he was deeply driven to do the best he could to apply the truth of the Bible. He held the truth of Scripture in one hand and the grace of Jesus in the other hand, and he used both to navigate through all the tough issues. Sometimes that meant he was not going to do certain things or have another discussion about the same issue. He was not someone to mess with when it came to sin; his leadership did not lack resolve.

He Came to Peace With His Role

Pastor Kent Carlson: Jerry and I had a conflict in the later years when I hired Mike Lueken [another Grace Baptist pastor]. There are things now that I would redo, but there was never anything acrimonious. I asked Mike if he was going to stay at Grace long term because if that was his plan, I did not want to get in the way of it. When he said no, I asked him to come out to California and plant a church.

Jerry did not like the way in which I brought out Mike, and he said that it bothered him. As a professional courtesy I should have talked to Jerry first before I talked to Mike. Even in this, he was mature and secure and did not make it all about him. Instead, he talked about how I could have done it better and about how I hurt him. I was the first pastor Jerry hired and, in some way, me hiring Mike felt a bit like a betrayal; but we talked it through and worked it all out.

During this time Jerry was coming into his leadership training calling and was coming to grips with that gifting: he was to pour into young guys, but not necessarily for the benefit of Grace. I think early on there was a sense that he would train these guys and then they would leave to serve in other places. All the guys Jerry trained had, humanly speaking, some leadership chops and abilities, but they left. He was training and leading men who were first-chair guys, and the more chops the leaders you hire have, the more space they will need. There is only so much space in a church. Jerry was a high-functioning, high-quality leader, who had set the pace and direction for what he felt God wanted to do at Grace.

I think God used this whole situation with Mike's departure to help Jerry see another layer of his calling. I think it was a process for him to learn that training leaders was his calling, his legacy. As the years went on, he embraced this fully and took great and appropriate pride in having young pastors move on. And that was impressive.

It Felt Like He Handed Me the Baton

Pastor Mike Matheson: I think I had a chance to meet Jane and Jerry the Sunday I was at Grace interviewing for the discipleship pastor position. My initial impression of him was that he was trying hard not to be imposing. He just really wanted to be known as "Jerry who sat up in the pews upstairs."

When the previous lead pastor stepped down and I took on an interim lead pastor role, Jerry started interacting with me heavily—although I don't know who reached out first. Not only that, but I became aware that he began meeting and talking with people he saw as influential at Grace and who he had influence with, people who had been at the church a long time. He saw it as something he wanted to do to convince them that he thought I should be the next lead pastor.

I know it was always his biggest regret that he felt he did not do a succession plan well. That bothered him throughout his later years. His son-in-law, Tim, trying to be encouraging, told me that one of the reasons he felt Jerry passed when he did was because he was so confident that Grace was back in the right hands. Jerry was always very encouraging and very clear about his support of me.

In our relationship, it felt like he was the lead pastor for thirty-five years and then he handed me the baton.

Just a Jar of Clay

Pastor Danny D'Acquisto: There are very few people who had as big of a platform as Pastor Jerry had. There are also few pastors who have had the type of success he had or who can label what God has done over such an extended period. So, the temptation when meeting Jerry was to assume he was something more, something bigger than an ordinary man.

In middle school I saw him as this big pastor. Then as I got to know him over time I thought, *No, not really.* Now, certainly he was a uniquely gifted man and a very special person, but I was struck by how ordinary he was. From this I learned that I did not have to try to have an influence like he had or to try to mimic him.

In some people's lives the power of the gospel is very evident, and Jerry was one of those lives. He was always just his ordinary self but clearly filled with the all-surpassing power of God (2 Cor. 4:7).

Chapter 9

THE MARK OF MISSION:
Witnesses to the
Ends of the Earth

"But you will receive power when the Holy Spirit comes on you;
and you will be my witnesses in Jerusalem, and in all
Judea and Samaria, and to the ends of the earth."

ACTS 1:8

To Pastor Jerry missions was the work of the church. Disciples of Jesus Christ are to make disciples of Jesus Christ by sharing the good news of the Son of God's perfect life, sacrificial death, resurrection, current reign, and return. Every time one disciple is made, one faithful God worshiper is gained.

"You are worthy, our Lord and God, to receive glory and honor and power, for you created all things, and by your will they were created and have their being" (Rev. 4:11). Jerry was looking forward to heaven and worshipping King Jesus with people from every tongue, tribe, and nation who were rescued (Rev. 7:9–10).

During his pastorate, Jerry ensured 25 percent of the Grace Church budget was dedicated to supporting missionaries and mission work and taking the gospel across the world. Hundreds of Grace members went on hundreds of mission trips. He also encouraged young people to go on the mission field and willingly and joyfully took time to mentor anyone who had a heart for mission work. Along with his role as the Grace Church senior pastor, Jerry simultaneously served on the South America Mission (SAM) board of directors and as its chairman of the board for many years. SAM is a mission organization that ministers in Bolivia, Brazil, Colombia, Paraguay, and Peru.

Driving Through Central America

Ralph "Easy" Worsham: Three or four times when we were growing up, we drove from Panama to Texas to stay with our Aunt Velma for the summer. It was an eleven-day drive and we did it in a small Ford Galaxy. We saw miles and miles of Latin America as we drove.

When we went through places like El Salvador and Nicaragua, we saw people living in extreme poverty. I remember a deep sadness coming over Jerry. Once when we were staying at a hotel in El Salvador a bad earthquake hit. There were many older people there who had no one to help them and that deeply troubled Jerry.

He was very compassionate. I think he saw them like sheep without a shepherd.

A Heart for the Lord's Heart

Grace Harding: Jerry always had a heart for the heart of the Lord, and the Lord's heart is that the entire world would know and believe in Jesus as Savior.

My dad, Pastor Gordon Gustafson, was a missionary in the Philippines. Our family couldn't stay there for health reasons, so we moved to Panama.

My dad had been at Pearl Harbor and had a heart for servicemen to know God. When he preached to the congregants at our church in Panama, he told many military stories and his love for mission work came through. Jerry heard my dad's preaching, and it was one seed of many that God planted in Jerry for mission work.

Dad was also huge on discipleship, which is a part of The Navigators'®[25] focus. Jerry loved my dad, became deeply dedicated to discipleship, and was a supporter of The Navigators®.

Curundu's Love of Mission Influenced Jerry

Johnnie and Ruth Jenkins: "Pastor Leidig was the pastor of Curundu Protestant Church when Jerry, Jane, Ruth, and I were all there together, and he put a strong emphasis on missions. He regularly gave the congregation public presentations of mission activities and challenged us toward mission work," Johnnie said. "It instilled a love for mission into us all."

"We were not attending Curundu long before the church started supporting us as missionaries financially, and they asked us to help at their Bible youth camp right away," Ruth said.

"Missionaries from Wycliff, New Tribes, Central American Mission, and four or five other groups worshipped at Curundu. This led to congregants developing personal connections with many missionaries," Johnnie said. "This was a powerful influence on Jerry's love of mission.

"I was reading something from the church recently and they still have the same strong emphasis on mission," Johnnie added. "They want to get the Word of God out into the world."

"Curundu Church sparked Jerry's love of mission. It was a good start, but he was always looking outward," Ruth said. "God knit something into Jerry's heart that made him very people and mission oriented."

---

[25] The Navigators® is a ministry that shares the gospel of Jesus and helps people grow in their relationship with him through Life-to-Life® discipleship. For more information visit www.navigators.org.

Woven Together

Pastor Jason Esposito: I think missions and developing leaders were woven together for Jerry. He was open to trying new things to reach lost people, like using our new church building as a homeless shelter. He hired young and inexperienced staff members, trained them to do ministry, and then never held on to them like they were his to keep.

Even when I went to him to tell him that I felt God wanted me to plant a church, he said, "Hey, you should connect with the North American Baptist church-planting people."

I know there were things he wanted for those of us he mentored. When staff positions at Grace were available, it wasn't that he did not want us to stay or did not try to get us to stay longer in various positions. Even though he may have offered a position or suggested it, he always wanted us to do whatever we thought the Lord had for us to do for the good of the kingdom.

Inseparable

Don Amundson: To Pastor Jerry, mission and the gospel were inseparable. He believed that we needed to take the gospel to other parts of the world. I remember him talking about South America being primarily Catholic and how they were not hearing and receiving the complete gospel, and this was why he was so passionate about us going there.

Mission *Is* the Mission

Joe Kobriger: To Pastor Jerry, mission was the mission of the church. It wasn't a program or an area of focus; it was the mission.

The church is to be about spreading the truth of Christ throughout the world and making more disciples. Disciples make disciples. Jerry did not put mission in its own category. He knew the reason why we are here as a church is to grow the kingdom of God.

Scripture is clear. Acts 1:8 says we are to be God's witnesses to the ends of the earth. Jerry knew that, lived that, and saw that as his mission as a pastor. We are not just to stay in our Jerusalem.

Great Commission

Pastor Rusty Hayes: Jerry was obedient to the Great Commission (Matt. 28:18–20). He believed you needed to disproportionately promote evangelism in your church if you are going to succeed at the Great Commission because evangelism, by its nature, is uncomfortable to people. If you don't mention it, people will not naturally share the gospel.

Deep Concern for Lost Souls

Terry Kultgen: Jerry's heart was for the lost souls. He wanted his flock to mature and to be transformed spiritually, but he had a deep, deep concern for the lost and dying people. I think this is part of why he made mission a priority.

Mission Is the Heartbeat of God

Pastor Brian Petak: I was a mission pastor for twelve years, and I would never have gotten into mission or had the heart for it without Jerry's influence.

I had been at Fellowship Bible in Nashville for many years as a worship pastor, and the church asked if I would be willing to oversee mission. My first thought was, *I don't know; I'm wired as a worship pastor.* Then I decided I wanted to combine my worship skills with mission. I started something called *Worship Global.* We took mission teams all around the world with the focus of worship and exalting the glory of God.

This was all because of Jerry's influence. Jerry had a great love of mission. I am sure it is simply because mission is God's heart; God is a God of mission, but also because Jerry is part Panamanian; he was not even born in North America. He was a man of the full council of Scripture and mission is the heartbeat of God throughout Scripture from Genesis 12 forward.

Time Is Short

Pastor Jason Montano: One of the strategies Jerry got the most push back for during his later years at Grace was his EQUIP model. People wondered why Grace was developing these great leaders who would all leave. I lamented leaving Grace, and in many ways, Grace is still my church, but I knew I had been discipled to make disciples.

When you plant a church, you can create your own culture, and at Mosaic Church we utilize Jerry's EQUIP model. We find leaders, we send leaders; we find pastors, we send pastors; we find missionaries, we send missionaries. We are not going to hoard any of them. Time is short. The church isn't a gathering spot for hens and chicks. It exists to take the gospel out where it is needed. Jerry got this; he understood the mission.

Sharing the Gospel

Pastor Isaac Miller: Pastor Jerry had an intense desire to share the gospel often. It wasn't just an occasional thing or some information to share when the opportunity presented itself. He was deliberate about sharing, and he wanted us to be more deliberate and intentional about making disciples. The way I shared the gospel changed because of his influence.

Non-Negotiables

Pastor Dave Kehrli: One could not be in regular contact with Jerry Worsham and not understand that evangelism and discipleship are at the heart of the gospel of our Lord Jesus. Jerry's fervency for wanting people to come to faith and then grow in that faith were two non-negotiable things to him.

The necessity of missions was always at the forefront of his life and message. Taking the Great Commission (Matt. 28:18–20) seriously is not an easy task, but a necessary one. Reaching the nations for Christ and sharing the good news with every tribe, language, and people group was integral to who Jerry was.

When he preached the Word of God, he would always close with applications for our lives. His challenges to the Grace congregation were practical and included local evangelism and evangelism to the ends of the earth; to him both were non-negotiable, a given.

It Is All Connected

Pastor Chris Amundson: Jerry's love of mission wasn't for the love of mission; it was for the Great Commission (Matt. 28:18-20). And his love of developing leaders wasn't for developing leaders; it was for the Great Commission. And his love of children wasn't for the love of children; it was for the Great Commission. Everything Jerry did flowed from one thing. It is all really connected.

South America Mission

Kirk Ogden: The first time I met Jerry I was about ten years old. I was a missionary kid in Columbia where my parents were serving with South America Mission (SAM). Grace Baptist sent Kent Carlson [one of its pastors] to be part of a mission project, and Pastor Jerry came down to visit him. As a young boy, I was really impressed with Kent, so when his pastor came down, it was exciting to me. Over the years, I stayed in touch with Jerry from a distance because my father had become the director of SAM.

Pastor Jerry knew me through my parents and knew I was finishing up ministry with InterVarsity Christian Fellowship.[26] I interviewed at Grace and was going to take a mission director position in preparation for long-term international service. My wife, Emily, and I visited the church and started thinking about all the cold-weather clothes we would need. Then a mission opportunity came up in Bolivia, and we joined SAM instead of coming to Grace. It was supposed to be a short assignment with the thought it would be great preparation for a mission director role at Grace.

Pastor Jerry was always looking for future leadership for the church, and so he was willing to take the long-term view because he was interested in someone with mission field experience coming on staff. During our time in Bolivia, Grace had been supporting us as missionaries with the idea that they were making a future investment; they just did not realize where the investment would pay off. We were in Bolivia for about three years, and I was asked to take a role in bringing new, younger people into the mission. And with Pastor Jerry's heart for training young leaders, SAM, and missions, that idea was appealing to him, and he and the Grace leadership released us from our commitment.

Jerry was on the SAM board for more than thirty years—twenty-five of those years he was chairman of the board. My dad was the mission director and I was in senior leadership at SAM, and I would see Pastor Jerry regularly at board meetings.

When SAM needed some change, the board of directors unexpectedly asked my dad to step down from his role as the mission director. I

---

[26] InterVarsity Christian Fellowship is a campus ministry that establishes and advances witnessing communities of students and faculty. For more information visit www.intervarsity.org.

was offended for him, hurt for him. At the same time, they told my dad that they wanted me to take over as SAM director. There had always been questions about whether I really wanted to be the SAM director of missions and whether it would be good for the mission for me to succeed my father or if it would be better for them to hire someone totally new. I certainly wasn't comfortable taking that position in that way without a deeper conversation with Jerry. So, I booked a flight, came to Wisconsin, sat in his office, and talked to him.

Jerry had a posture that struck me. I knew it was a bit of a crazy idea to have me as the director, but I have become convinced that the craziness of it was part of God's purposes. My inadequacy became my greatest qualification. I was young and opinionated and a little wounded. I was angry about what had taken place with my dad, and Jerry left room for my anger in a way that enabled a process of open discussion and communication instead of the need to be right. This doesn't mean he got wishy-washy. Certainly, there was a little negotiation as we moved to an overlapping period between my dad leaving and me taking over, but the things underneath the conviction of the decision were still there. We got to discuss how relationships mattered amid this so we could see the way forward.

I shared my heart about what I did not think was done well. Dad being asked to step down was a board decision not a Pastor Jerry decision. I asked his perspective, and we talked openly about if and how we would be able to work together. It was a significant conversation. We negotiated a transition where I became director designate and my dad remained as director for one year.

During that year, Pastor Jerry and I began to talk regularly on the phone. It was always marked by him praying for me. That was the beginning of the formation of our deep relationship. Later, Jerry and I would speak monthly to review things and pray together. We would also get together at least three times a year for the SAM board meetings.

One of the things Pastor Jerry always focused on was keeping what was important in front of the Grace congregation. He translated this to SAM, but the ability to execute radical change and keep everyone informed in an organization that is dispersed was challenging.

I don't think everyone had as smooth a relationship as I did with Jerry. To this day I don't even understand why, but Jerry was always for me. And he really communicated a belief in my leadership of the mission and my instincts as a leader. I have tried to do a better job, especially as I get older, of investing in the younger generation like he did.

I think we underestimate the impact of our past experiences in shaping our future perspectives. Foundationally, I think Jerry had such a great love for mission because of his international upbringing, and because of that, he was an engaged pastor with a global perspective. He automatically included the idea of missions as essential to the role of his pastorship. It allowed him to send Kent Carlson on mission instead of keeping him at Grace Baptist Church. This then connected Jerry to South America Mission and got him on the board, with regular trips to Latin America.

I am not sure if he had a mission philosophy as much as he had a ministry philosophy and whether they were that segregated for him. I think it was a faithful application of his experience and what the Good Spirit continued to cultivate in him. Seldom do we see pastors who own the Great Commission (Matt. 28:18–20) as part of their church ministry. It is a lot of work, it is hard, and it is easier to do what is right in front of you.

One of the times I really noted connection between Jerry and me was when I quoted Psalm 127:1 that says: "Unless the LORD builds the house, the builders labor in vain."

South America Mission has the marks of our mission; they are the five characteristics we want to see exhibited as we minister: abiding, loving, redeeming, suffering, and growing. Pastor Jerry really resonated with these. He wasn't involved in writing them, but I thought of him while I was putting them together.

Missionaries can become so driven thinking things like: *God has given me something to do. I'm going to get it done. Either you are on my side, or you are in my way.* And so, we have a history sometimes, and in the church too, of getting done what the world sees as decent work but at the expense of honoring the Lord in our relationships. I think those five marks of our mission reveal what we want to see and what we want to get done, but also who we are going to be while we are ministering.

If I had to give a ministry philosophy for Jerry, I would say that it was remembering these five characteristics, and not just getting the work done, but allowing the Lord to do the work in us to build the house—that was the essential ingredient.

Jerry's conviction that there is salvation in none but Jesus was unequivocal. He was a thoughtful person who carried that to its logical conclusion and saw its foundations in Scripture.

Pastor Jerry got that mission was at the heart of the Bible. Even the fact that we have the Word is a mission to a lost people. God is communicating to us. Pastor Jerry understood that it wasn't just about me and mine, but to all people.

Today SAM continues to be a mission organization that is focused on the proclamation of Christ and the establishment of the church to make disciples in local communities. And that is not true today simply because of Pastor Jerry, but he was absolutely an essential part of maintaining an institution that is more than one-hundred years old. Many institutions have a tough time staying true to purpose, yet SAM's convictions continue to be reflected in who we are because of Jerry's leadership over so many years.

I think our board members, those who knew him, continue to see Jerry's leadership and his vision as kind of that North Star for what it looks like to be a board member and to lead even as we deal with challenges.

The Worsham Legacy Fund[27] was established at SAM and is used for leadership, governance, and collaboration. Almost all who have donated the most, are Jerry's fellow board members.

We Felt Spoiled

Paul and Laura Kienzle: In 1985 we were newly accepted appointees to South America Mission (SAM) and were raising support to go to Peru. We had only raised about 50 percent of our support and had exhausted every support outlet we knew. Laura sat and cried in our Iowa apartment and I comforted her. Then the phone rang.

It was Pastor Jerry Worsham from Grace Baptist Church in Racine, Wisconsin, calling. He explained that his church was looking for a young, green missionary couple who would be willing to come and begin building relationships with his congregation prior to leaving for the mission field.

---

[27] The Worsham Legacy Fund builds excellent leadership at all levels and cultivates stewardship through godly, organizational governance. All proceeds from *Hear Me Now* will be donated to this fund. For more information or to donate visit southamericamission.org/donate/ministries/worsham-legacy-fund/.

The SAM board of directors, to which Pastor Jerry belonged, gave him our contact information. He offered us an opportunity to interview with the Mission Team and share our testimonies. This started a beautiful relationship with Grace Church. Pastor Jerry had us stay with different church members every time we came to town. For us, he was God's hand of encouragement and challenge.

Pastor Jerry led SAM well, and he led Grace Church to love its missionaries. Grace was a church that had our backs, knew our names, formed a support team around us that would change our lives and the lives of our children, who visited us on the mission field, and who loved us through all our difficulties. We thought that all missionaries had this kind of support from back home, but we soon realized that was not the case. We became known as the "abundantly blessed missionaries" who had a congregation and a pastor with a mission spirit who understood that missionaries were an extension of the local body. We felt spoiled.

Jerry was the pastor who always asked us to do things that seemed a little harder than we thought we could manage. He took chances with us. We never really knew if he realized how unequipped we felt, but he demonstrated confidence in us and caused us to grow. He was a good coach who led us by example.

At times we felt we let him down, but he never gave up on us. Pastor Jerry was committed to raising up leaders. At times we would look at the other leaders he was raising up and feel exceedingly small and not as gifted. It was true; we were not as gifted in the preaching needed to lead a U.S. congregation. But Jerry looked deeper and asked us to pursue and cultivate the ways God had specifically made us and how he could use who we were for his kingdom.

He would say things like, "Paul, you are relational and funny. How do you see God using that as a gateway to sharing the gospel on the mission field?"

When we passed through times of struggle and depression, he would smile and say, "This is great! Brokenness is a blessing, and it will lead to connections with other people."

We are eternally thankful that he had the tough love to share things like this with us in our most critical moments.

During Jerry's pastorship, short-term mission teams partnered with us, and these partnerships helped us not only on the field but blessed us while we were on furlough.

We served with South America Mission with Pastor Jerry for our entire thirty-five-year tenure. We joined SAM when Jerry was one of the board members and later he became chairman. He never once divulged to us any SAM secrets or anything that would be inappropriate. He was a man of integrity through and through. We saw the respect that he garnered, the way others listened to his wisdom, and it made us so thankful to be from his flock in Racine.

We went to Peru in 1987 and had our first tenure in the jungle of the Ucayali River. Due to terrorism, the mission moved us to the town of Pucallpa after a year, and we changed our job description from river ministry to working with the physically disabled. We did our first three-year term, furloughed in Racine, attended Trinity, and then returned for our second term. We took our first-born child, Erica, back with us. She was just four-months old then and was continually ill. One year into that term, we began to question our desire to be on the field due to her health and our own confusion about what our calling was. *Were we to be short-term or career missionaries?*

Pastor Jerry visited us and counseled us to stick out our term, but we did not follow his counsel and resigned from SAM. This hurt him and put a large barrier in our relationship.

We returned to the USA and struggled with our *what's next*. We eventually rented an apartment in a Chicago suburb and worked, but we still felt sadness at losing our relationship with Pastor Jerry and our spiritual home at Grace Church. We felt we had disappointed him beyond repair. We did not feel loved or pastored during our weakest moments. After about four months, we received a call from him asking us to come to Racine for a series of Saturday mornings so we could process things and talk.

His initiative restored our relationship and eventually led us to realize God was not finished with us and was calling us to return to South America with SAM. Jerry showed great humility by apologizing for his part in our broken relationship, and we too apologized for our part. This was a turning point in our relationship as we all knew that we needed to work together to make our being on the field a reality.

Jerry invited SAM leadership to the old Grace Church on Northwestern Avenue. In his office, we talked through what a return to the field would look like, if our calling and motivation were sound, and how to make it happen. The mission decided they needed us to go to Bolivia and run the SAM guesthouse, and so with Pastor Jerry's blessing and support, we began to raise funds to return, this time with our three daughters.

We served in Bolivia from 1997 to 2012, and they were some of the most fruitful years of our overseas ministry. (After the guesthouse ministry, we did church planting, and in the living room of our home, a house church was born among the professional class.)

In November 2016 we were part of a Grace Church mission trip to Bolivia. There were many amazing moments on this trip, but two stand out regarding Pastor Jerry. First, he asked the mission to call a group of about fifteen national pastors and their wives together for a meal. After the meal, he shared a message with them. It was specific, pointed, intentional, and a call for them to keep on in times of hardship because sharing the Word of God is the most important calling that we have in this life. Pastor Jerry lived to make Christ known and to encourage and equip others to do the same.

Second, we all went to a local hospital to share the gospel with the patients and their families. We split up and went room to room, and near the end, we caught up with Pastor Jerry and Jane in a hospital room where very pregnant mothers were waiting to see an OB-GYN. Pastor Jerry had packed an exceptionally large EvangeCube[28] of which he was immensely proud. We watched him deliver the salvation message as he unfolded the cube. He asked questions and engaged the mothers. His face was radiant and he exuded joy as he shared the good news of Jesus Christ. We all stood back and marveled at what Pastor Jerry was doing; that moment was a prime example of what characterized all that he was about and all that he loved. He always had on his mind how he could disciple and impact others for Jesus.

Same Mission

Pastor Jason Montano: From Jerry I learned to celebrate and unite with other like-minded churches because we all have the same mission. To him it was never *Grace Church against the world.* Jerry united with people who would unite with him. I am involved with pastor prayer groups in my area, just like Jerry was.

Simple Living, Generous Giving

Kristen Pedersen (Pulda): I was always amazed at how simply Pastor Jerry and Jane lived, yet how far their generosity reached. I remember asking Jane one day, as she no longer had children living at home and she was retired from teaching, if she needed to go back to substitute teaching.

---

[28] The EvangeCube by E3 Resources is a seven-picture cube that simply and clearly unfolds the gospel of Jesus Christ. For more information visit https://www.e3resources.org.

She humbly told me that long ago she and Jerry decided how much money they would live on and that the rest they would give back to the Lord and mission work.

He Helped Make Up Our Support Deficit

David and Marilyn Simmons: Our first memories of Jerry and Jane are when Grace Church started supporting us as missionaries. We were on furlough and lacked the financial support we needed to return to the mission field in Peru. Through his connections with South America Mission (SAM), Jerry found out about our lack of funding, and because Grace and another church began supporting us, we were able to return to the mission field.

We have very fond memories of Jerry's field visits. At one conference he was the keynote speaker, and he gave a sermon from Jeremiah 2:13: "My people have committed two sins: They have forsaken me, the spring of living water, and have dug their own cisterns, broken cisterns that cannot hold water." He reminded us to be careful not to look for fulfillment and happiness outside of the Lord, but to look to him to fulfill all our needs.

Even though Pastor Jerry was the chairman of the board of SAM, he was more like a pastor to us. He was always kind, always caring.

David was a SAM pilot for thirty-two years and had the privilege of flying Jerry around when he visited Peru. His ability to speak Spanish was a huge advantage in interacting and preaching to the people wherever he went.

When David became the field director to SAM Peru, Jerry took time to meet with him regularly via Skype to encourage, mentor, and pray with him.

We will never forget his laugh and the sparkle in his eyes. We appreciated his faith and positivity.

He Was Passionate About Mission

Eric Ernst: I moved to Racine in the summer of 1977 to work with InterVarsity Christian Fellowship at the University of Wisconsin—Parkside. I visited Grace Baptist Church because it was part of the same North American Baptist Conference that I had been associated with during the previous two years I had spent in Milwaukee. I attended an evening service, and afterward Pastor Jerry greeted me with his warm smile, asked me what I was doing in Racine, and made me feel totally at home. In fact, I believe the words he said to me were, "This is your church now." I was convinced!

When I met Jerry, I was already 90 percent committed to serving as a foreign missionary. Shortly after coming to Grace, I got engaged to Marlies. Jerry did our premarital counseling and was a great mentor to us early in our marriage. Marlies was open to missionary service but not as convinced as I was. Jerry's passion for missions and for mentoring others into missionary service was certainly instrumental in God's leading us to serve as missionaries.

Jerry was warm, encouraging, wise, godly, and always thinking of how to help others know Christ and grow as his disciples. His people skills were incredible. He had a way of asking tough questions that opened you up rather than shut you down.

Jerry was always full of enthusiasm and joy as he engaged in mission work. You could tell it was his passion. He knew people without Christ were lost and introducing them to the Savior is the most important thing we can do.

Jerry was convinced of whom Jesus Christ is and what he did to save us on the cross. His worldview was totally in line with Scripture. He knew the Great Commission (Matt. 28:18–20) was not given to just the Apostles but to all the church through all ages until Christ returns. He was rock solid on that, and it drove him to promote missionary outreach to the ends of the earth. Because he knew he couldn't do everything, he focused Grace mission efforts on Latin America with the goal of doing that well. His mission was accomplished! Yet, Grace also supported missionaries serving on most continents and among some of the least-reached people groups.

Grace sent out Marlies and me to serve as missionaries in Paraguay in South America with SIM[29] [formerly known as Sudan Inland Mission] not his beloved South America Mission!

When I first met Jerry, I had a lot of passion and biblical and theological knowledge. I thought black and white and was a bit "in your face" as I confronted what I saw as biblical error. Jerry showed me how to be both firm and gracious at the same time. He had the ability to ask tough questions and broach sensitive topics with people in a disarming way that was fabulous. This was a great gift that made him such an effective pastor and mentor.

His people skills were contagious. He helped me grow in practical, people-ministry skills. I grew in my understanding of people and how to effectively minister to them. On a personal note, he also helped me to be more sensitive to my wife, seeking to understand her perspective.

He was a pastor to Marlies and me throughout our missionary journey in South America. He took the time to visit us and was a tremendous source of encouragement. He and Jane prayed for us and they faithfully supported us through monthly giving for more than thirty years.

Jerry encouraged us to always be involved in ministry that plants, grows, and empowers the church in its ministries locally and to the world. He knew the greatest ministry impact comes through the church.

The Making of a Missions Trip

Jen Binkley (Worsham): My dad's passion for missions definitely influenced me. My senior year in high school, I begged my dad to let me

[29] SIM helps prepare and journey with Christians sent by churches to make disciples of Jesus Christ around the world. For more information visit www.simusa.org.

join the team from Grace that was going to Columbia, South America. (I had spent the previous summer in Ecuador for nine weeks with Teen Missions International.[30]) My dad said the trip was just for men in the church, and I argued that I should be able to go. I told him I would be praying that not enough men would sign up, and sure enough, not enough men signed up and I was allowed to go!

Mike and Julie Lueken [one of the Grace Baptist pastors and his wife] agreed to go so there would be another female on the trip. My dad also removed himself from the position of team leader so I would not have to report to him.

We Need Mechanics

Darrin and Nanette Roetman: When we first came to Racine, it was because we were looking for a house to rent. Darrin had been hired as an aircraft mechanic for Midwest Airlines in Milwaukee.

We drove past the old Grace Baptist Church on Northwestern Avenue and said to one another, "This is where we should go to worship the Lord this Sunday." The church sanctuary was full of people, and we sat in the second row, close to the pulpit. It just so happened that we sat right behind Pastor Jerry and Jane. Pastor Jerry turned around and said, "I don't think I've ever met you. I am Pastor Jerry." He shook our hands and we introduced ourselves.

"What do you do for a living, Darrin?" he asked. Darrin responded that he was an aircraft mechanic. Pastor Jerry said, "Ah, we need aircraft mechanics on the mission field."

This brief response spoke directly to Darrin's heart. Since he was a young boy, he had wanted to become a missionary.

---

[30] Teen Missions International exists to launch youth into lifetime mission involvement by training, discipling, and mobilizing them to impact eternity around the world NOW. For more information visit www.teenmissions.org.

We have now been on the mission field in Rennes, France, working with French and international students for many years.

Pastor Jerry and Jane have always supported us as missionaries by praying for us, encouraging us, and by even supporting us financially.

We Will Go for Just One

Debbie Palmer: It was such a miracle I got into dental school. I was going to Marquette University in Milwaukee to be a dental hygienist, and somehow, I got into the Marquette University School of Dentistry because someone else cancelled! I remember praying and asking God to help me *be* the person that I *pretended to be.* I knew God wanted me to serve him.

After I graduated, I was teaching Sunday school at another Racine church, and I had some missionaries from Indonesia speak to my class. I told them to call me if they ever needed someone to help and they called me. I went to Indonesia and then got involved with Word of Life Fellowship[31] doing summer camps.

When I came to Grace, Pastor Jerry asked me to be on the Mission Board. I got to know all the missionaries, and I wanted to have the genuine care and love for the missionaries that he had. I felt like a sponge and desired to absorb all the things he knew about missions and all the things he said.

I loved that Pastor Jerry wanted a high percentage of the Grace Church giving to go to mission work. I've now been on more than thirty mission trips including Romania, Spain, Poland, and many trips to Guatemala.

When we went to Guatemala, we had to take all these supplies and medicines. It was hard to do, but we did not care! Jerry reminded us

---

[31] Word of Life Fellowship is a non-denominational Christian organization creating faith-defining experiences that give students and families the chance to encounter God and grow in their spiritual walks. For more information visit www.Wol.org.

that if just one person decides to become a follower of Christ on a trip, it is worth it. Jesus rejoices over one sheep that comes back to the Father (Matt. 18:12–14).

Jerry supported sending teams from Grace to many different countries, and there have now been thousands of people who have received Christ during these trips. Many of those saved during Grace trips began attending Bible clubs, went to Bible school, planted churches, and then became missionaries themselves. Often when we went back to the same place the next year, a church would be planted from those who got saved the year before.

Just Give It to Her

Joe Kobriger: I came to Grace Church in 2003, divorced, and as a single dad. Jerry got to know me and got to know my family. He knew my kids by name and would ask, "How's Dillon? How's Peyton? How's Reannyn?"

My wife, Sheri, and I met at Grace, and Pastor Jerry married us. We both wanted to do a mission trip with our kids. After this trip and seeing my interest, Pastor Jerry asked me if I wanted to come onto the Mission Team. I was floored. Grace was a huge church at the time and I had only been there four years. The Mission Team was a big responsibility, and it had a huge budget to manage. On this team I got to know Pastor Jerry even better.

During one team meeting, there was discussion about a student who was requesting funds for a summer mission trip. As a team we were talking about it and saying, "We have no more money in the budget. What do you want to do? Where can we take the money from? Should we do that?"

Pastor Jerry listened to us all and then his response was, "Oh, just give it to her. She's going to do excellent work. The Lord will provide. Don't worry about it."

Just those words....

I've seen and heard lots of things to the opposite of his statement since I've been on the Mission Team throughout the years. People worry so much about provision, and there was Pastor Jerry, the guy in charge of the whole church, showing us faith.

It is a simple story, but I thought, *Man, this guy is awesome. Faithful.*

God Will Provide

Jack Bell: Once when Pastor Jerry and I were meeting, we started talking about life work. I told him that when I retired at age sixty-two, I wanted to go into full-time ministry. I had worked in sales and had a high salary, so I was concerned about provision.

All along Pastor Jerry just kept telling me, "God will provide. You want to make disciples; he will provide."

Jerry was full of support for me at every stage of my ministry. I even had an office in the church for a while. (I had to move out because people would wander into my office and I could not get anything done. There were so many interruptions! I learned the life of a pastor is one of interruptions, and yet they keep going and going.)

Pastor Jerry encouraged me, supported me, and even offered clerical support from the Grace staff when I needed extra help. His name is on my commission badge, and that is special to me.

Mission Is God's Heart

Maria Rosa Griffin: I think those who love the Lord know mission is God's heart. To me, Pastor Jerry's support of mission was just another sign of how much he loved the Lord. The Bible says you will recognize disciples by their fruit. I saw in his love for mission his love for God's heart. And he wanted Grace to have this same love.

He Never Compromised His Witness

Jerry Morrison: I was the manager of the Grace softball team for a couple of years, and Pastor Jerry was our pitcher. I had played softball with many Christians who totally forgot about their witness when they stepped onto the field. Not so with Pastor Jerry. Softball was about competition, but it was about fellowship and camaraderie as well. He made sure we never forgot our witness and reminded us that we were ambassadors for Christ while we were on the field and everywhere we put our feet.

Bible Study Fellowship
Was a Mission Field

Patti Booth: When we moved to Racine, there was no Bible Study Fellowship (BSF) class here so I got involved in the Christian Women's Club. This was a women's outreach with a big luncheon and study. They asked me to be their prayer advisor.

I was also asked to teach at Grace Baptist, and they gave me three choices: I could teach an exercise class, teach from a book, or teach the Bible. I choose teaching the Bible, and I followed the format I had been taught at BSF because it was the only format I knew.

At this time, a prayer group began in Racine to pray about bringing a BSF class to the area, and many churches and groups were not happy. In fact, I got called on the carpet by the Christian Women's Club. Someone asked: "What are you doing bringing another study here?"

Women from other churches and even one person from Grace asked me the same types of things. I was asked, "When you have a ministry at Grace, why are you bringing another ministry to Racine?"

I said, "I am not bringing it. If God opens the door for Bible Study Fellowship to come to Racine, we will go through that door."

I was not prepared for the enemy to attack the way he did. These people couldn't see beyond their own churches and ministries. I couldn't understand it. I had been in BSF in many other states, and Bible churches always loved BSF, but not here.

Many of the evangelical churches in Racine felt threatened by BSF; Pastor Jerry never felt threatened. In fact, he was the total opposite and looked at BSF as a mission to the community of Racine.

Jane shared that about the time my husband, Chris, and I moved to Racine, someone from Grace who had moved away became involved in BSF in her new hometown. She told Jerry and Jane how BSF was a Bible-teaching organization.

Becoming the Racine BSF teaching leader was a huge commitment, and I had a list longer than Moses on why I could not step up. Jane and Pastor Jerry were always encouraging; they listened and were careful to let God be the one who called me to do the ministry.

Pastor Jerry always said to me, "Patti, you are an arm of Grace." I don't want to use the word proud, but I think he was thrilled about Grace women being part of BSF. I wasn't representing Grace at BSF, but so many women came to Grace Church after being in BSF.

I remember meeting with Jerry after my first year of teaching. I felt like a failure because there is so much that a new teaching leader needs to learn and do. And I felt like I did not get it right for God. I think I went into a little depression. I did not recognize it because I am not a depression-prone person, and yet, I met with Jerry and he identified it.

"Patti, I think you are feeling depressed," Pastor Jerry said to me. "But let me tell you that God never asked you to be perfect. He asked you to be available and faithful."

When people would say about BSF that we were "stealing their sheep," Jerry would say, "No, BSF is just growing grass."

He knew BSF was mission work, and mission work was God's work. Therefore, Bible Study Fellowship coming to town never threatened him. Others were all so scared about what this ministry was going to do to *their* ministries. He wasn't; he saw it all linked together as kingdom work.

(*Author's Note: Patti Booth served as the Racine Bible Study Fellowship teaching leader for twenty years. During this time, thousands of women and preschool-age children systematically studied the Bible. She also trained hundreds of women to teach and lead women and children through the Bible. Pastor Jerry Worsham's support was instrumental in bringing BSF to Racine. Today, there is both a women's and men's class in Racine.*)

You Stay Focused

Joe Kobriger: After Pastor Jerry retired, he said things to me about mission that more scared me than inspired me, things like, "God has plans for you."

In 2016 Gimy and Cristina Caballero wanted some people from Grace Church to come to Bolivia, and my wife, Sheri, and I agreed to take a team. It turned out that Pastor Jerry wanted to go on that trip. Paul and Laura Kienzle, retired South America Mission missionaries, also wanted to go on that trip. Then Jane Worsham decided to join us. While we were there, I listened to many conversations between Jerry and Danny D'Acquisto, who was the Grace director of mission at that time, about the tribulations of mission work. I was also talking to them about why we do mission.

Jerry looked at me and said, "Joe, the Lord has great things for you in missions at Grace Church. You just stay focused."

I had no clue what he meant; it just scared me. Mission is a funny thing. It is not what everyone is excited about.

After this, Danny asked me to be chairman of the Mission Team with him. When he left to do the Redemption Church plant, I was asked to keep things going until the next mission pastor was hired. From there

I became a missionary mobilizer and made mission my full-time work. It is obvious Jerry had insight into where God was working in my life. It was so prophetic, and I don't think God is even done yet with our mission work at Grace church.

(Author's Note: Joe has retired from his job as a mission mobilizer. In 2022, he and Sheri became part of the Grace Church staff as the co-directors of missions.)

Mission DNA

Sheri Kobriger: It was well-known that the Grace Church budget was so mission focused because of Pastor Jerry. It is the DNA of what he did and what we still do as a church. I can visualize the many times we had all the country flags on the sanctuary stage. We talked about mission, promoted mission, and had mission Sundays. It was a regular part of the rhythm and heartbeat of the church because of Pastor Jerry.

God Used Park Basketball
for His Kingdom Plan

Jim Kerkvliet: As the varsity girls' basketball coach at Racine [Washington] Park High School, I would organize events that included the parents of players. Pastor Jerry and Jane's daughter, Jen, was on the team in the late 1980s. I had occasion to meet Pastor Jerry and Jane at a preseason meeting and at a parents' night meeting.

I had many types of conversations with players' parents in my years of coaching basketball. Quite often these conversations focused on all the reasons why the parents thought their daughter deserved more playing time. Pastor Jerry and Jane never once questioned the amount of playing time Jen got. Their comments only consisted of how they enjoyed watching the games and how much Jen enjoyed being part of the team. Jen was a pleasure to have on the team. She displayed a winning combination of attitude and effort. While she was not a starter, she contributed great support for the girls who got more playing time than she did. We did not know it at the time, but God had a kingdom plan for my wife, Steph, and me which began with Jen joining the Park girls' basketball team and her parents becoming loyal team fans.

After Jen graduated from Park, my next encounter with Pastor Jerry and Jane was at a wedding. Steph was working as a sign language interpreter at a co-worker's wedding that Pastor Jerry officiated. At the reception, Pastor Jerry and Jane invited Steph and me to sit with them during dinner. Before this wedding, we only knew the Worshams as nice people who enjoyed being fans of Park girls' basketball and to whom we were drawn to because of their warm and friendly personalities.

Steph and I had previously discussed attending a church to enhance our marriage because we were struggling with several issues. Up to this time, neither of us had attended any church in years. During our dinner discussion with Jerry and Jane, we mentioned our interest in attending a church. Pastor Jerry extended an invitation to attend a service at Grace Baptist.

At Jerry and Jane's invitation, we did attend a service very soon after the wedding. We felt very welcomed, and immediately after the service, Pastor Jerry rushed out to find us, to say hello, and to invite us to attend again. Both Pastor Jerry and Jane were very genuine and welcoming, and we felt very comfortable talking to them.

We became regulars at Grace Baptist. Not only did attending church influence our marriage, but Jane and Jerry were also excellent role models of a loving and covenantal marriage.

After attending church for a few months, Pastor Jerry and Jane invited us to join a couples' Bible study they were starting. I was learning about how to have a relationship with God by listening to Pastor Jerry preach on Sundays. The Bible study gave Steph and me an opportunity to delve more deeply into the Bible and share experiences with other couples.

Growing up I knew who Jesus was, but I did not have a relationship with him. Pastor Jerry guided me on how to have a relationship with Jesus. I had been taught throughout my youth that I had to be good. If I was not good, I needed to go to confession as soon as possible and then perform the penance that I was given to have a clean slate with God until the next time I messed up. I usually felt like God was mad at me after I messed up. My upbringing encouraged me to believe it was necessary to ask for salvation again and again. Pastor Jerry taught me that Jesus offers salvation once and for all. All I needed to do was accept the free gift of salvation. If I messed up, I needed to ask for forgiveness, but I did not need to ask for salvation again. There were times when Satan would provoke guilt trips in me, but conversations with Pastor Jerry helped me to see God's truth in those trying times.

Two Unique Tour Guides

Larry White: On a mission trip to Panama, the team was in two different vans taking a tour through the city. Jerry and I were with the luggage in one van and Jane and everyone else was in the other van.

Jerry was telling me things like, "This is where I took Bible study; this is the church where I became a minister; this is the church where Jane and I got married; this is where we first met."

We made a quick stop and I went to the other van and asked if they were getting a good tour. I told them Jerry was giving me a tour talk of all the places he had been. And everybody in Jane's van started to laugh. Jane was telling them where they made out and where they went on dates. I was thinking, *Jerry! You did not tell me this good stuff!*

Next Steps

Jack Bell: Pastor Jerry was a champion of following up with new believers and he thought follow-up was a weakness of the local church.

Next Steps[32] is a ten-step ministry created to help new believers in their walk with Christ. Pastor Jerry did not help write the material, but he looked it over, helped inspire its use, and helped lay out the key features. There are sections on fellowship, worship, corporate prayer, and mission opportunities. Maxine Omdahl [another Grace Church member] and I assembled and developed *Next Steps,* and Jerry encouraged us at every step.

Once the program was finalized, I invited Pastor Jerry to come to one of The Navigators® regional training meetings in the Twin Cities. He invited a pastor from Bolivia to accompany him. This catapulted the *Next Steps* ministry into South America Mission.

Jerry's leadership and shepherding impacted me profoundly as this ministry developed. It is now used in seven countries, in five languages, and in 2,000 churches.

They Need to Know Jesus

Joe Kobriger: I learned from Pastor Jerry to always be Jesus-focused on mission trips. It would have been easy to get off track because we were traveling to Third World countries to help people who needed our help. There were widows and hungry kids and people in desperate situations.

For Jerry it was always about, "These people don't know Jesus. They need to know Jesus."

He, of course, wanted us to help people who needed help, but his first and primary focus was always all about sharing the good news of Jesus. He wanted the entire world to know Christ.

---

[32] For more information on *Next Steps* visit https://nextstepschurchministries.com.

From Concrete to the World

Joe Van Bree: A few weeks after my wife, Kathy, and I started attending Grace, Pastor Jerry was looking for someone to repair an area of concrete plank. I told him I would do it, and that was the start of my working relationship with him.

Shortly after, he invited me to go on a mission trip to Columbia to help rebuild the second floor of a school. That trip was cancelled due to missionary kidnappings in other areas.

Not long after this, Pastor Jerry asked me to go to Bolivia to help rebuild an earthen dam that had let go and flooded three Indian villages. I agreed and Kathy went too. This trip was the start of our mission service for the kingdom of God. Because of Pastor Jerry's invitation and encouragement, I have been on thirty-eight mission trips and Kathy has been on twenty-six. We have served in Panama, Costa Rica, Bolivia, France, Guatemala, and the Dominican Republic.

He Was Down in the Dirt Digging

Larry White: I wanted nothing to do with the first mission trip to Panama that Pastor Jerry invited me to because I thought we would be going door-to-door to witness. Jerry assured me this trip was a construction trip, and then he introduced me to Joe Van Bree who was involved. After hearing more from Jerry and Joe, I agreed to be part of the trip.

Pastor Jerry led by example. On the trip in Panama, he was down in the dirt digging holes. Someone as important as he was in the world was humbly digging holes in the dirt. This trip really opened my eyes to God's presence in him and his devotion to mission work.

After this, he suckered me into another trip. He told me that we were going to build buildings. I said, "That is not a mission trip."

He said, "Okay, Larry. Then just say we are going down to build a building so people there can come to the building and learn about Christ."

I agreed to his terms but still joked with him that it was not a mission trip. Pastor Jerry just kept saying how important mission work was, and I bought into it.

Instrumental in the Launch of Youth For Christ

Jon Nelson: In 1984 I left the produce business to become the associate pastor of the Community Church of the Nazarene in Racine and to help plant the church. I met Pastor Jerry Worsham my very first week on the job. He was part of the Racine Pastors' Fellowship that met the first Thursday of every month at the old St. Luke's Hospital cafeteria.

Jerry asked me what I was going to do in my job. I said as associate pastor I would do a lot of follow-up and discipleship work, but that I also wanted to start a youth ministry. He immediately hooked me up with the Grace Baptist Youth Pastor, Dave Garda. Dave and I became close friends, and he helped me get started in youth ministry. We did many things together including forming the Racine Youth Network. It was like a youth pastors' version of Racine Pastors' Fellowship, and I also became very good friends with Jerry and other Grace staff members.

Fast-forward nine years. By this time, I had served twice as the interim pastor of the Community Church of the Nazarene, and I was sensing it was time for me to move on. I resigned from my position at the church. I knew it was time for something else, but I wasn't sure what that *something else* should be; I was thinking that it would take three or four months to find a new position.

Shortly after I resigned, I got a call from the Youth For Christ[33] (YFC) regional director saying he was getting ready to shut down the local chapter in southeastern Wisconsin, but a pastor told him that he should talk to me first. I told Pastor Jerry right away and asked him to pray for me and what my involvement might be.

---

[33] For more information about Youth For Christ in Southeastern Wisconsin visit www.youthforchristwi.com.

As the months went on, YFC began to look like something I might do. In the meantime, the head pastor of Community Church of the Nazarene resigned, and they asked me to consider being the interim pastor again. I requested a few weeks to think about it, then I agreed, but I told them that I did not want to be considered for the head pastor position.

During this time, I started to learn more about what it would be like to restart YFC because absolutely nothing was going on. They had no board, no activity, and lots of debt.

Jerry and I met on a regular basis to talk about YFC. He said to me, "Jon, you are the guy to do this."

I told him I appreciated his support, but I had never raised funds before, I had four children, and my oldest was going to be a senior in high school. I told him I was not sure how this is all going to work out, and I felt anxious about taking the position.

Jerry said, "Jon, this is what I am going to do. I will serve on your board for one year, and then I will find a replacement from Grace to take my spot. And in the spring of 1994, all the Grace Baptist Church Easter offerings will be dedicated to restarting Youth For Christ. We will also put you in our mission budget."

I can't remember what the dollar amount was, but it was extremely generous monthly support. I told him, "Wow, man! I really appreciate that!"

Without Jerry's support and prayers, I know that I did not have the courage to step out and do the restart of YFC at age forty-one with much uncertainty. Grace Baptist's and Jerry's support were critical. Grace was the first church to put YFC in its mission budget.

I needed to have $20,000 in the organization's checking account before I could start working full time. We started fundraising in February 1994, and with Grace's generosity, by April we already had $35,000! Jerry also introduced me to a couple attending Grace who became believers in Jesus through YFC in the 1960s, and they made a significant yearly financial contribution.

I think our very first meeting was also at Grace. We had no board, so Jerry helped recruit people. The first board had to vote themselves in.

As promised, when Jerry's board term was up, he introduced me to Chris Booth, a local business owner and elder and leader at Grace. Chris came on the board, served on the board for years, and was also our chairman numerous times, as well as a generous financial partner.

Jerry helped me to grow and keep growing. He instilled in me the steps to take to start something from scratch. When he came to Grace Baptist Church, it was a very small [historically] German Baptist church.

People have said that it is easier to give birth than to raise the dead. Pastor Jerry took a position at a decades-old church and he was able to re-energize it to become the Grace Church we now know. It really is amazing! Usually once a church hits a downward spiral, it is hard to revitalize it. He taught me to take YFC from dead to alive just like he did at Grace.

Two to three years into YFC, things were really starting to happen. I needed more staff, and Jerry knew this. I was struggling to find people who would be willing to raise support and come on staff.

I was sitting in my office, and a young lady came in. I did not know her, but it turns out she was Jerry and Jane's daughter Jen. She had just graduated from Anderson University and told me that she had gone through national level training for YFC. She was going to go out of the country and minister, but she had back surgery, and they did not want to send her. So, after talking about a position for an hour or so, we decided that she would raise support and come on staff full time at YFC. She had a vast network of people who would support her and came on staff in a matter of months working between Mitchell and McKinley. So, there was that connection with Jerry Worsham too.

Later, Chris Amundson came on our staff and worked for us as a single guy, and when he got married, he and his wife, Dawn, did an awesome job for YFC at Park High School. Later Grace hired him as its youth pastor.

Thousands of students have been impacted through YFC. We keep records, and we share the gospel with between 1,000 and 2,000 students a year. If you multiply that over twenty-eight years, we have reached between 28,000 and 56,000 students with the gospel of Jesus Christ since 1994.

YFC was going to happen with or without Jerry Worsham or me. Yet, God chose to offer it to us, and we both decided to accept the offer. *Instrumental* would be how I would describe Jerry's role in YFC. Without his support, I did not have the faith and resolve to do it. Jerry's support was critical for me. When he laid out what he would do for me, I told my wife, Brenda, we needed to do this. And it is not a two-year project; it is a five- to ten-year project, at least.

Pastor Jerry Worsham's marks are all over YFC—much more than he ever realized.

Christ for Children International

Jane Worsham: Christ for Children International (CFCI) was a board both Jerry and I had the privilege of serving on for thirteen years.

With a great burden for impoverished children, Dr. Lyle Dorsett and his wife, Mary, started CFCI in Fresnillo, Mexico. Dr. Dorsett was a popular professor at Wheaton College, and Mary was a Bible study leader. Both encouraged many students to pursue mission work; our daughter Janna was one of them. She served for two years on the CFCI founding team.

During our annual trips to Fresnillo, Jerry and I helped with team building and teaching. We were blessed to watch God transform lives in the poor and undeveloped nearby community through the work of the CFCI missionaries. We also had the privilege of bringing many Grace Church students and members with us and exposing them to international mission work.

What a joy to be part of the CFCI mission: "Share the gospel of Jesus Christ with all children, and develop in them the principles of Christian discipleship, including providing food and clothing for children in need."

As they were fed and clothed and the love of Christ was shared in clubs, hundreds of children and entire families became followers of Christ. Eventually a national church called Iglesia del Gran Pastor[34] was established in Fresnillo and continues to thrive.

Marina Ministry

Patti Booth: My husband, Chris, and I would get up on Sundays, go to church at Grace, and then head to the Racine marina to go boating. One day Chris noticed all the boat slips from Illinois and all the out-of-town people who were not going to church.

"I don't think God gave us a boat just to give us a boat," Chris said to me. So, we talked with Pastor Jerry and launched a Marina Ministry with Grace coming alongside us.

Pastor Jerry taught at the Marina Ministry in its early years and recruited others to come and teach. We did this ministry for twenty-five years.

Use Your Gifts Inside and Outside the Church

Dr. Paul Durbin: Through his preaching, Pastor Jerry moved me to live out my faith. He explained faith was not something to bottle up

---

[34] For more information visit www.facebook.com/IglesiaDelGranPastor.

but something to share with others. I was spurred to share any gifts and talents given to me to glorify God inside and outside the church.

An opportunity arose for me to be part of a mission trip to Mexico. I thought this trip would be a wonderful opportunity for one of my children to serve with me, and Pastor Jerry really encouraged this. He had a tremendous heart for mission work and emphasized how important it was for Grace to be a mission-minded church.

God closed the door on this trip but instead opened the door for me to go to Belize. This trip really changed my life in an incredible way. I saw poverty like I had never seen before. Our team ministered to people and shared the gospel. While we were there, we met a woman named Loretta Moody who lived in the jungle. She was married and had fourteen children. She covered her neck with a large bandana. When she took it off to show me, it revealed a massive enlargement of her thyroid gland. She said she had it for about five years and it was growing, but she did not trust the doctors there to do the surgery. I told her I would see what I could do about getting her to the United States for the surgery. God opened that door, and a fellow Grace member who was a surgeon did Loretta's surgery in Racine.

It turned out she had very aggressive thyroid cancer, and she stayed with my family for six months. Grace Church, and in particular Pastor Jerry, provided so much love and support to Loretta and to my family. Loretta loved Pastor Jerry and his messages. She eventually did pass away three years later due to this very aggressive cancer, but she had a reasonable quality of life for most of that time and had that extra time to be with her family.

Since I first went to Belize, I have taken a mission trip annually with at least one of my children (until the COVID pandemic occurred in 2020). We have done three mission trips to Belize, and nine medical and dental trips to Guatemala.

Pastor Jerry would also often preach that we needed to share Christ with others in our city. So, I prayed for an opportunity to serve locally in Racine with my family. A fellow Grace member was serving dinner once a month at HALO, a Racine homeless shelter. When I heard about that, I decided to join her doing music and praying with the residents. Our family has been serving at HALO once a month ever since. God has moved in a powerful way through HALO and impacted many lives for Christ.

Baseball

Tony Ferraro: Pastor Jerry had just come on board as Grace's pastor [in 1976] and a picnic was held at Sanders Park. Jerry and Jane came up to talk to my wife, Jeanne, and me. When Jerry introduced himself as the new pastor, my mouth dropped because he was just so young looking. He and Jane both looked like teenagers!

Pastor Jerry had no issues that I was Catholic and Jeanne was Baptist. He was never judgmental. He accepted our church relationship. There were many people who did not.

Jerry was a big baseball fan. We talked baseball the first time we met at the picnic, and then he went out in the field to shag fly balls.

Years later when he was going to Cuba, we supported his trip. He came to me and said, "You know, Tony, there is a baseball pitcher from Panama City named Mariano Rivera who is a Christian. He authored a book on his baseball career and his Christian life [*Mariano Rivera: Playing with Purpose*]. I want to get this book and distribute it to the people in Cuba."

I told him the support money is yours to do with what you want. He was so conscientious in asking permission to use the funds this way.

He took copies of a Spanish version and was knocking on doors and giving out the book to reach people for Christ.

Welcome Younger People

Larry White: Once I witnessed an older couple complaining to Pastor Jerry that the music played during the Sunday service wasn't old, gospel, organ music. Jerry firmly told them the bottom line is that we must attract and welcome younger people into the church. He was always looking for ways to make the younger crowd fit in the church.

Hosea Musical

Phil Adams: A musical like *Hosea* was not something a church did in the early 1990s. It was an edgy outreach, yet Jerry got behind it. From the get-go, he gave us carte blanche musically to perform. He had questions, but he let us do it. His words were always, "We are here to bring glory to God."

Substitute Preacher

George Gorton: I first met Pastor Jerry when I was attending a meeting in an emerging Spanish church. On various occasions he would speak at that meeting. When I talked with him about it, he said this forming church could not afford to call their own pastor at the time, so he helped when he could preaching in Spanish.

Gracefully Fit

Loreen Radke: Gracefully Fit was a women's exercise ministry held three mornings a week that drew women from all over the Racine area. Attendees would exercise, fellowship, and hear a brief devotional message. The fact Pastor Jerry approved a budget for exercise equipment and music showed his support for sharing Christ in all different settings.

It Bothered Him

Lee Smith: I think Pastor Jerry was so mission focused because the thought of someone, anyone not knowing Christ just bothered him.

Middle School Madness Is Born

Jon Nelson: Every year while the younger kids at Grace Church were participating in Vacation Bible School (VBS), Pastor Jerry and Jane led a group of sixth, seventh, and eighth graders in their own, age-appropriate VBS. They were doing high-energy things with the students as well as breaking them into small groups for discussion about Christ.

Jerry told me to come by and see what they were doing with the students because I had shared an idea that I had for a summer day camp for Racine area middle school students.

To help my idea along, he told me that the next summer instead of Grace hosting a VBS for middle schoolers that they would send them to the Youth For Christ (YFC) day camp. This is how Middle School Madness was born, and it is still running today.

Pastor Jerry encouraged me to advertise it throughout the year at the YFC middle school ministry locations. There were times when there were more than two-hundred students attending.

His Passion Became Mine

Denise Pipol: I am grateful to Pastor Jerry for being so enthusiastic about mission and evangelism and purposefully leading Grace Church to value these. His passion for mission and evangelism has become a passion in my life and the life of Grace Church. Had I not been in a mission-minded church, I may have never been able to serve in the way I believe God has called me.

Pastor Jerry came to support us at one of our annual fundraisers for the medical and dental mission trip to Guatemala. I pointed to the multitude of people from Grace and other churches who were there and now involved in the trip and mission work because of his faithfulness.

You Don't Cut the Mission Budget

Patti Booth: Pastor Jerry was committed to keeping a large part of the Grace budget going toward mission work. The Great Commission says, "go and make disciples" (Matt. 28:19a) and Pastor Jerry always took God at his word.

"You cut spending from other places. You don't cut the mission budget," Pastor Jerry often said.

Equal in Christ

Maria Rosa Griffin: I first met Pastor Jerry when he came to a SAM (South America Mission) meeting in Florida. He was Latino, so I started talking to him in Spanish. He was very young looking, and he was very kind. You know when you meet someone and you can sense something about their spirit? I sensed he was faithful and could be trusted.

Pastor Jerry invited Cristina Caballero [missionary to Santa Cruz, Bolivia] and me to come to Grace for the church and us to get to know each other. He wanted to support us as missionaries. We stayed with Jane and him when we came. I think it was for about ten days or so.

I started to know him and Jane more staying there. Also, his daughter, Janna, spoke Spanish and she took us places. The atmosphere of the house was very peaceful, they were all very kind, and I feel like they really took care of us even though we were strangers and could not speak much English. They embraced us and made us feel welcome, like part of their family. At that time, I had not seen my own family for almost four years, and I longed to go back to Bolivia to see them. The Worshams met that longing for family for me.

Later Grace Church supported us with a lot of money. Christina's and my life were really marked by Pastor Jerry and this support. We were so grateful to God for how he was using Pastor Jerry and a church that did not even know us well to support us. It overwhelmed me with God's love and God's care. God was teaching us to really trust him, and he gave us Pastor Jerry and Grace Church so we would know how he loves, gives, and is faithful.

I saw Pastor Jerry as a brother in the Lord. In this, he had immense value. I saw him as very humble. He was a very important person but treated me as more important than himself.

In Bolivia you see an American person, a white person, as way up high, better than you. Sometimes people make you feel you are below them. Pastor Jerry was never like that. Even though I exalted him and his family, they never made me feel down low. They made me feel equal in Christ.

Christina and I were two little nobodies. Pastor Jerry came and said, "Okay, we are going to support you and help you." It was just like Jesus does for us.

Later when I met and married Cole, I told him in America I was a lemon in the middle of watermelons, comparing the size. God was working on my self-esteem. I had incredibly low self-esteem growing up until I met Jesus. And Jerry was like Jesus. He esteemed everyone greater than himself.

No Place for Idle Conversation

Pastor Dave Kehrli: Pastor Jerry equipped people to serve in so many ways at Grace Church. His pastoral counsel was biblically based and challenging. He wanted us all to submit to the will of God in our work and lives because this was his way of life.

Jerry and I went to Cuba in 2016 for a two-week, short-term mission trip with East-West Ministries International.[35] He and I were roommates for that trip, and it was such a blessing to share special times of prayer with him in the quietness of our room.

In twelve years on the mission field, I have never been involved or witnessed such an incredible moving of the Holy Spirit. Our small group of eight men saw more than 450 Cubans make a profession of faith in the Lord Jesus and accept his gift of forgiveness. I was just amazed at how God was convincing these people to place their faith in Christ.

On our way back to Wisconsin, we were held over in Miami for hours waiting on our flight. During these long hours, our group saw a distressed traveler and her young child also trying to get a flight out of Miami. We rallied around her plight and began to pray for her situation. When the airline finally agreed to place them on a flight that day, we let out a loud round of applause for the favorable decision.

She found a seat next to me. Since I spoke Spanish better than most of the men in our group, I started to inquire about what she believed about spiritual matters. During our conversation, God was working to help convince her of the need for forgiveness and to trust in the saving work of Christ. Jerry was sitting on my other side and following our conversation intensely and feeding me questions. I can still feel his elbow in my side urging me to just keep talking to her about Jesus. He wanted me to remember that there was no place for idle conversation when there was an opportunity for helping a person with their eternal life.

This story typifies how Jerry never separated his calling as a pastor from his everyday life as a witness for Christ. Living for Jesus everywhere was his privilege. He never missed an opportunity to be God's messenger.

---

[35] The mission of East-West Ministries International (East-West) is to mobilize the body of Christ to evangelize the lost and equip local believers to multiply disciples and churches among the unreached. For more information visit www.eastwest.org.

Bible Smugglers

Levi Binkley: In middle school I was really interested in spies and wanted to work at the Central Intelligence Agency. I did an end-of-the-year history speech on Brother Andrew who smuggled Bibles into the Soviet Union.

When I found out that my grandpa smuggled Bibles into Cuba, I could not believe it! It was so amazing to me, and I couldn't get over it. He told us about the exciting things that happened on that mission trip and the run-ins the team had with the Cuban government. The team was constantly being watched to see what they were doing.

I would flex that my grandpa was a Bible smuggler to my friends and talk about it often. One year my grandpa got us matching shirts that said, "Bible Smugglers." I loved wearing mine.

Another year I wrote a paper for my literature class about my grandpa's experience in Cuba. I was very proud of the title and my literary prowess; the title was, "My Grandpa: A Cuban Criminal for Christ."

From Meeting to Missionary

Craig Rebro: Just for background's sake, I think it's important to explain how I ended up knowing Pastor Jerry. I grew up in a family that did not attend church regularly. We would go to church on Christmas and Easter and for weddings and funerals. My dad would claim to be Catholic and my mom sort of Methodist. Unfortunately, this became an excuse for us to not worship anywhere. I attended Catholic grade school for three years and went to church during the week there, but we moved when I was entering seventh grade, and I began attending public school, ending my mid-week church service attendance.

A funny side note, when I was in fifth and sixth grade, we lived in a neighborhood where missionaries surrounded us. I never really understood what "being a missionary" meant other than they invited me to Bible studies with their kids, and they made my parents uncomfortable.

One time, my dad lost his job, and they all came over in a group to pray for him. If I recall, my dad did not want them to pray for him.

Also, one of the missionary kids was adopted from some South American country, and I remember him being very unruly. Once in winter we were playing outside in the snow. The boy and his sister had sticks, and he hit me in the face. I chased him down and let him have it. As I look back now, I realize missionaries are normal people just like anyone else!

After high school I attended university and still had not encountered the Lord. Although in hindsight, I can see the hovering of the Holy Spirit was always there. I seemed to be protected and come out of situations much more favorably than my friends. I tried to be a good person, but faith wasn't a part of my life.

After I graduated I met Brenda, who later became my wife. She went to the same university, but we had never met there. While dating, she invited me to the Catholic church she had attended all her life. Of course, I said "yes" because I really liked her. This is where a spark of reconnection with Jesus happened. I felt totally awkward not knowing the prayers but eventually felt like church was a good thing.

After we were married for a few years, we both had encounters with the Lord. Brenda's encounter came while she was in a car driving home. Mine came later when I was alone in a Texas hotel room with a Gideon Bible. God spoke to me through John 3:16, and I was prompted to fall to my knees and pray. I remember calling Brenda and telling her that "something happened." At the time, neither of us knew what being born again was.

Somewhere along the line, about seven years after she was saved, Brenda's brother gave her a study Bible. Most Catholics don't read the Bible, so this was fresh territory for her. In about a year, Brenda read the entire Bible, including all the study notes. She would show me passages as she read that would spark conversations about inconsistencies we noticed between the Bible and Catholicism.

We were also listening to Christian radio and ended up at a concert hosted by Grace Church. We really liked the vibe of the worship and kept seeing our neighbor, Rob Blascoe, who was a Grace Church elder at the time, everywhere. It was funny because we hadn't seen him or his wife, Carol, in the neighborhood for a few years before that. We set a coffee date with them at our house, and at the end of the conversation, they asked us where we worshipped. We told them, but then we asked them if we could come to Grace. They said something like, "Well, that was easy." God had clearly been orchestrating all these events.

I'd like to say that our entry into Grace was easy and wonderful, but it wasn't for me. Brenda thrived and quickly joined in with the ladies. I was working, so my exposure was on Sundays only. I carried some of my parents' Christian prejudices with me, and so I viewed the "born again" crowd with caution. I was afraid I would become one of those crazy Christians. With this attitude, I struggled to connect, and to Brenda's dismay, she submitted to visiting another church in Oak Creek since she desperately wanted me to be the spiritual leader of our household. That Sunday, the pastor preached about the local church being your family and to not church hop because no family is perfect. I was deeply convicted as it felt as if he was speaking directly to me, and this was the turning point for me to get over myself.

The next day I called and asked for a meeting with Pastor Jerry. He reminded me of my maternal grandfather, slightly unassuming but with an incredible shepherd's heart. I went into his office and I think it was the first time a man truly just wanted to sit, listen, and know about me. I explained to him my struggle with connecting at church, and he gently suggested that I get into a small group. As we chatted, I explained that I had a few friends who might be interested. At the end of that conversation, he released me to start a men's small group with Rob Blascoe.

We did a Bible study using *Experiencing God.*[36] I still quote from that study: "See where God is working and come along side of Him." I also remember an older man on the video sharing something like, "When he has a need, he just prays for it, and God provides." At that time, I thought that statement was crazy, but since then I've experienced God's amazing grace in that same way many times.

After my meeting with Jerry and the men's small group, I began serving on the Grace Outreach Team and Mission Team and got involved in other church initiatives. Pastor Jerry taught me how important being on mission is, but it was that very first meeting with him that springboarded me into fully walking with Jesus. It was the turning point in my Christian walk. It was extremely important to me for a man to have taken the time to sit with me, unhurried, and I sensed he cared about everything that I was saying. I walked away feeling cared for, like I belonged, and like someone believed in me.

Because of Pastor Jerry, my spiritual father, my life changed completely. I watched him be a shepherd. I watched him believe in people and empower them. He opened the door for me to have a deep relationship with Jesus that has since taken Brenda and me into full-time mission work in South Africa. Now ordained, I preach, help run a church, oversee all the small groups, am actively involved in church plants, and care for more than 1,200 orphaned and vulnerable children and widows.

How many people have made decisions to follow Christ just because we are in Africa? I would say dozens at least (we don't count), but our hearts are really for the discipleship that comes after the decision for Christ. We do life with the people that give their lives to Jesus. In this current missionary season, I don't think a week passes where we don't have people in our home who spend one or more nights with us.

---

[36] Henry T. Blackaby, Richard Blackaby, and Claude V. King, *Experiencing God: Knowing and Doing the Will of God* (Nashville, TN: B&H Publishing Group, 2008).

For Brenda and me, it took seven years after we made decisions for Christ before Pastor Jerry and others pulled us into the fold to show us the "now what" that comes after being saved. Jerry's legacy in my life is to NOT allow the flock to wander around aimlessly. This big lesson affects my daily ministry the most.

He Invited Me to Learn

Pastor Danny D'Acquisto: I remember seeing Pastor Jerry from a distance as a young kid. The most intimate personal interaction I had with him was when I was in college as part of a church plant, and we were trying to figure out how to do leadership. We were specifically trying to figure out what our Elder Board should look like. I emailed Pastor Jerry; he invited me to come to Grace and meet.

In our meeting, I told him that I wanted to spend my life in ministry like him. He told me to get a job at a church and to go to seminary. I thought I would get a job at a Milwaukee church, but it turned out that Grace Church employed me as the communication director.

I sought out Pastor Jerry again, though he had retired, when I transitioned from the communication director position to the mission director position. I spent a lot of time trying to figure out what was going on. There was a lot there. Occasionally, I would pull Jerry aside and ask him about the missionaries. Eventually, I started going to his house to talk. After a few visits, he said, "Why don't I just take you to Peru?"

He had some business to deal with there for South America Mission (SAM) and he brought me along. He had a leadership development fund that went toward pouring into guys on the mission field or in a ministry setting. This fund paid for the whole trip.

He appreciated when he saw me wrestling with things and trying to get a grasp on an area that he was super passionate about. It was great for me to have someone to go to who had his history and perspective.

Much of what we talked about in Pucallpa, Peru, was the challenge of connecting cross-cultural ministries with the life of the local church. There are so many layers between the two, and there are complex things going on in the field. He stressed that I must learn to discern what is going on in the field or otherwise I am just having the church send money.

He was on the SAM board at that time, and I got a perspective of what mission leadership was like and glimpses into his personality. We stayed in a cabana in the jungle. I got to sit with him on the porch, stay up late, and talk about life and ministry.

I am preaching in Colossians and wrapping up chapter four where Paul is talking about knowing how to answer each person; speaking and walking with wisdom; speaking graciously; and having speech that is seasoned with salt (Col. 4:6). This was Jerry, and it was a huge leadership skill. He was very intuitive when it came to people. I don't know how he juggled his daily life while being head pastor of a large church and leading a mission organization, but I think this intuition about people was a big part of it. Jerry knew when someone needed to be admonished or encouraged or just given a high five. That is not always intuitive for leaders, but he knew how to do it.

Before the second mission trip I went on with Jerry to Bolivia, he humbly and adamantly said, "I don't want to go on the trip if it will take away from your leadership in any way."

I was the Grace mission director and team lead for the trip. He knew because he was on the SAM board, that even if he did not want to have a leadership role, he would still have one. Missionaries knew him and wanted to talk to him.

"Let's not worry about it," I said. "Just come on the trip."

This trip was very different from our first trip together where he poured into me and let me ask a ton of questions. By the time I really got to know Jerry, it was his later years, and gentleness was a hallmark of his character; people at church and in the field knew him as a very gentle shepherd. What I saw in Bolivia added great substance to this. Jerry was gentle, yet he still had strong opinions about what should be done for the sake of the mission. The world's perception of a gentle man is that he will take the path of least resistance; I did not see that in Jerry at all.

On our Peru trip I watched him have pointed conversations with people on how to do things well for the sake of the mission; on our Bolivia trip he was more in the background and let me deal with things, have the pointed conversations, and put into practice what I had watched him do.

You Will See Them Again

Jack Bell: I went on a mission trip to Cuba with Pastor Jerry, four or five former Grace Church elders, and pastors from other churches. In preparation for our trip, we planned a simple and clear gospel message.

Pastor Jerry was in his element and had a heyday! He had men that he had invested in throughout the years with him in a foreign, communist country and was sharing the gospel. In the week we were there, 450 people came to Christ! Pastor Jerry was beaming.

One of the pastors from the other churches asked us, "What is it with all you guys and Pastor Jerry? You all have this deep, devoted love and commitment to him. We have never seen anything like this before."

Someone answered him that it was extremely easy to follow Pastor Jerry because he was the real deal; he was exactly who he asked us all to be.

At this time, Pastor Jerry was having some serious health issues, and Dave Kehrli, who is a pharmacist, was there to be his right-hand man and watch his health. Jerry went to this flea market to buy a hat, and somehow we lost him. No one had seen him for a while and none of us could find him, and we were getting really concerned. Finally, up walks Jerry leaning to the right a bit and physically zapped of energy. He did not look good, but he was extremely excited because he had found gifts for all his grandkids. At the hotel, he rested up and was fine.

When we were getting ready to go home, I was suddenly overwhelmed emotionally and started to cry. Pastor Jerry came over and gently asked, "How are you doing, Jack?"

"How do you do this, Jerry?" I asked. "How do you do ministry with all these people and leave them when they have such difficult lives?" It was sad to me because we had shared the gospel with them, watched them come to Christ, and we would never see them again.

I did not have the deep emotional relationship with Pastor Jerry men like Dr. Cohill or Craig Vaughn had. I would not just stop by his house and chitchat. But in that moment, he put his arm around me and he said, "I know how very hard this is for you to leave them, Jack, but because of what God did here, you *will* see them again."

Cuba

Craig Vaughn: The sponsoring mission organization for our trips to Cuba was East-West Ministries International, and the trips were life changing for those of us who went. Many of us went twice and Pastor Jerry went back a third time without us. He could not get enough.

We went to share the gospel under the guise of a building ministry, and we were instructed about what to do and what not to do. One thing you could not do was pass out Bible tracts unless someone specifically asked for materials. I don't know if Jerry forgot or if he was being defiant, but let's just say he got into a bit of trouble for passing out material in a public place!

Our leader from East-West Ministries International did not know all of us and was having trouble corralling us to give directions. Jerry sees this guy with his hands full trying to lead our group of leaders and he walks up to him and says, "Listen, if you are having trouble with getting these guys in order, you just let me know. They'll listen to me."

On our first trip, I got detained in customs and I was concerned because I was being interrogated in a room with customs officers. The second time we went into Havana, they were checking us over good. On this trip Jerry took a backpack full of baseballs and books and was planning on using them to start conversations about Jesus. Baseball is a big deal in Cuba, and Jerry knew it would help him connect. He figured they would talk a little about baseball and then he could talk about why we had come there from America.

A customs officer came in and began going through all of Jerry's bags. Jerry struck up a conversation with him in Spanish, and he asked Jerry about the baseballs. I am not sure what Jerry said to him, but finally he let us through.

Jerry was not in the best health, yet his energy on these trips was surprising. It was endless. It was supernatural. We would have to say, "Jerry, calm down!"

He was so passionate in the field and had no time to waste; he was there to touch as many people as he could with the news about Jesus in the time we had there.

On our second trip, Jerry was my roommate. He did not sleep at all, so I did not sleep well. The best part of rooming with him was our times of nightly prayer. We sat on the ends of our beds and he would ask me, "What is going on your life that I can pray for?" I would answer and then I would ask, "What is going on in your life that I can pray for?" We prayed for one another and we prayed for the people of Cuba, for gospel seeds to be sown, and that the church there would grow, thrive, and flourish.

Jerry would wake up in the morning and say, "Let's go! Let's go!" Even with his health issues, he did not want to sit around. He wanted to go place to place, house to house, to share the gospel with people. Sometimes there was a lot of walking involved. We each went out with an interpreter and would scatter. It was amazing to see Jerry in that element; not as the pastor of a church in Wisconsin, but as a follower of Jesus in another country, talking in Spanish, and telling people about Jesus.

And he also took the opportunity while we were there to meet with pastors to encourage and pour into them as leaders. He had a way of doing it one pastor to another.

Jerry also counseled me while we were there. I marvel that we were sitting in a room on the island of Cuba, and he was giving me parenting advice. He told me that as my girls grew into women, I needed to let go a little bit.

"Now you're becoming more the coach, mentor, and giver of advice," he told me. "You need to step back and let go."

He knew I needed to hear that. I am always thinking about what he told me there; my tendency is to get more involved. His advice was to step back, and he was right.

Why Is Mission Work So Important?

Pastor Danny D'Acquisto: Jerry and I had a lot of fruitful dialogue about his philosophy of mission. Part of what I was wrestling with as the mission director at Grace was that the unfolding work in the New Testament is focused on making disciples and multiplying churches. That is what happened everywhere the apostles went. Often in the mission world, there are a million good things that can be elevated and planting churches becomes peripheral; it is one of "many good options" that are all "good options." Jerry helped me wrestle through all these good options.

I was in seminary and I saw that mission was the mission, and I got to talk to a guy who was heavy in missions saying, "Yes, I see this too." It was good for me, really reassuring.

Jerry shared what he saw with increasing clarity over the course of his career and ministry. When first answering the question, "How are we supposed to take the gospel to the nations?" he said he would cast a wide net. But over time, he saw that making disciples and planting churches was central to mission. It was not the only thing we were to do, but the primary thing we are after, and this core belief was a neat way for us to connect.

Posthumous Church Plant

Pastor Jason Montano: I speak often about Jerry to our church leadership team. I tell my staff what he told me: we are not here to entertain Christians or to build something for ourselves; we are here to advance the gospel and to reach lost and broken people in our community and across the world.

Jerry Worsham indirectly planted Mosaic Church. Isn't it cool when you think about that? He even posthumously planted a church!

I took everything I learned from Pastor Jerry Worsham and I lean into what is good. Jerry's mission is continuing forward because it is the Lord's mission and we believe in it.

Chapter 10

THE MARK OF PRAISE:
For the Praise
of His Glory

*In order that we ... might be for
the praise of his glory.*

EPHESIANS 1:12

If you attended Grace Church on a given Sunday during his pastorate, you could always spot Pastor Jerry seated up front on the right-hand side of the sanctuary. Week after week he worshiped God with his hands raised high. He sang and worshipped with boundless joy and gave God glory in his life.

God's glory was one of the driving forces of Jerry's life and nothing impeded his worship of King Jesus—no anxieties, no worries, no illnesses.

Joy

Johnnie Jenkins: Joy was typical of Jerry. He always had a smile on his face, a joyful spirit, and lips that uttered continuous praise to God. You knew he loved the Lord and his kingdom, and his love was contagious and overflowing. He cared about God and he cared about people. My wife, Ruth, and I would often pray that his joy would be contagious and spread.

Glorify Was His Word

Pastor Mike Lueken: I would say this from the highest hill, the goodness of Jerry Worsham exceeds that of most people I have met: the depth of his goodness, the depth of his devotion, the depth of his love for God, and his absolute quest to honor and glorify God.

Glorify was his word. He wanted to glorify God; he talked about wanting to glorify God in all he did; he talked about the glory of God; he talked about everything and everyone being for the praise of God's glory.

He would pray at the end of a sermon or at the end of a service for God to be glorified. You could just see the genuineness of his ferocious, relentless passion to live a life that pointed other people to God and showed other people how good God is.

Driven by Praise

Phil Adams: Jerry was a paradox: he was extremely simple but at the same time very profound. He stressed, Don't preach about prayer unless you are passionately committed to prayer. Don't preach about being in the Word unless you are reading it, devoting your life to it, pouring yourself into it, fully giving yourself over to it, and being led by the Spirit through it.

He would worship alone, pouring himself out before the Creator. In today's church many are driven by methodology, personality, and strategy. Jerry was driven by praise.

Worship Was His Lifestyle

Pastor Brian Petak: Sometimes Jerry would forget to turn his microphone off when we were singing during services. He did not have a great voice, but he had so much passion for God. I have images in my mind of him standing in the front row of the church with both of his arms raised. He was a fully embodied, engaged worshiper, and his worship became even more evident in how he lived. For him, worship was a lifestyle. He stressed that our lives of worship cannot be separated from what we say and how we live. We had many conversations about this. He wove discussions about worship into staff meetings, prayer meetings, and sermons.

Hands Raised in Praise

Lorain Worsham Evans: Jerry worshiped and honored the Lord God Almighty. His hands were always raised in praise, and he really walked the walk. When people think of my brother Jerry, they get a picture of what a man of God should be like.

Praise Gatherings

Patti Booth: Pastor Jerry was big on praise gatherings. We went to these with him and Jane in Indianapolis for seven or eight years.

Through exposure to these, Pastor Jerry had Grace Baptist Church change its music from a traditional style utilizing a choir and organ to more contemporary praise and worship music. As the first Racine church to make this shift, Grace received a lot of criticism. Pastor Jerry stayed the course. It was all about praising God.

Pastor Jerry's Praise Led to Church Growth

Phil Adams: Pastor Jerry said you could never expect a church to grow past its leadership, and his growth in worshipping God was one thing that allowed Grace Church to become what it became.

He wanted us to have hearts that met with God and to allow us the freedom to see God and to worship him with our personality. People at Grace were free to be who they were without condemnation for their outward expression. He gave messages like, "No matter whether you have your hands raised or at your side, you lift your heart to God. There are different personalities, different expressions. It doesn't matter."

It was a time that God was having his way with the whole congregation. How could you explain people wanting to sit behind a glass partition? There were forty or fifty chairs placed back there and people could not even see what was going on in the sanctuary. It was a fire hazard, but we had to do this just to fit people in the building. And the people were worshipping even there. It was a movement of God. That is the only way to explain it. It sure seemed like a revival. It is the only thing that I've ever experienced like that. I have experienced great growth in churches in short periods of time that were more manufactured. But this was organic.

It did not matter what was going on, Pastor Jerry would always say, "Well, you know, we are just Grace. We are here to honor God. It is about glorifying our God."

What You're Meant to Do

Harold Pinto: I'll never forget a trip with Pastor Jerry to Paraguay. I had received a spur-of-the-moment invitation to speak to a group of young people at the church we were visiting. I wondered what to say, so I asked Jerry what he thought I should talk about. He said, "Tell them to live lives that will bring glory to God because that is what we are meant to do."

To Pastor Jerry, once we had our lives transformed by faith in the death of Christ on the cross and his resurrection from the dead, it is no longer about us. Everything is about God and his glory.

He encouraged us to seek the Holy Spirit's direction, support, and answers for how to live through the study of the Scriptures and prayer. This was all so we could reveal God's truth, reflect his grace, and bring him glory as we are meant to do.

God's Shapes Through Struggles

Paul and Laura Kienzle: From Pastor Jerry we learned that every bit of suffering and brokenness has a purpose. No matter what, it provides an opportunity to glorify God and is a blessing from God.

When Paul came to Jerry once in tears to let him know he was struggling with depression and wanted help, Jerry smiled and said, "This is a great thing."

Although this might appear uncaring, it really showed great compassion. Pastor Jerry always turned darkness into opportunity and praise. He was a man of hope. He saw the way God's hand shapes people through struggles.

The excitement that he showed to Paul in this moment gave him strength to face the struggles ahead.

A Culture of Praise

John Czerwinski: Jerry worshipped. Every Sunday. Each service. He made it clear that prayer and worship were a priority. He said that he could not walk in *after* worship and then preach as some do. His disciplined life of prayer and worship translated to a church that knew no other way. I do not think we or even he understood the leadership impact of his Sunday morning worship. He actively participated in corporate worship because he understood Romans 12. The added blessing was the culture of praise he cultivated at Grace Church.

He Did Not Want Barriers

Peter Jundt: Being part of the Worship Team and working with the Drama Team, I recall how Pastor Jerry let people experiment. We were able to be creative. He would not put things in boxes or say, "You can't do it that way! You can't worship that way!"

Not that he would ever tolerate sin, but in the formats we used, the types of music, the dramas, the Christmas skits, we could be serious or funny. He was not afraid to let people laugh in church. Oh, the horror of it! He wanted people to worship God and he did not want barriers erected.

Power Under Control

Lee Smith: I heard a sermon when we were living in Peoria, Illinois, about humility being power under control. This described Pastor Jerry. He was a powerful man, yet under the control of the Holy Spirit and always seeking to glorify God first. This was evident in everything he would do.

No One Represented Jesus Better

Joe and Sheri Kobriger: "I have never met anyone who represented Christ better than Pastor Jerry Worsham. I am sure Jerry would not want to hear that and would deflect all the praise to God," Joe said.

"We loved him for so many reasons but certainly because he represented Christ to us and brought Jesus into the room," Sheri said. "He poured into all of us, so we can now go and represent Christ to a lost and dying world."

Come Holy Spirit

Maria Rosa Griffin: Pastor Jerry never tried to put the methods people used to praise God in a box. He let the Holy Spirit work. He embraced people whose worship style was very free in the Lord. This showed me that Pastor Jerry wanted the Holy Spirit. He was a pastor of balance. He recognized people's different views on the Holy Spirit and never went to the extreme or caused disunity.

That's Why I Could Not Sing

Phylis Hessenthaler: Though we were members of a Bible-teaching church, our daughter wanted to know what other Christian churches were like. She and I spent a year visiting different churches one Sunday a month until I decided we had seen enough.

When my daughter pleaded for just one more, I agreed to take her to a church less than a mile from our home: Grace Baptist Church. It was strikingly different from any church we had visited. The place was packed; the music was vibrant; and the pastor taught in such a way that I did not want him to stop. A rare thing indeed!

My husband, John, had not taken part in our monthly church visits, but he agreed to come and see what I was so excited about. When we visited Grace again, I did not pay much attention to John until we started singing. I took note of him then because he was not singing along. When we got home, I commented that I knew he had not liked the service because he would not even sing.

"I loved everything," John responded with tear-lined eyes. "That is why I did not sing; I could not sing!"

Pastor Jerry led in worship and praise, and he truly shepherded our souls.

Look at What God Has Done

Yvonne Manning: There is always a piece of our humanness in what we do; I do not think there is a godly man in the Bible who did not have this. But Pastor Jerry would always say, "Look at what God has done!" He had his humanness, but his motivation was to honor the Lord and to live to please his Heavenly Father.

The Worship Team always had a special view of him during services. In his early years at Grace Baptist, he would be taking notes, jotting things down, working through things he wanted to tell the congregation. Later, our view of him was with one hand raised, which later became two hands raised, full out praising his God. I will never get that image of Pastor Jerry out of my mind. I know he is doing this right now, and one day I will be doing it with him!

Sold Out for Jesus

Scott Demarest: Pastor Jerry was sold out for the Lord. There was no confusion, no questioning, no doubt about his position; he was going to obey the Lord and give him the glory in all things.

The Arms Raised Higher

Jane Worsham: The brain surgeries Jerry had in 2018 damaged the language part of his brain [aphasia]. He understood well, but could not speak, write, or answer direct questions without difficulty. He had endured so much loss, but that did not keep him down.

What spoke most to me during this time was how joyful, worshipful, and fully in tune with Jesus he was. The Holy Spirit was more alive in him, his sense of worship was more intense, and he raised his arms higher. It did not matter where we were—inside our home, sitting outside in our backyard, walking at a park, or sitting under palm trees in Mexico—he raised his hands and worshipped God.

Jerry lived his whole life for the praise of God's glory, and now he is in the very presence of that glory! To me, it seemed appropriate to put the words "Rejoicing in the Glory of God and in Jesus the Lamb" on his tombstone.

Chapter 11

THE MARK OF DYING:
To Live Is Christ

*For to me, to live is Christ
and to die is gain.*

PHILIPPIANS 1:21

As Christians become more like Jesus Christ, they die little deaths to themselves every day. It is in dying that we learn to really live.

"So here's what I want you to do, God helping you: Take your everyday, ordinary life—your sleeping, eating, going-to-work, and walking-around life—and place it before God as an offering" (Rom. 12:1 MSG).

Pastor Jerry put his whole life on the altar and trusted God to do what was best. He served seventeen of his thirty-five years as Grace Church senior pastor with progressively debilitating heart issues.

God Works in Mysterious Ways

Ralph "Easy" Worsham: I did not get to see Jerry much in person in his later years, but he was the one who always held our family together with his love and compassion. And you could see these in him from his early years.

"God works in mysterious ways," Jerry would say often. I did not fully know what he meant until later when we visited our younger brother, Arvin, who was sick and dying of cancer. It sunk in that Jerry's approach toward me all my growing up years was kindness, and I did not see it.

Our parents brought us up in the way of the Lord, and Jerry loved our siblings and me. No matter what he was doing or how busy he was, he would help me every time I called him. I would ask him about the things that were happening between my son, Nathan, and me. I helped too, but Jerry was instrumental in bringing him to the Lord.

When Jerry passed away, Nathan saw the funeral service and what people said about him and said, "Man, Uncle Jerry touched thousands of lives. He was gifted, and he was a blessed man."

A Powerful Observation

Johnnie Jenkins: If you knew Jerry then you observed that it is possible to handle suffering in a godly way, with a smile, with a joyful spirit, and with the joy of the Lord as your strength. That is a powerful, powerful observation.

From watching Jerry, I took to praying this way: "Lord, when it comes time for me to suffer, let me do so joyfully, representing you with a spirit of joy, acceptance, and praise."

Like Jerry, I want to sing of the mercies of the Lord forever even in my discomfort (Ps. 89:1).

Thick Skin, Soft Heart

Pastor Jason Montano: I asked Jerry how he made it in ministry for thirty-five years. "You get a thicker skin but a softer heart," he told me, and you could see it in his eyes when he talked about ministry.

You can spot the look of someone who has been to war. When war veterans come home, they have the look Jerry had. He had been through it all, and he would never tell you about it. He would never tell sob stories. He never got shaken, and he always loved. He knew God was looking at his heart.

He Had To Peel off His Role
From His Identity

Pastor Mike Lueken: About four years before he died, Jerry and Jane were in California visiting Kent Carlson and his wife, Diane, and my wife, Julie, and me. We were all sitting around the kitchen table talking. Jerry shared that leaving Grace Church as pastor was one of the hardest things he ever had to do. He told us that he would drive into the parking lot on Sunday mornings and would sit in the car until everyone got in, and at other times he would have to leave because he was sobbing so hard. He had pastored for so long, had a role and a voice in people's lives for so long, and now that was gone.

I also think what made things hard was that people did not think about Grace Church without thinking about Jerry Worsham. And that was no longer the case. He had to peel off his role from his identity. The pain came in recognizing that his identity, in a large part, had been wrapped around his role as pastor. With that gone, he had to crawl back to truths like: I am a child of God and the beloved of God.

I remember Jerry turned to Kent who was getting ready to leave Oak Hills Church and asked him how he was feeling as things were getting close. Kent gave some casual answer and Jerry looked right at him and said, "Kent, this is going to be the hardest thing you've ever done. I think you are underestimating how difficult it is going to be."

Jerry even shepherded us through this experience. I think if you would have asked him five or six years before he was getting ready to leave Grace how he thought it was going to be, I think he would have said, "It will be easy, not that hard." He grew from everything the Lord brought his way.

The Sovereignty of God Was His Theme

Dr. Robert Gullberg: Jerry was big on the sovereignty of God. It was one of his themes throughout his life as a pastor. I can't even tell you how many times he used the term "sovereignty of God" in his prayers, his preaching, and his everyday conversations. There wasn't a prayer he gave that did not acknowledge that God was in control of everything that happened. This is really where faith starts: understanding that everything that happens in life is about God, from creation of the world to your life on the planet.

I was his doctor beginning in 1988. When he was younger, he was relatively healthy, and despite some issues, his heart was stable for decades. The last five to seven years of his life he had some special problems that required subspecialty care, super specialists. Through it all, he suffered well for Christ and did not complain, which is tough. I think part of this stemmed from his trust in God's sovereignty.

One of the first verses I taught my children was Philippians 2:14 [ICB], "Do everything without complaining or arguing." We want to complain when we are hurting and going through physical pain.

Pastor Jerry taught us well going through all he did. I am sure he expressed frustration. Nobody is perfect when they are going through tough times. Ultimately he accepted everything as part of God's plan for him.

I Am a Man Under Authority

Craig Vaughn: When Jerry was having health issues and was hospitalized, he taught us through his difficulties.

During this first go-round with his health, I was chairman of the Elder Board. Thankfully, his issues were minor and he was released from the hospital, but it was his intent to go back to the pulpit and preach the next Sunday.

The elders discussed the situation and we unanimously decided that Jerry should not preach for his own good. I think his girls were even saying, "Please don't let him preach!"

As chairman of the board, I had to knock on his door, sit with him in his living room, and tell him our decision. He really wanted to preach. I had to tell him, "Jerry, you are not going to preach on Sunday."

He looked at me, processed things, and pushed back a little. I told him the elders said that he should rest and that his health was more important than whether he preached. I assured him that we had the preaching covered.

"I've always said that I am a man under authority," he told me. "Therefore, I will submit to your decision."

He did not realize that even in that moment he was teaching and modeling submission to authority.

Bonus Time

Pastor Greg Smith: I saw Jerry as a person passing through, someone who embraced that he was here to make an eternal impact. He knew his ministry was God's ministry and that in his grace, God used humans, but humans come and go.

Jerry may have had more of an awareness that life was brief because when I was at Grace, he had a stroke that looked like it was going to take him out of ministry. Any time after was bonus time! [And it ended up being fifteen years.]

Run the Race With Perseverance

Pastor Cole Griffin: Jerry was very purposeful in everything including exercise. His routine included a regular run through Graceland Cemetery, where he is now buried. He told me he loved running there not only because it was beautiful but because it was a reminder to him that life was short and he had goals to complete for the Lord before his life ended.

He ran daily until his doctor told him he could not run anymore because of his cardiac issues—he really grieved this. He started walking instead of running and that became a love of his. He and Jane walked together until the very end of his life, and that was a very special thing for them both.

I Kept It All in My Heart

Debbie Palmer: I wanted to be like Jerry in my suffering and have his outlook. He genuinely loved and cared for people so much that he never made himself the focus, even as sick as he was. There was never, "Woe is me!"

In all his suffering, if you did not know he was sick, you would never know. He always had a big smile on his face. He knew God had a plan and he was fine with it.

I had several heart issues when I was younger, and when I got cancer, I initially thought I was having more heart issues. When I was diagnosed my prayer was, "Whatever you decide God. You are in control, and I am fine with whatever you want."

Everything Pastor Jerry said about suffering through the years was not lost on me; I kept it all in my heart. It wasn't just one thing he said that helped me; it was everything.

Every believer wants to go to heaven, but no one is in a hurry to get there.

Pastor Jerry taught his people to storm the gates of heaven in prayer because God is the Healer. I know people stormed heaven's gates for me. This was the blessing of cancer; knowing people loved and prayed for me. I appreciate things more, and I look at things differently now. I got all the beautiful blessings while I was alive.

He Was Not a Lamenter by Nature

Pastor Kent Carlson: Maybe I just wasn't close enough to see it or maybe it just did not exist, but Jerry was never discouraged or depressed. His thought was always, *What is the right way to behave?* In the Psalms we can read about tremendous anger, crying out to God, questioning, lamenting, and arguing. That was not Jerry. He was not a lamenter by nature.

Sometimes when I would listen to him during all the medical struggles and church struggles, I felt like I wanted him to be sadder, more discouraged. That could just be my junk. Jerry took things as they came and took the hand he was dealt. He was always positive, always smiling.

A few times I got the sense from him that what he was facing was not what he had planned. He was such a vibrant, dynamic, energetic person. And in the end when he was still preaching, the sharpness wasn't there. He felt his body was betraying him and knew he could no longer do everything he used to do.

Jerry Did Not Go Sideways

Pastor Jason Esposito: Toward the end of his career after decades of leading and pastoring, Jerry's energy wasn't there and physically he was tired. In my estimation three things led to this: physical exhaustion and illness; staff challenges that brought some disappointment; and then just the cumulative effect of day-to-day ministry. These might make some pastors go sideways. Jerry did not go sideways.

He Would Not Take the Effortless Way

Pastor Mike Lueken: Two big reasons Jerry and Jane stayed at Grace after he retired were his great love for the church and the people there that they had done life with, went on trips with, and were in a small group with. If they had left, they would have lost their community.

I also speculate that they stayed because leaving Grace might be good and easier, but it did not make it the right decision. Jerry intuitively knew that if he could not go to Grace, it was a reflection on him, and he would not take the effortless way out. He wanted to surrender to God and watch him transform things.

God Allowed It; I Will Not Complain

Jane Worsham: Jerry's seventeen years of heart issues caused him to struggle with depression twice in his life as heart problems and depression often go hand in hand. At one point the doctors convinced him to take some antidepressants which energized him enough to have several additional years of mission work, including going on three mission trips to Cuba.

The second short bout with depression came when he got the initial news after his brain surgeries that he would never be able to operate at a missionary board level again. However, after only one day of being very down, Jerry perked up and said, "God allowed it; I will not complain." He spoke truth into the situation and he purposed not to complain, though every now and then I would hear him say to himself, "Stop it, Jerry!"

He accepted his limitations, proceeded to freely talk to anyone and everyone, and learned that nothing can take away the glorious gift of the presence of Jesus and his constant companionship.

Jerry basked in God's presence daily for extended periods of time, ending with prayer and hands lifted in worship. With his speech problems, I asked teasingly if he was speaking in tongues when he prayed. He would just smile with a glimmer in his eye, and say, "Maybe."

No Longer Just Scripture on a Page

Sheri Kobriger: I remember when preaching became a struggle for Pastor Jerry as his heart issues and the medications he was prescribed increased. He contended with low energy, lack of sharpness, and a decrease in the clarity of his speech. I was amazed and thought, *The message is still just as strong as it ever was!* The Lord enabled him to speak the Word with great authority even though he struggled physically.

For a man who spent his whole adult life loving the Word of God, preaching the Word of God, and sharing the Word of God, a struggle with speech must have been very hard. I wonder if the enemy whispered to him, "It is just speaking; everyone can speak." I cannot imagine his human struggle in all this. It had to take a lot of humility for him to die to himself, get up to the podium, and still do exactly what the Lord had given him to do.

Paul's words, "My grace is sufficient for you, for my power is made perfect in weakness" (2 Cor. 12:9) come to me when I think of Pastor Jerry in his last years because he lived out these words. As I watched him, God made these words very real. It was no longer just Scripture on a page. Sometimes we repeat Paul's words in passing, but Jerry lived out his suffering with beauty and showed us all just how sufficient God's grace truly is.

At Home in Church

Pastor Chris Amundson: Pastor Jerry would be at church with Jane every week even when his memory and his ability to communicate were getting limited. He was always happy to see everyone. There was still joy there. I think he sensed that he was still at home at church and was happy to talk to people.

His call to ministry, which happened much earlier in his life, was still alive until the day his body gave out. This made an impression on me that I will never shake. Even in his limited capacity, he still gave everything he could.

He Had the Spirit of the Lord

Lorain Worsham Evans: Jerry got through all his suffering and struggles because he had the Spirit of the Lord. He knew no matter what, he could do all things through Christ who gave him strength (Phil. 4:13).

I understood a lot of his suffering because I had a brain tumor. When I had surgery, I had to relearn many things just like Jerry did. The struggles he had with his speech, his pronunciation, and his disability were much worse than mine. I watched him grab onto the Lord Jesus Christ for strength and ability to make it through.

I prayed and prayed for Jerry like he always prayed and prayed for me. Prayer was our foundation. When you go to the Holy God of Israel and are uploading your prayers to him, you trust he will take care of you. He will comfort you. He will uphold you by his righteous right arm.

When he died, I know that the Lord said to him, "Well done, good and faithful servant!" (Matt. 25:23a).

When I Am Weak, Then I Am Strong

Eric Ernst: Pastor Jerry knew what God's will was and faithfully focused on accomplishing it. He poured his life into others and mentored everyone in very personal ways. He exuded joy even during difficult circumstances. It makes me tear up when I think about how faithful he was in continuing his cross-cultural ministries even though he had physical issues that would have stopped most human beings in their tracks.

In watching his suffering, what I learned from him would be summed up in the words of the Apostle Paul, "For when I am weak, then I am strong" (2 Cor. 12:10b).

You Saw Learned Contentment

Terry Kultgen: In his later days, Jerry's speech capabilities had diminished. He understood what we were saying, but he lacked the ability to have an extensive conversation any longer. He would often break into Spanish. Jane would chuckle. I would chuckle. Jerry would chuckle. He would say, "I ca-ca-can-can't say it."

There was no sense of *poor me*. Never. Paul talks about learning to be content (Phil. 4:11-12), and you could see learned contentment in Jerry. It was like, "I don't like what I am going through, but God is with me."

I Saw My Eyes in Pastor Jerry's Eyes

Diane Peterson: I was diagnosed with chronic fatigue syndrome and Lyme disease, and I remember seeing my eyes and the look of being ill in Pastor Jerry's eyes. I knew how hard it was to try to live as who you once were but no longer are.

I know his living only came through the Lord's strength and simply trusting God alone.

The Inner Man Is Growing Strong

Jack Bell: The massive thing Pastor Jerry communicated to me about suffering is that God allows it to solidify character. Even in suffering, God brings glory to himself.

"We bring glory to God throughout our life and in our death," Jerry told me. "The inner man is growing strong, while the outer man is fading away."

I Loved Seeing His Name
on Our Calendar

Michelle Bush: I first met Jerry on December 13, 2011. His primary cardiologist Dr. Short referred him to our center [Aurora St. Luke's

Medical Center in Milwaukee]. We got to see him every six months or sooner depending on how he was doing. I loved to see Jerry's name on our calendar for an upcoming visit. I enjoyed speaking with him and Jane.

I knew Pastor Jerry followed God the very first time we met as he spoke about his faith and his calling. We always had nice visits and conversations that revolved around Christ.

Dr. Tajik, the heart specialist, asked Pastor Jerry the same thing every visit: "What is the word of the day?" Jerry would spend a few minutes preaching the Word of God to us both. It was awesome!

He also shared often about his church and his many mission trips. He encouraged our love of Christ through the way he freely shared at every visit. In all the years we treated him, he never once complained but instead praised God for his health, his family, and his friends. He was always so joyful even during his last year or so when he would talk to us both in English and Spanish.

Preaching Jerry and Balcony Jerry

Jim and Debbie Arndt: "We know two parts of Pastor Jerry—the Pastor Jerry preaching from the pulpit and the Pastor Jerry living out everything he had preached from the pulpit. We nicknamed him *Balcony Jerry* in his later years because that is where he sat and worshipped at Grace when he retired. For us, those were the greatest years. We got to know *Balcony Jerry* on a more personal level. We spoke with him and Jane every Sunday," Debbie said.

"Sometimes for fifteen, twenty, or thirty minutes," Jim added.

"When we first met Jerry, Jim told me he reminded him of a car salesman. Remember that?" Debbie asked Jim.

"Well, you know that is because he was always smiling and was super friendly like a car salesman. But Jerry was very sincere," Jim said. "Our first few weeks at Grace, I did not know what to make of him. I thought, *How can someone be this nice and friendly? This just can't be real!* Turns out that it was real. Pastor Jerry acted and preached the same way for thirty-five years."

"Pastor Jerry was selling God's Word with his preaching and his life," Debbie said. "And nothing spoke stronger. His life example will carry me to the end of my days. Even in the hospital he was so gracious, still putting others first. It was never about him," Debbie said. "It was always about glorifying God. This was his number one priority."

Free to Be Himself

Larry and Maggie White: "In Pastor Jerry's later years, he started to reveal things that he had previously wanted to keep more private. He felt freer to talk and did not feel he had to be a perfect person. I think that is what he always liked about Larry; Larry did not act like a perfect person, and he always just let Jerry be who he was," Maggie said.

"We were blessed to have him come swim at our house in the last few months of his life. He came to our house because it was the early months of COVID, and he and Jane couldn't go anywhere public. It was good exercise for him," Maggie said. "They would come over a couple times a week for a few hours."

"I never saw Jane get mad at Jerry until then," Larry said. "He would come over on all his meds. And when he was swimming, Jane would say, 'Okay, Jerry, I think that is enough swimming now,' and he would say, 'No. Not yet,' and keep going. She was very protective of him.

"Jerry would never say anything bad about anybody," Larry said. "He was protective of people. But the last couple months of his life, I would say, 'This is going on. Don't you hate that?' He would say, 'Yes! Don't you?'"

"And Jane would be saying, 'Shush! Jerry, stop it,'" Maggie said. "Pastor Jerry had a goofy side to him that Larry brought out. This is what made Larry and Jerry's relationship so special."

God's Timing

Pastor Isaac Miller: Pastor Jerry was so confident in where he was going when he died. He knew God had a time ordained for him. I guarantee he and Jane struggled, were sad, and wept about it; but at the same time, their confidence was in the Lord and they fully trusted in him.

Suffering Did Not Stop Him

Patti Booth: Though a positive person, Jerry went through a time where he did not have that; he was very quiet for a season. Heart attacks and medicine can do that. Jane would share more about things going on behind the scenes. When he was preaching toward the end, Jane would always pray he could remember.

Jerry did not talk about his suffering much. It never stopped him. It did not even stop him at the very end of his life.

Basking in His Love

Scott Demarest: My eyes sting every time I think of the last time I spent with Pastor Jerry. Several of us who had served together with him on the Grace Elder Board during his transition into retirement were invited to the wedding of a dear friend's daughter. My wife, Cynthia, and I drove to Racine from Tennessee and were thrilled to be reunited with many friends from Grace.

As God would have it, our seating assignments for dinner placed us right next to Pastor Jerry and Jane. Jerry was a bit self-conscious about the effects of his brain surgeries because it was sometimes difficult for him to get the words out, but we thought he was doing amazingly well. He just beamed as he visited with friends and enjoyed the celebration with Jane. I spoke with him at length, and he expressed how thrilled he was that this group of leaders who meant so much to him were reunited.

At least three times during the night Pastor Jerry turned to me with eyes as big as saucers and said, "Isn't this great? Isn't this just wonderful?"

It was a joyous occasion, and the memory of seeing Pastor Jerry so happy and animated still causes me to get a lump in my throat. I loved Pastor Jerry and had tremendous respect for him. It was wonderful to see him so happy as he basked in his love for the people who had shared so much with him.

Content Because of God's Sovereignty

Pastor Rusty Hayes: Jerry's belief in the sovereignty of God was a big part of his contentment in suffering. He and Dr. Cohill, who was an adamant Calvinist and his best friend, would have lively discussions about man's responsibility versus God's sovereignty and authority.

Jerry had this mentality: Work like it all depends on you; pray like it all depends on God. If you are doing the work, you must rest in the Lord to take care of everything. This is the way he lived.

Jerry had a Charles Spurgeon view of sovereignty. When Spurgeon was once asked, "How do you reconcile God's sovereignty with human will?" He said, "I never try to reconcile friends."

Pastor Jerry was extremely comfortable with both of those doctrines and saw them as friends. He knew God worked everything out; some things are part of the mystery of God. He rested in the Lord and came back to God being in control.

Hug Ministry

Deb Hilker: It is hard to imagine what my spiritual life would have been like without Pastor Jerry. He was my pastor for twenty-five years.

He hugged me differently after his last stroke. He would look for me to hug me. Jane said he went looking for other people to hug too. Toward the end of his life, he would get words and phrases mixed up, but he never forgot who we were. He praised God and loved people to the very end.

A Special Visit

Geri Baumblatt: After Pastor Jerry had all his heart trouble and brain surgeries, he had to learn to speak all over again. Jane was marvelous in how she cared for him.

Despite what happened to him and his brain, he was so happy and fun. Jane and Pastor Jerry came to visit me after I broke my hip; after all he had been through and was going through, he was coming to visit me! He gave me a hug and said I love you or something like that and it so surprised me. He was extra jolly and happy this visit.

There Is Hope for Me

Lee Smith: I struggled for a lengthy period with the whole *prayer thing* Pastor Jerry preached on. This had to do with God telling me that I was a Pharisee—I liked to study the Word of God, but I didn't love people or care about them enough to pray. That's who Pharisees are. They major on the minors and minor on the majors. Unfortunately, that was who I had been for a very long time.

I heard funny stories about the young, aggressive Pastor Jerry, but I never saw any of that. All I saw was the truth and grace pastor, and I knew that it was God who grew him into the pastor he became.

That tells me that there is hope for me! Someday down the road maybe someone will say they don't know the *Pharisee Lee*, but they do know this other Lee that God is working on. One of those hopeful things for me was knowing how Pastor Jerry learned to live for Christ and die to himself as his life went on.

Stay the Course

Janine Carls: Pastor Jerry lived life with the essence of gratitude. He was genuinely grateful for everyone he met and always found a reason to thank them and bless them with his smile, his joy of the Lord, and his enthusiasm for Christ.

He was always rising above the challenges in his life. Paul's words "give thanks in all circumstances" (1 Thess. 5:18a) remind me of him. He never complained and he always found reasons to see God in every circumstance. If he was in the hospital, he was witnessing. When he was well again, he shared a God story that came from his time in the hospital.

Health issues that would have stopped many of us in our tracks did not stop Pastor Jerry. He fought hard to recover each time he faced a setback. And when he was well enough, he went right back onto the mission field locally or globally. After "retiring" from Grace Church, he remained active in South America Mission.

Many of us ask the Lord to use us, and we wait for clarity. That wasn't Pastor Jerry's style. He went out knowing God would use him, and he depended on God for every step.

Remembering Pastor Jerry as I saw him every Sunday during the year of COVID makes me tear up. He was at church with the body despite the risk; and he was smiling and greeting everyone. And this was impressive as his ability to communicate clearly declined when his health declined. But even this did not stop him. He had confidence that his smile and his faith in God would deliver the message he had just for you unimpeded by his difficulty speaking. I believe he knew the grace that he had extended to others would now be extended to him.

When I think of Pastor Jerry, I think of staying the course; he did this all the way to the very end. It can be said of him, "Well done, good and faithful servant!" (Matt. 25:23a).

No Complaining

Maria Rosa Griffin: Pastor Jerry never complained. That is a sign for me of those who really are God's children. I see that in other seniors whom I am close to. Like Pastor Jerry, they don't complain about when or how they are suffering; yet you know they are suffering. Pastor Jerry had great peace and extraordinary joy, and that only comes from the Holy Spirit. He had great perseverance, and I want to be like that. I don't want to complain.

To the End

Trish Baccash: After words became elusive for Pastor Jerry, on the occasions when he would see me at church, he would lay his hands over his heart and then point to me. Even now, I tear up as I can picture him doing that.

I have a star by Psalm 119:112 in my Bible which says, "My heart is set on keeping your decrees to the very end." Pastor Jerry certainly fulfilled this verse.

A Thorn

Phil Adams: For many years Pastor Jerry had bad cases of gout, and one time he told me this was a thorn in his flesh. Gout was very difficult, very painful, and can affect how you live out your life. He told me he had to guard his heart; be in the Word of God; entrust himself to God, his plan, and his sovereignty; and not let suffering dictate to him how he would live his life.

He Loved the Lord

Jessica Schultz: Pastor Jerry was transparent about his heart issues. He often shared his amazement about the technology and advancements in his treatments. On occasion before his retirement, he would express his exhaustion and frustration when his heart condition interfered with his preaching. Yet, I learned that having a strong prayer life, a close relationship with Jesus, and a supportive family gave him strength to keep going.

He was just a simple and happy man with integrity and lofty standards who loved the Lord!

People Had to Be There

Lee Smith: Even Jerry's memorial service, how people all *had* to be there, demonstrated how one person living for the Lord impacts how people live. It made you think, *Wow! I wish I could be like that or more like that.*

Paul said, "Follow my example, as I follow the example of Christ" (1 Cor. 11:1). You can look at Pastor Jerry and say, he is someone who followed Christ, and I want to be like that and follow in his footsteps.

His Memorial Service
Accurately Depicted Him

Larry White: I think the most accurate depiction of Jerry was his memorial service because all these people told how he impacted their lives. How many pastors came out of Grace Church because of Jerry? Win. Build. Equip. He believed in that. He would win people over, he would build them up, and he would send them out into the world. At his service, so many people said that was what he did for them.

My brother-in-law doesn't go to Grace Church and neither does my sister, but they came to Pastor Jerry's service because we were such close friends with Jerry and Jane. My brother-in-law said he had never been to a service like that where someone had impacted so many lives. He said, "I can't believe we have been here for two hours. I feel like we just got here. I could listen to this forever."

A Piece of Jerry

Nancy Henkel: Pastor Jerry was so good. Everyone watched him, took a piece of him, and learned to be more like Jesus because of him. In the end after giving so very freely of himself, he had nothing left; his body, his brain, and his human strength failed. He freely laid down his life to serve the Master. He gave and gave until it hurt and he got to go home to Jesus.

He Modeled Christ to the End

Craig Vaughn: Jerry had heart issues for years and endured a long season of difficulty and suffering. He certainly would not have been able to do all the things he did were it not for Jane standing by his side.

As elders we cried together at times about Jerry. Once we were in his hospital room when Jane was taking a break. I said, "Jerry, I'll do most of the talking." It was a way I could give back to him for all the times he ministered to me.

The Apostle Paul said he was content in all circumstances; he knew suffering and hardship; he knew plenty and want (Phil. 4:11–12). There was a sense of contentment in Jerry. I'm sure he did not like what he was going through and did not want to go through it, yet there was peace and contentment and joy in all the suffering. He was modeling, teaching, and demonstrating what it was like to serve and follow Christ until the end.

It was sad to me that he gave his whole life to ministry and to the church as a shepherd, but he only got to live a few years in retirement. It also makes me sad that he is not here anymore to go to and to process things with. He was the one I would always turn to when I needed to talk to someone. I miss him.

A Walking Miracle

Pastor Dave Kehrli: Jerry powered through physical and emotional issues at the end of his life with grace and purpose. As a pharmacist, I was amazed seeing the list of medications that he took daily to keep his heart and other major systems operating. Jane called him a walking miracle, and that was not an exaggeration but a testimony of his will to serve God with every ounce of life and breath the Almighty allowed. Jerry went on three, short-term mission trips to Cuba even with these severe limitations, and it served as a powerful witness to those who knew him. This type of attitude is what guided our beloved pastor to live out the verse, "For to me, to live is Christ and to die is gain" (Phil. 1:21).

Super Bright Flame

Yvonne Manning: Pastor Jerry's illness kept him in a place of humility and trusting God. When his health declined, it was a sad thing for everybody. I know it was hard for Jane, but I remember thinking about how some candles are not long burners; they have a little, slight flame when they burn. Pastor Jerry was like a super bright candle with a flame that shone so brightly for Jesus that he just burned more quickly.

God knew Jerry's overall life plan and span. It was like God was demonstrating he was not going to burn Pastor Jerry out, but that he was going to light a fire in him and make him a seed planter and a seed harvester and bless him because he was so hungry for and so disciplined for him.

Absolutely Delightful

Pastor Kent Carlson: In his last years after his stoke, Jerry and Jane came to California when I was retiring from Oak Hills Church. Mike Lueken was here, and all of us were hanging around together.

Jerry was on new meds for the medical issues he was having and he was a different dude. He had no governor, no filter; he got colorful, and it was absolutely delightful. It was embarrassing to Jane, but we loved it!

Later I was visiting Wisconsin and we were at my in-law's house. Jerry had brain surgeries and could not form words. He prayed and his prayer wasn't making any sense, just words here and there, but it was still delightful. He would acknowledge what was going on, but the spirit that he maintained was always positive. Sometimes I would worry about that because Jerry had a huge weight on him about what was appropriate and what was not appropriate behavior and how to publicly present.

This is why the unfiltered way he was in his later years was so delightful to see. Nothing dark or evil came out, just pure fun. I loved this snapshot of his playfulness because I am overly playful to a fault.

The Mark of Someone Who
Made an Impact

Pastor Danny D'Acquisto: Jerry is gone, I miss him, and he comes to mind often. This is the mark of someone who has really made an impact. I think often of his longevity, his endurance, his dependence on the Lord, and how he would share the gospel by all and any means necessary.

Jane's Strength

Pastor Mike Matheson: Jane was the quiet strength behind Jerry. What surprised me was how she always seemed to place herself behind him, especially in public settings to watch him and make sure things were okay. Then as his health declined, she took on a little of a motherly role. I even remember times when Jerry would come into my office and talk to me. And she would say, "Jerry, come on! Enough. We've got to go."

I am sure it will be said quite a bit about how remarkable it was that Jerry never complained. Equally remarkable is how Jane never did either. Jane was suffering too, having hopes and dreams die, and she was every bit as strong and as positive as Jerry was.

When you think how you are going to spend your early seventies, you don't think you'll spend it caregiving. I think in many ways their retirement was not what they expected.

One thing I really appreciated, especially when things got bad for Jerry physically and his speech was difficult, was that Jane brought me in and made sure I had time with Jerry.

I remember going up to the hospital in Milwaukee to visit him. I was there with Jane, Craig Vaughn, Dr. Gullberg, and one or two other guys. They were there for a while and were getting loud. Jerry was getting excitable, and Jane asked everybody to leave, but then she asked me to stay. I don't know why she asked me to stay, but it gave Jerry, Jane, and me our separate time in that hospital room.

Jerry had electrodes on his head and was speaking half Spanish, half English. Jane was interpreting for him. I will never forget that time. It was a sweet time. I distinctly remember him saying in that conversation, "I love you." He even kissed me on the cheek.

Beyond Doubt

Luke Binkley: Grandpa always told us that when he passed and went to paradise that he wanted his passing to be a time of extraordinary joy, not a time of sadness. He was very content with where he was in his life, and he knew beyond any doubt where he was headed.

He would remind us that he wanted us to tell people everything he did and said, all of it, because he believed in the true gospel of Jesus Christ. He wanted everyone to know the hope he had.

His whole life was for the gospel, and he would want it to continue to be shared. If his life was used as an instrument to grow God's kingdom after his passing, he would be happy.

My Role Model to the End

Caleb Augustyn: I saw Grandpa in the physical state he was in toward the end of his life and how frustrating it was for him to lose his speaking ability, and I cannot begin to imagine his suffering. Yet, the way he carried himself during it all was almost shocking.

Every time my family went to Wisconsin to visit, he had a big smile on his face. Grandpa would try to talk to us and be involved in whatever we were doing. I would have never known how tough it was for him by how he acted. Even in his immense suffering, I can look back on how he handled it and say that my grandpa was a guy who did it right.

He shared that knowing there was a kingdom to come and that he would live eternally with Jesus was what helped him hold it all together. He exemplified joy right where he was knowing that he was going to such a better place.

This is just another example of Grandpa being a role model to the very end.

I Don't Know Where My Life Would Have Been

Pastor Mike Lueken: Just a few times in my life I've attended a memorial service where it is a never-ending downpour of exquisite reflections on the person's good life—the quality, the depth, the impact, the influence, and the beauty. The sharing isn't forced or made up, with people wondering what kind thing to say. The words are on the tip of every tongue, embedded in their life and their DNA due to the person's remarkable life and influence. My wife, Julie, and I felt that at Jerry's memorial service from the very beginning to the very end.

To have Jerry in my life at such a pivotal time as a voice, a presence, and an example was a profound blessing for me. I am deeply grateful to God for it. Jerry incarnated so many aspects of a God who

THE MARK OF DYING: To Live Is Christ

started to look very, very good because of how Jerry reflected his character. I don't know where my life would be if my path had not crossed Pastor Jerry Worsham's.

What Pastor Jerry Believed
By Pastor Danny D'Acquisto

I had the privilege of becoming very close with Pastor Jerry Worsham toward the end of his life. He was in his late-sixties and early seventies; I was in my mid-to-late twenties. Suffice to say, he was not necessarily "in process" anymore. He was very settled about what he believed. I remember a handful of times, during a discussion we were having about a complicated doctrinal topic, Jerry would give me one of his very loving, gentle looks. I call it the, *Danny, I had these debates thirty years ago, and I'm pretty settled about this* look. I got the hint. We moved on.

But since I had this incredible window into Jerry's later life and doctrine, I consider it an honor to reflect on his beliefs and do my best to summarize them here. At risk of sounding trite, it seems appropriate to begin with Jerry's deepest, most sincerely held belief: **Jerry Worsham believed in God.**

Now, when I say that I do not just mean, "Jerry was pretty sure that God existed." No, no. It was far more than that. Jerry *believed in God* in the same way that a man lost at sea *believes* in his life raft. He's not just casually convinced that it's real. That much, he is certain of. (If it were not real, he would be dead.) Far more importantly, the sea-stranded man *depends and relies* on that life raft with every fiber of his being. This is how Jerry believed in the one true and living God.

Not long before he died, Jerry and I met regularly to talk about life, doctrine, and ministry. By the second or third time we met, I finally realized what was going on. I typically came into our meetings with a lot of energy, eager to process my ministry strategies with Jerry. I was preparing to plant a church at the time, and I had a lot of thoughts and questions for him. I wanted to know how he thought I should go about my life's work, which was just beginning. It was hard for me to imagine a better use of our time! But Jerry was not very interested in all that. After spending about ten minutes talking with me about fund raising or leadership development, Jerry would very politely dismiss my next question in a way that made it clear: "That's not what we'll be talking about today." Then, he would ask me a soul-penetrating question about my spiritual life and relationship to God. (These subtle redirections taught me quite a bit about what it means to be a pastor.)

During one meeting, I remember discussing a book that Jerry had assigned me to read: *E.M. Bounds On Prayer.* I read it; I thought it was fine. Bounds made some great points and a few not-so-great points. But when we met to discuss the book, Jerry said something to me that I will never forget. In fact, for me, this one comment personifies Jerry. It will always be how I remember him. Toward the end of our conversation, he set the book aside and leaned in, slightly closer. It was clear; we were not discussing the book anymore. But I could tell, whatever we were about to discuss *really mattered.*

In the most sincere and weighty way, he said, "Danny, you need an *intimate* prayer life with God."

There was nothing earth shattering about his words. This was not necessarily the kind of mantra that might spark a modern-day Reformation. Coming from one pastor to another, you might even say it was common sense. And yet, somehow, it felt like Jerry had just unlocked his chest, opened a little imaginary trap door, and given me a sneak peek into the most precious spiritual secret of his entire life—the one reality which, more than anything else, sustained and empowered his incredibly fruitful marriage, family, life, and ministry. It was not a leadership strategy or philosophy of ministry; it was not some other pastor worth emulating; it was not even some rare, highly-sought-after personal quality. It was God. **Jerry Worsham Believed in God.**

This deep, personal belief that Jerry had in the God of the Bible was also the gravitational center of every other conviction he had. In short, Jerry believed in God's **Word**, God's **Son**, God's **Gospel**, God's **Family**, and God's **Glory**. Let's take each of these beliefs in turn and briefly consider how they shaped his life—and the lives of so many others, including myself.

God's Word

Jerry believed that the Bible is far more than just a collection of ancient religious texts. He believed it was a personal revelation from God himself—a divine word from heaven—and he gave much of his life to preaching and teaching it. For that reason, most of our conversations also revolved around the Bible:

- "Do you think speaking in tongues is still a valid spiritual gift that we should all hope to experience?" (1 Cor. 12:27–30)

- "Do you think the 'husband of one wife' qualification for elders means that divorced men should *never* serve as elders?" (1 Tim. 3:2 ESV)

- "What do you think that whole thousand-year reign of Christ is all about in Revelation 20?"

Scripture was the basis of Jerry's entire worldview, and the ultimate measure of truth in his life. He knew it well, he read it often, and he taught it with winsome persuasiveness. More than anything, Jerry wanted the God he believed in to speak and to change people's lives.

This is what happens, I'm convinced, when men like Jerry read God's Word, grasp it, explain it, and apply it to life today. "But as for you, continue in what you have learned and have firmly believed, knowing from whom you learned it and how from childhood you have been acquainted with the sacred writings, which are able to make you wise for salvation through faith in Christ Jesus" (2 Tim. 3:14–15 ESV).

Jerry was an incredibly gifted communicator, that's true. But more importantly, he was convinced the words of Scripture were God's words, and God's words mattered far more than his own.

God's Son

The more you read and understand the Bible, the more you will come to see that all sixty-six books are working together to point us to one man—Jesus Christ. Jerry knew this truth well and he cherished it.

It's a profound mystery, but toward the end of the Bible we learn that God is both three and one. *How can that be?* Anyone who is honest will tell you that they don't really know—it is beyond our comprehension—but it is clearly what the Bible teaches. Moreover, the Bible also claims that one of these three persons of the Godhead took on human flesh and became man. His name, of course, is Jesus.

Jerry believed that Jesus is, on one hand, truly human—just like us—and, on the other hand, the God of the Bible. He is not just some of each either, but all of both at the very same time. Another mystery!

After rising from the dead, Jesus appeared to two of his disciples as they walked along the road to the city of Emmaus. Somehow, Jesus kept his identity hidden from these men, and he asked them why they were so sad. They explained that their Messiah had just been crucified, and even worse, his body was now missing (Luke 24:13–24 ESV). Jesus' response is quite enlightening:

And he said to them, "O foolish ones, and slow of heart
to believe all that the prophets have spoken! Was it not
necessary that the Christ should suffer these things and
enter into his glory?" And beginning with Moses and all
the Prophets, he interpreted to them in all the Scriptures
the things *concerning himself.* (Luke 24:25–27 ESV,
emphasis added)

This is an incredible claim; make sure you don't miss it. The first
five books of the Old Testament, the Pentateuch, were often referred to
as one work: "the book of Moses" or here just "Moses." (Moses is understood to be the primary author of these books.) The last sixteen books
of the Old Testament are all prophetic books, written by prophets who
spoke on God's behalf to the nation of Israel. In other words, in Luke
24 Jesus is basically saying, "Listen guys, the whole Old Testament has
always been about me! Here, let me show you...."

Most people are familiar with Jesus. They know him as some stoic,
religious figure. They may even have some vague sense that he really
existed—but most of them don't believe *that.* Jerry did. Here's how the
apostle Paul describes this Jesus in his letter to the church in Colossae:

He is the image of the invisible God, the firstborn of all
creation. For by him all things were created, in heaven
and on earth, visible and invisible, whether thrones or
dominions or rulers or authorities—all things were created
through him and for him. And he is before all things, and
in him all things hold together. And he is the head of the
body, the church. He is the beginning, the firstborn from
the dead, that in everything he might be preeminent. For
in him all the fullness of God was pleased to dwell, and
through him to reconcile to himself all things, whether on

earth or in heaven, making peace by the blood of his cross. (Col. 1:15–20 ESV)

At the very center of Jerry's life was this transcendent, resurrected God-man. He believed that Jesus was God in human flesh; the second member of the Trinity; fully God and fully man, yet without sin. And that belief changed everything!

God's Gospel

One of the most fascinating things about Jesus is that he came preaching a message about a "kingdom."

> Now after John was arrested, Jesus came into Galilee, proclaiming the gospel of God, and saying, "The time is fulfilled, and the kingdom of God is at hand; repent and believe in the gospel." (Mark 1:14–15 ESV)

Back in this day, a "gospel" was simply a message of good news from a king to his subjects. As a citizen of an ancient kingdom, you might expect to hear a gospel from your king announcing, "We won the battle!" or "A new son has been born, as heir to the throne!" But in this case, at the very beginning of Jesus' earthly ministry, the good news was that "the kingdom of God [was] at hand"—which is to say; it's very close, not far.

In one sense, the entire Bible is the story of God ruling and reigning over his creation as king. First, he created all things (Gen. 1). Then, he created human beings in his image to rule over all things, and he gave Adam and Eve "dominion" (Gen. 1:26–28). *Dominion* is what a king has over his kingdom. It is the right to rule. In short, then, God created human beings so that, through them, he could rule over all things—as a king rules over a kingdom. But of course, we ruined this by rebelling against him.

From Genesis 3 on, human sin wreaks havoc throughout all of creation, until the whole thing is filled with sinful, raging "nations"— mini-kingdoms—that wage war against each other and fill the earth with violence. God's solution to this was to raise up a nation for himself: the nation of Israel.

There are many twists and turns in Israel's history. It all started with one man, Abraham, and his wife, Sarah. They do eventually multiply into a great kingdom. Some of their kings were very good, like David; some were pretty terrible, like Saul. But all of them were very complicated and imperfect. By the end of the Old Testament, though, the kingdom of Israel collapses. The citizens of God's kingdom were scattered and sent off into exile—without a king or a kingdom.

With all this in mind, when Jesus showed up saying "the kingdom of God is at hand" it was a big deal. To many, this meant, "All right guys, we're getting this whole story back on track! Pagan emperors will not rule God's chosen people anymore." A Jewish man like Jesus preaching a message like that could easily be misconstrued as a religious zealot planning a coup against the Roman Empire. But the truth was, Jesus' message was much bigger and far more transcendent than that.

The irony of Jesus' message about God's kingdom was that he certainly didn't *seem like* a king at all. He didn't have any political power or authority in the world; he didn't even have many possessions. But he claimed he had the authority to forgive people's sins (Mark 2:5 ESV) and he did heal the sick (Matt. 15:30 ESV) and perform many different miracles (Matt. 8:26 ESV). Jesus was a very strange king with a very strange message. Most people didn't get it. Even God's own covenant people, the Israelites, were not expecting a heavenly king like this, who would bring them back to God's good design for creation. Many of them were just hoping for an earthly king, like the ones who ruled the other raging nations. So, when Jesus kept insisting that he was God's Son and the king of God's people, eventually, they accused him of blasphemy. And even though he was without sin, they had Jesus killed.

At first, it may be hard to see how this is "good news," but it is the message all Christians now preach and refer to as "the gospel."

It turns out, when a heavenly king like Jesus comes to the earth, he is not exalted or celebrated. He is brutally murdered. And not for anything he did—he was sinless—but instead, Jesus was executed *in our place*. He died *for our sins*, as a substitute, so that we can be redeemed and rescued from our sin. Here's what the apostle Paul has to say about this gospel:

> Now I would remind you, brothers, of the gospel I preached to you, which you received, in which you stand, and by which you are being saved...For I delivered to you as of first importance what I also received: that Christ died for our sins in accordance with the Scriptures, that he was buried, that he was raised on the third day in accordance with the Scriptures, and that he appeared to Cephas, then to the twelve. (1 Cor. 15:1–5 ESV)

Jerry wanted to use any means necessary to relay the message of this gospel, so that everyone could hear it, grasp it, believe in it, and gain eternal life.

God's Family

Oh, and it just keeps getting better. It turns out God is using the good news of this gospel to do something very specific in the world. Remember, before Christ came the world was filled with sinful raging nations. Well, another name for someone who is a citizen of one of these nations—not God's nation, Israel—is a "Gentile." And in Ephesians 2, the apostle Paul reminds the Gentile members of that church: "Remember that you were at that time separated from Christ, alienated from the commonwealth of Israel and strangers to the covenants of promise, having no hope and without God in the world" (Eph. 2:12 ESV).

That's bleak. But then, right away, he also explains how the good news of God's gospel has radically changed their hopeless situation: "But now in Christ Jesus you who once were far off have been brought near by the blood of Christ" (Eph. 2:13 ESV). And he goes on to further reassure these Gentiles: "So then you are no longer strangers and aliens, but you are fellow citizens with the saints and members of the household of God" (Eph. 2:19 ESV).

In other words, the Father sent his Son, Jesus, to gather us into their heavenly family. It doesn't matter what nation we come from. The whole point of Jesus' death and resurrection was that it has the power to redeem sinful people *of all nations* and gather them into a new kingdom and household. *God's household.*

In fact, in the very next chapter of Ephesians, Paul explains that this is the *mystery of the gospel:* "This mystery is that the Gentiles are fellow heirs, members of the same body, and partakers of the promise in Christ Jesus *through the gospel*" (Eph. 3:6 ESV, emphasis added).

The way this works is that sinful people all around the world hear the message of God's gospel, they believe it, they place their trust in Christ alone for the forgiveness of their sins, and then they are baptized into the church. Baptism welcomes us into this new heavenly family. It has a way of spiritually associating each believer with Christ's death and resurrection: "Do you not know that all of us who have been baptized into Christ Jesus were baptized into his death? We were buried therefore with him by baptism into death, in order that, just as Christ was raised from the dead by the glory of the Father, we too might walk in newness of life" (Romans 6:3–4 ESV).

But this "church" we are baptized into is not just meant to be an idea or a theory. It is a real heavenly community, but it does actually exist here on earth. Even today, it is the collection of all true local churches made of people who believe and preach this same gospel.

Jerry was the pastor of one of these churches. And he was not like today's celebrity pastors, with suspect character, who use their local church as a platform for their own "brand." No. Jerry was hired as the pastor of Grace Baptist Church in Racine when he was twenty-nine years old. He preached the gospel and faithfully baptized new believers into that same church for thirty-five years. He knew us. He loved us. He was there for us. And it was not just because he was a good guy—although, he was that too— but it was because he believed that the God of the Bible sent his Son to gather us into his family by the power of his gospel.

And even then, if you can imagine, Jerry believed there was a much *bigger* purpose in mind.

God's Glory

What is the real point of all this? *Why* did God create all things and then reveal himself to us in the pages of Scripture? *Why* did he send us his Son? *Why* did his Son have to die? *Why* did he rise again? *Why* do the people who believe this travel the world telling others about it? *What is the point* of these local churches that preach this stuff and call others to believe it?

Paul put it this way when describing the motivation for his ministry in his letter to the church at Corinth: "For it is all for your sake, so that as grace extends to more and more people it may increase thanksgiving, *to the glory of God*" (2 Cor. 4:15 ESV, emphasis added).

In other words, God is doing all this so that he can be glorified and we can enjoy him in all the ways he intended. This is the arrangement we had in the beginning, when he created all things and declared it all "very good" (Gen. 1:31 ESV). Back then, we had an intimate, personal knowledge of him that gave life and meaning to everything else. He dwelt with us; we were his people. This is what we lost when Adam and Eve tried to become their own little gods. And this is why our world is so deeply broken today.

In a way, God's glory—his *big-dealness*—is now concealed. It's hidden. Most people can't see or appreciate it at all. It is only in the person and work of Christ that this mystery of God's eternal glory is revealed.

> In him [Christ] we have redemption through his blood, the forgiveness of our trespasses, according to the riches of his grace, which he lavished upon us, in all wisdom and insight making known to us the mystery of his will, according to his purpose, which he set forth in Christ as a plan for the fullness of time, to unite all things in him, things in heaven and things on earth. (Eph.1:7–10 ESV)

> Now to him who is able to do far more abundantly than all that we ask or think, according to the power at work within us, to him be glory in the church and in Christ Jesus *throughout all generations, forever and ever. Amen.* (Eph. 3:20–21 ESV, emphasis added)

The death and resurrection of Jesus is God's plan to bring all of creation back to its original purpose, as a cosmic stage where his glory can be put on full display for all to see and enjoy.

It was this passion for God's glory *among all nations* that compelled Jerry to give much of his life to cross-cultural missions, especially as chairman of the board for South America Mission (SAM). He used to tell me, "Danny, it's good to have a ministry passion *outside* of your church, something much bigger and farther-reaching than your role as a pastor. It gives you a certain perspective and keeps you focused on the big picture."

Jerry had an incredibly fruitful ministry, and he led an incredibly successful church—but that was not the "big picture" for him. For Jerry, the "big picture" was God being glorified throughout all the earth. The "big picture" was people of every tribe, nation, and tongue coming to know, trust, and follow the Lord Jesus.

As Christians, these are the kinds of people we should find, cherish, and follow—those whose vision for God's glory far outweighs their own interests and agendas. There is nothing more refreshing than to meet and get to know a person like this. Jerry was one of the finest I've ever met. He knew exactly who he was; he was content with who God made him to be; but more importantly, he longed for God to be glorified far more than himself.

What Jerry Now Sees

It brings me great joy to think that everything Jerry once believed, he can now see and experience firsthand in a way he never could during his earthly life. Paul writes in 1 Corinthians 13:12 (ESV), "For now we see in a mirror dimly, but then face to face. Now I know in part; then I shall know fully, even as I have been fully known."

Jerry's faith has become sight. I can only imagine the satisfaction that would come from the powerful realization: *It was all worth it! I gave my life to the glory of God, and now look!*

I long to experience that myself someday, in no small part because of Jerry's influence. I can't wait to see him again, to worship with him, and to thank him for passing on his precious beliefs to a young, aspiring pastor like me.

All glory be to God!

Pastor Jerry's Favorite Things

Books

- *A Godward Life: Seeing the Supremacy of God in All of Life,* John Piper

- *Daily In His Presence,* Andrew Murray

- *Desiring God: Meditations of a Christian Hedonist,* John Piper

- *Experiencing God: Knowing & Doing the Will of God,*
  Henry & Richard Blackaby, Claude V. King

- *Future Grace: The Purifying Power of the Promises of God,* John Piper

- *God's Wisdom for Navigating Life,* Tim Keller with Kathy Keller

- *Happiness,* Randy Alcorn

- *Heaven,* Randy Alcorn

- *Humility: The Journey Toward Holiness,* Andrew Murray

- *Knowing God,* J. I. Packer

- *Let the Nations Be Glad! The Supremacy of God in Missions,* John Piper

- *Living A Prayerful Life,* Andrew Murray

- *More Precious Than Gold: 50 Daily Meditations on the Psalms,* Sam Storms

- *One Thing: Developing a Passion for the Beauty of God,* Sam Storms

- *Ordering Your Private World,* Gordon McDonald

- *Practicing the Power: Welcoming the Gifts of the Holy Spirit in Your Life,* Sam Storms

- *Rebuilding Your Broken World,* Gordon McDonald

- *Safely Home,* Randy Alcorn

- *Streams in the Desert,* L. B. Cowman

- *The Case for Christ: A Journalist's Personal Investigation of the Evidence for Jesus,* Lee Strobel

- *The Grace and Truth Paradox: Responding with Christlike Balance,* Randy Alcorn

- *The Hidden Life of Prayer: The Lifeblood of the Christian,* David McIntyre

- *The Ministry of Intercession,* Andrew Murray

- *The Pendragon Cycle Five Book Set (a series of historical fantasy books), Taliesin, Merlin, Arthur, Pendragon* and *Grail,* Stephen R. Lawhead

- *The Pleasure of God: Meditations on God's Delight in Being God,* John Piper

- *The Supremacy of God in Preaching,* John Piper

- *The Testament,* (a fictional adventure story), John Grisham

- *The True Vine: Meditations for a Month on John 15:1-16,* Andrew Murray

- *Trusting God: Even When Life Hurts,* Jerry Bridges

- *The Valley of Vision: A Collection of Puritan Prayers & Devotions,* edited by Arthur Bennett

- *Waiting on God: A 31-Day Adventure into the Heart of God,* Andrew Murray

- *What's So Amazing About Grace,* Philip Yancey

Sermons & Songs

https://graceinracine.com/jerryworsham/

- "Amazing Grace (My Chains Are Gone)" – Chris Tomlin

- "Be Thou My Vision" – 4Him

- "Behold Our God" – Sovereign Grace Music

- "Blessed Be Your Name" – Matt Redman

- "Glorify Thy Name" – Maranatha! Acoustic

- "Great Is Thy Faithfulness" – Carrie Underwood with CeCe Winans

- "How Great Is Our God" – Chris Tomlin

- "How Great Thou Art" – Carrie Underwood

- "I Can Only Imagine" – MercyMe

- "In Christ Alone" – Travis Cottrell

- "It is Well With My Soul" – David Phelps and Guy Penrod

- "My Praise" – Phillips, Craig and Dean

- "Turn Your Eyes Upon Jesus" – Lauren Daigle

- "With Lifted Hands" – Ryan Stevenson

- "Wonderful Merciful Savior" – Kari Jobe

- "You Are God Alone" – Phillips, Craig and Dean

Sayings

- A church building is a consumable resource.

- Avoid micromanaging.

- Being in the center of God's will is more important than being in the center of a tropical climate.

- Coffee is good. Coffee is bad. Coffee is good. Coffee is bad.

- Delegate.

- Discipline is a necessary part of church life.

- Easter is our Super Bowl!

- Effective leadership encourages others to serve fully.

- Every man is afforded two blind spots: Go Braves! Go Packers!

- Exalt God's character in your brokenness.

- God is always doing something new.

- Have you seen our grandkids?

- Hide God's Word in your heart.

- Hire help for household and automotive maintenance and worship leading.

- Honor your mother and your wife's mother.

- In our brokenness we serve out of humility.

- Invest in the lives of your kids.

- It is your job to lose.

- It takes a team.

- Live life in light of eternity.

- Ministry is all about swimming: jump in, panic a bit, tread water, then swim.

- Ministry is important but never more important than family.

- Mission work is God's work.

- Often God's truths are caught not taught.

- Pray without ceasing.

- Prayerlessness is a sin.

- Protect your staff.

- Sometimes the donkey is the best part.

- Sometimes women lose control at retreats—sometimes it's the pastor's wife. It's always the quiet ones who initiate it.

- Take every opportunity to show off your grandkids.

- That's ministry!

- The success of your staff wives has a direct bearing on the success of your staff.

- This world is not my home.

- To move mountains, you need to know the mountain mover.

- Trials in this life are real but temporary.

- We are all created to worship something.

- We don't know how prayer works; we just know it does.

- You can't outgive God.

- Your neighborhood is your mission field.

AND ...

There are no superstars here. We are ordinary people with an extraordinary God!

Pastor Jerry's Life and Ministry Timeline

- Jerry Worsham born, Ancon, Panama, December 15, 1946

- E. Jane Hesters (Worsham) born, Maxwell Air Force Base, Montgomery, Alabama, September 24, 1948

- Jerry born again, age eight, Curundu Church, Panama Canal Zone, 1954

- Jerry graduated from Balboa High School, Panama Canal Zone, 1965

- Married E. Jane Hesters, December 20, 1968

- Earned undergraduate degrees in history and psychology, Asbury University, Wilmore, Kentucky, 1969

- Served as Youth Pastor, Curundu Church, Panama Canal Zone, Summer 1968, 1969; and June 1970–September 1971

- Janna Worsham born, Ancon, Panama, December 15, 1970

- Served as Youth Pastor/Associate Pastor, First Baptist Church of Elmhurst, Illinois, 1971–1976

- Earned a master's degree in biblical studies, Wheaton Graduate School, Wheaton, Illinois, 1972

- Jennifer Worsham born, Elmhurst, Illinois, October 23, 1973

- Earned a master's degree in family counseling, Loyola University, Chicago, Illinois, 1975

- Ordained at First Baptist Church, Elmhurst, Illinois, November 2, 1975, with Reverend Milton Leidig speaking

- Hired as Senior Pastor of Grace Baptist Church, Racine, Wisconsin, September 1976

- Joined the South America Mission (SAM) board in 1983 and served as a board member or board chairman until 2016

- Grace Baptist Church purchased sixty-two acres of land to build a new church building, September 11, 1995

- Grace Baptist Church changed its name to Grace Church, January 24, 1998

- Grace's new building opened and could accommodate 1,830 worshippers, March 14, 1999

- Janna Worsham married Tim Augustyn, July 19, 1996

- Jennifer Worsham married John Binkley, May 29, 1998

- Granddaughter Karis Augustyn born, December 21, 1998

- Grandson Luke Binkley born, February 9, 2000

- Grandson Caleb Augustyn born, March 2, 2000

- Grandson Clay Augustyn born, June 29, 2001

- Granddaughter Kaya Augustyn born, January 27, 2003

- Grandson Levi Binkley born, June 2, 2003

- Godson Carter Stafford born, April 30, 2014

- Retired as Senior Pastor of Grace Church in 2011

- Entered heaven's joy, August 17, 2020

Contributor Index

- Bell, Jack – Grace Church member and elder; currently Next Steps Church Ministries/The Navigators®, www.nextstepschurchministries.com

- Bell, Julie – Grace Church member, Children's Director

- Bickle, Reannyn – Grace Church member

- Binkley (Worsham), Jen – Pastor Jerry's daughter

- Binkley, John – Pastor Jerry's son-in-law

- Binkley, Levi – Pastor Jerry's grandson

- Binkley, Luke – Pastor Jerry's grandson

- Booth, Chris – Grace church member and elder

- Booth, Patti – Grace Church member; Bible Study Fellowship teaching leader, Racine women's class

- Boscha, Al – Grace Church member

- Bryson, Kiyomi – Grace Church member

- Bush, Michelle – Nurse Practitioner with Dr. Tajik, heart specialist

- Cape, Amy – Grace Church member

- Carls, Janine – Grace Church member, Office Manager

- Carlson, Pastor Kent – Grace Baptist Church member, Minister of Youth & Music and Janitor, Minister of Youth; currently Pastor Emeritus at Oak Hills Church, Folsom, California, and Regional Minister and Consultant in Leadership Formation and Emerging Ministry Leader Engagement for the North American Baptist Conference

- Clark, Fay – Curundu Church, Panama Canal Zone, youth group member

- Cole, Pati – Curundu Church, Panama Canal Zone, youth group member

- Czerwinski, John – Grace Church member, Director of Worship & Music, Minister of Music & Worship, Director of Worship Arts

- D'Acquisto, Pastor Danny – Grace Church member; currently Pastor of Redemption Church, danny@redemptionbrookfield.org

- Hayes, Pastor Rusty – Grace Baptist Church member, Associate Pastor, Adult Ministries Pastor; currently Founding and Senior Pastor of Renovation Church, www.therenovationchurch.org

- Henkel, John – Grace Church member

- Henkel, Nancy – Grace Church member

- Hessenthaler, Phylis – Grace Church member

- Hesters, Allan – Pastor Jerry's brother-in-law

- Hesters, Bryan – Pastor Jerry's nephew

- Hilker, Deb – Grace Church member

- Hilker, Jon – Grace Church member

- Jacobson, Rob – Grace Church member

- Jenkins, Johnnie – Life-long friend of Pastor Jerry and Jane Worsham

- Jenkins, Ruth – Life-long friend of Pastor Jerry and Jane Worsham

- Jenks, Michelle – Grace Church member, Associate Director of Student Ministries; currently Grace Church Lead Pastor Assistant, www.graceinracine.com

- Jundt, Heidi – Grace Church member

- Jundt, Peter – Grace Church member

- Kehrli, Mary – Grace Church member

- Kehrli, Pastor Dave – Grace Church member and elder, Pastor of Missions

- Kerkvliet, Jim – Grace Church member

- Kerkvliet, Stephanie – Grace Church member

- Kienzle, Laura – Grace Church member, missionary to Peru and Bolivia through South America Mission (SAM)

- Kienzle, Paul – Grace Church member, missionary to Peru and Bolivia through South America Mission (SAM)

- Kincade, Lisa – Grace Church member

- Kind-Bauer, Kim – Grace Church member

- Kobriger, Joe – Grace Church member; currently Grace Church Co-Director of Missions, www.graceinracine.com

- Kobriger, Sheri – Grace Church member; currently Grace Church Co-Director of Missions, www.graceinracine.com

- Kottke (Vaughn), Kelsey – Grace Church attender

- Kultgen, Debbie – Grace Church member

- Kultgen, Terry – Grace Church member and elder

- Lindsey, Melissa – Grace Church member

- Lueken (Cohill), Julie – Grace Baptist Church member

- Lueken, Pastor Mike – Grace Baptist Church member, Intern Pastor, Special Ministries/Youth Pastor, Associate Pastor; currently Senior Pastor of Oak Hills Church, www.oakhills.org

- Magruder, Bob – Grace Church member and elder

- Manning, Yvonne – Grace Baptist Church member, Counselor

- Matheson, Pastor Mike – Current Grace Church Lead Pastor, www.graceinracine.com

- Mathew, Amy – Grace Church member, served on prayer teams with Pastor Jerry including the Prayer Furnace, Convoy of Hope, and Lead Pastor Prayer Shield

- McGuire, Cathie – Grace Church member

- Miller, Pastor Isaac – Grace Church member, Fifty-six Ministry Director, Associate Director of Children's Ministry, Minister of Children's Ministry, Pastor of Children's Ministries

- Montano, Pastor Jason – Grace Church member, Director of Junior High Ministries, Minister of Student Ministries, Family Life Pastor; currently Lead Pastor of Mosaic Church, www.mosaicwi.com

- Morrison, Jerry – Grace Baptist Church member, Board of Deacons member

- Nelson, Jon – Executive Advisor of Youth For Christ of Southeastern Wisconsin, www.youthforchristwi.com

- Nobles (Czerwinski), Hannah – Grace Church attender

- Ogden, Kirk – Executive Director of South America Mission (SAM), https://southamericamission.org

- Palmer, Debbie – Grace Church member

- Pedersen (Pulda), Kristen – Grace Church member

- Petak, Pastor Brian – Grace Baptist Church member, Junior High Director, Assistant Worship Director, Worship Director; currently Lead Pastor of The Ascent Church, www.theascentchurch.com

- Petersen, Pastor Dan – Grace Church member, elder, Elder Council Chairman, Production Assistant, Senior Ministry Chaplain

- Peterson, Diane – Grace Church member

- Pinto, Harold – Grace Church member and elder

- Pipol, Denise – Grace Church member

- Radke, Loreen – Grace Church member, Family Life Ministry Assistant

- Rebro, Craig – Grace Church member, missionary in Mpumalanga, South Africa, through Sinani – NPO and Church Unlimited

- Roetman, Darrin – Grace Church member, missionary in Rennes, France, through CRU

- Roetman, Nanette – Grace Church member, missionary in Rennes, France, through CRU

- Rush, Stacie – Grace Church member

- Rush, Tim – Grace Church member

- Schackelman, Suzanne – Grace Church member

- Schultz, Glenn – Grace Church member

- Schultz, Jessica – Grace Church member, Children's Ministry Administrative Assistant

- Simmons, David – Aviation missionary to Peru through South America Mission (SAM)

- Simmons, Marilyn – Missionary to Peru through South America Mission (SAM)

- Smith, Karen – Grace Church member

- Smith, Lee – Grace Church member

- Smith, Pastor Greg – Grace Church member, Pastor of Student Ministries; currently Student & Missions Pastor at West Evangelical Free Church, www.westefc.org

- Stanwood, Bob – Grace Church member

- Stanwood, Lori – Grace Church member, Director of Women's Ministries

- Stewart, Cindi – Grace Church member

- Stewart, Jeff – Grace Church member and elder

- Stewart, Samuel – Grace Church attender

- Toutant, Juliana – Grace Church member

- Van Bree, Joe – Grace Church member and elder

- Vaughn, Craig – Grace Church member, elder, Elder Council Chairman

- Vaughn, Lori – Grace Church member

- White, Larry – Grace Church member

- White, Maggie – Grace Church member

- Worsham, E. Jane – Grace Church member, Pastor Jerry's wife

- Worsham Evans, Lorain – Pastor Jerry's sister

- Worsham, Ralph "Easy" – Pastor Jerry's brother

Also available from
KAREN LYNN SYTSMA

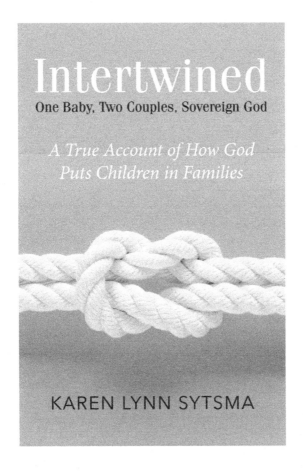